D1216989

25 Greatest Sports Stories
in the History of Indiana™

The 25 Greatest Sports Stories in the History of Indiana™ is a thoughtful collection of reflections on why we are and always will be loyal sports fans in Indiana.

Forewords by Bob Hammel, Angelo Pizzo and Bill Benner

- Featuring essays by Hall of Fame Sports Journalists and a
special contribution from Joe E. Kernan, who served as the 48th Governor of Indiana -

The Storytellers

Who better to tell the Greatest Sports Stories in the History of Indiana, than some of the greatest sports journalists of our time. Storytellers are prized. They help us recall, celebrate, and maybe even painfully remember outcomes of memorable sporting events. They spend countless hours in research, waiting for an interview, and on a keyboard (or in some cases a typewriter) making final edits, so we can recall the story. There are times we may not even agree with the narrative, but one thing is for sure: without sports journalists to tell the story, we could not fully celebrate the victory, or in some cases heal from a big loss. They are scribes of our rich sports history, which by example of this book stand the test of time.

Our effort to make this book a reality, started with finding some of the best sports journalists of our time throughout the state of Indiana (plus a few young stars on the rise from our state colleges). Thanks to the following contributors who have made this book a prized possession!

Bob Bridge	Pete DiPrimio	Rex Kirts	Blake Sebring
Conrad Brunner	Bob Hammel	Dave Krider	David Woods
Curt Cavin	Lynn Houser	Tom Kubat	And two rising journalism stars:
Mike Chappell	Zak Keefer	Mike Lopresti	Ashley Steeb & Matthew VanTryon

M.T. Publishing Company, Inc.™

P.O. Box 6802, Evansville, Indiana 47719-6802
www.mtpublishing.com

Copyright © 2017
Indiana Sports History, LLC
All rights reserved.

Library of Congress Control Number: 2017902929

ISBN: 978-1-945306-57-0

Graphic Design by
Alena L. Kiefer, M.T. Publishing Company, Inc.™

No part of this publication may be translated, reproduced or transmitted in any form or by any means, electronic or mechanical, including photocopying and recording, or by any information storage and retrieval system, without expressed written permission of the copyright owner and M.T. Publishing Company, Inc.

The materials for this book were compiled and produced using available information. Although every reasonable effort has been made to be as accurate as possible about descriptions of events and photos, discrepancies in recorded history and human error are always possible; therefore, neither M.T. Publishing Company, Inc. nor anyone involved with the creation of this book shall be held responsible for any inaccuracies in the content.

Printed in the United States of America.

Contents

A Foreword by Angelo Pizzo

Indiana and sports. Why is the connection so powerful?

When I was growing up in Bloomington, Indiana, a question like that never occurred to me. Why is the sky blue? Hey, it just is.

Some of my earliest memories are of walking a few blocks from our first house in town and watching Indiana University basketball and football teams practice. Then, at age 6, my father taking me to my first basketball game in a magic place then called "The Fieldhouse."

From that moment on, I was hooked. Attending grade school back in the '50s, I just assumed the sports teams of every kid's childhood pretty much defined his life. At 10, I went to my first Indianapolis 500. To the world, it was the epicenter of everything happening on every May 30, but for me it was a track only 50 miles away and the Memorial Day ritual became my norm. I never missed another one until I left for grad school in California at 22.

Indeed, it was then, when I left my homeland and traveled west, that I first began to realize everywhere wasn't like Indiana. My first clue was my fellow students' usual response to hearing I was from Indiana:

"Oh, basketball!"

And/or:

"The Indianapolis 500!"

Occasionally:

"Notre Dame football!"

That's when I became aware that the national identifying signifiers to my home state all had something to do with sports.

By contrast, had I mentioned any other Midwest state – Illinois, Missouri – who knows what I'd have heard back then but I'll bet it wouldn't have involved sports.

You've seen those puzzle maps of the United States, each state represented by an illustration, a symbol . Indiana's was a race car. I don't recall any other state having a sport as its symbol. Even Texas, the football state – had an oil well.

Living in California is when and where I learned to appreciate the very special relationship between the people of Indiana – Hoosiers – and basketball. That unique bond of state and sport was what David Anspaugh and I tried to capture in our 1986 movie, Hoosiers. The enthusiastic national response – a surprise even to David and me – to that film afforded us an opportunity to try our hand again, this time with another sport and another unusual bonding – Notre Dame football, in our film Rudy.

Still Indiana. And still big, across the country.

When Hoosiers was pulling in people from Maine to Montana, people often asked: "What makes Indiana and basketball so unique?"

I never came up with a definitive answer, but I've found a few clues.

James Naismith invented basketball in 1892 for a young class at the Springfield, Mass., YMCA. One of his students, Nicholas McCay, began his own career at the Crawfordsville, Indiana, YMCA in 1893, introducing the game to the locals. It not only took root, but expanded throughout the state, the beginning of a love affair that still lasts.

I believe there are a few reasons why basketball flourished so well here. Around the turn of the century, Indiana's economy was almost exclusively agricultural, with a relatively few cities but hundreds of tiny farming towns and hamlets. The cities had high schools with football teams. The small towns had very small high schools, and along came this new game that required just five players for a team, not football's 11 or even baseball's 9.

Another plus for the new game: basketball was played in the winter, not in fall when the harvests had to be collected.

And no small factor in the almost instant popularity of basketball in Indiana was pure, undeniable, chest-popping community pride. The young men wearing the colors of the local school became, in effect, representatives of the communities. Generally conservative, quiet farmers could – and did – calmly walk into hot, bright gymnasiums on a winter night and become out-of-control lunatics. Pride in the basketball team tied all levels of a community together, ameliorated all differences. Bitter political or religious rivals who wouldn't speak to each other on sidewalks stood shoulder to shoulder on Friday nights rooting for their team, and nothing in the world mattered more.

High school basketball players were their knights in shining armor, their standard-bearers. During most of the 20th century, in Indiana not one community-building factor was more important than the basketball team.

Travel our state and you'll still see it. Drive into any small town that some time, some year with some group of hometown kids had big success in the state tournament and you'll probably learn about it. In Milan, after their state championship victory, the water tower was painted STATE CHAMPS 1954. And 62 years later, the tower's still there. And the pride. A museum dedicated to that team is the most visited place in the town.

I look back at my youth in Bloomington and recall what I still love to experience today. When the Indiana University basketball team is doing well, I and my whole town buzz, in a great mood, buoyant. And, oh, the converse: when the team is foundering, the general mood is foul, glum -- the winter darker, longer.

I'm too young to remember 1940 and '53, but when Indiana won national championships in 1976, 1981 and 1987, the entire town rode a week-long high, a months-long smile.

Psychologists and sociologists would study us and conclude Indiana and sports are about pride and tribal togetherness. We'll buy that. We connect through our teams and our sports, and we love them, win or lose. And when we go out in the world and say we're from Indiana and people say back to us, "basketball and the Indianapolis 500" – there comes that grin.

We say with pride, "Yes, that's us."

– Angelo Pizzo

A Foreword by Bob Hammel

As a boy growing up in Indiana and in a sports-conscious home, I really envied my Dad. I read of the Golden Era of sports in the '20s and wished, oh, I wished, that I had been lucky Dad and been around to feel the imminence and eminence of Babe Ruth and Lou Gehrig and those '27 Yankees, to be around when Red Grange and the Four Horsemen, Knute Rockne and George Gipp were creating college football lore, when golf had Bobby Jones and tennis had Bill Tilden and basketball – Indiana high school basketball! – had the Wonder Five at Franklin and Johnny Wooden as a player and Frankfort with Everett Case as a dominant power. Lucky Dad.

Now I look back and realize I was complaining when I had Ted Williams and Joe DiMaggio, and Jackie Robinson – Blanchard-and-Davis and Johnny Lujack, not to mention George Taliaferro who as much as any single athlete made me at 8 an IU fan for life. And I was just learning to remember when Broc Jerrell and Evansville Bosse were kingpins, and Jumpin' Johnny Wilson, then Bill Garrett were electrifying Marches at Butler Fieldhouse, so idyllic a palace in radio days.

As the phases of my own life advanced, I experienced the young Willie Mays and Mickey Mantle and watched them ripen into legends. I celebrated IU's 1953 NCAA championship, and Milan's 1954 state championship – and the Oscar Robertson magic.

By then, I had stopped envying Dad and just begun to realize that every era is golden, every hour has its moments and its heroes. And when Title IX, fathered as it was by Hoosier Birch Bayh Jr., doubled the number of opportunities and achievers and full-fledged stars …

That is why there is a book like this, to advance toward our Bicentennial with an appreciation of the glories of our times, and the times before right here around us in our unique and blessed state. And to pass those stories on, to new generations who will live out their own wonderful times.

We did it here through the eyes – and the minds, and memories, and diligent research – of people who spent their own lifetimes making legends: the men and women who make up the Indiana Sportswriters and Sportscasters Association.

Journalism is the working term for the art of covering stories, the news of that day.

"The first draft of history," someone called the stories told in the newspapers on the doorsteps of generation after generation of Hoosiers. And that's not a bad term, because first drafts always are subject to improvement and updating, to relegating or upgrading as the future provides perspective. What's big in the morning paper – or as a news flash on TV – might be meaningless as further events come or might, in retrospect, be far grander than first thought.

Perspective. That was the purpose when the daunting challenge of looking back through history and picking the 25 best sports stories ever to happen in Indiana was placed before the ISSA membership.

It's not an altogether new experience for people like that. Every day of their career they reported to work inundated by events of every sort that happened overnight, or in the latest news cycle, and they had to rank them 1-through-whatever in importance and public interest – and do it quickly, and boldly, unhesitatingly, and go to press, or on the air.

And always there is second-guessing. By the public. By the journalist, personally. Why didn't this get the biggest headline? Why wasn't this covered at all?

You're about to dive into a 120-year pool of this kind of thing. Be ready to absorb and to learn, to question and to criticize. But above all to treasure and recall, and smile.

Enter these pages understanding all of us tend to rank what we see and experience as better than what we read about from the past. A Roman poet named Lucretius a century before Christ wrote an ever-living poem called "On the Nature of Things" that showed our myopia is not new:

A fair-sized stream seems vast to one who until then
Has never seen a greater; so with trees, with men.
In every field each man regards as vast in size
The greatest objects that have come before his eyes.

"The greatest objects that have come before his eyes" – your eyes, the best that you have seen, and can't imagine there was ever anything better. It's just human nature – must be in there somewhere as a law of physics or something: More senses are tapped when you live something rather than hear about it.

So the attempt was made as much as possible to capture the memories through journalists who did live through historic times. Not many are around who saw Ray Herroun take the first checkered flag at Indianapolis on Memorial Day 1919, so some researching, some digging, some interviewing had to be employed … which is also "not a new experience" for the people who put this together.

What we who did the judging entered was a gold mine, nuggets all around: our take-home limit 25. The 25 shiniest and best. So we left behind some beauties.

But we all came out realizing that as Hoosiers we have been bountifully blessed with sports people and events and achievements and performances.

In Indiana, The Golden Era of Sports began early and seems to be unending.

And fun to experience, to read about, and to remember.

And cheer, and maybe even boo. We're all die hard fans at heart. And experts.

That's all in Hoosiers' blood. And it has made for great stories – way more than 25, over all these years. But these will do for starters toward making you feel blessed.

– **Bob Hammel**

None of us, of course, choose the time we are privileged to walk the face of this earth.

And without being able to foresee what will evolve after I check out for the final time, I nonetheless declare that as a Hoosier and both follower and chronicler of sports for the past half-century plus, there is little doubt that I have lived in our state's grandest era.

As a youngster, I listened to the crackling radio call of the 1953 Indiana Hoosiers of Don Schlundt and Bobby Leonard winning the national basketball championship. A year later, now watching black and white images on a Crosley television set, I witnessed the Miracle Men of Milan capture the state basketball championship, a victory that still inspires us – and Hollywood – all these years later.

As a young scribe for *The Indianapolis Star*, I was assigned to become the beat writer of the Indiana Pacers, then toiling in the fledgling American Basketball Association and coached by that same Bobby Leonard I idolized as a boy. The ABA-dominant Pacers soon would join the NBA, become Indianapolis's entrée into big-time professional sports and eventually serve as the platform on which a fearless gunslinger would play. Reggie Miller. Eight points in 8.9 seconds.

In 1976, I was in Philadelphia watching the basketball team of my alma mater, Indiana University, put an exclamation mark on perfection, a feat still unmatched in the intervening years.

My time with *The Star* – and later, as a columnist for the *Indianapolis Business Journal* – coincided with one of the most remarkable success stories in American sport: the renaissance of the state's capital city using sports as the catalyst for an extraordinary makeover.

Facilities went up (and in the case of Market Square Arena, the Hoosier Dome and the Indianapolis Tennis Center, went down) and enabled Indy and its bold visionaries to attract events no less grand in scope than the Pan American Games, NCAA Final Fours, Olympic trials, and world, national and Big Ten championships.

Indy even snagged the NCAA itself, beating out a field that began with 50 suitors hoping to lure the association from Kansas.

Oh, then there was the night that the Mayflower vans departed a Baltimore suburb and dropped the Colts and the National Football League into our laps. Not only had Indy had the audacity to build a football stadium without a team to play in it, but it had adorned the Hoosier Dome with blue seats, a serendipitous stroke that further convinced Bob Irsay to bring his football club to the Midwest.

Of course, that eventually led to the presence of a certain quarterback here in our town, and all Peyton Manning did, with the help of Tony Dungy and others, was lead the Horseshoes to the Super Bowl championship. Manning's influence was so profound that some dare to say Indiana has become a football state.

Oh, and speaking of Super Bowls, Indianapolis hosted one and did it so successfully the NFL re-wrote the bid manual for future cities.

Meanwhile, a fellow from Terre Haute – Tony Hulman -- resurrected the Indianapolis Motor Speedway from post-World War II ruin and set the stage for his heirs to turn it into the finest motorsports facility on the planet, an evolution that continues to this day and brought first NASCAR and later Formula One. And while IndyCar racing has ebbed in the national consciousness, the Indy 500 remains the world's largest single-day sporting event.

Butler passed the torch from an elder legend, Tony Hinkle, to a legend in the making, Brad Stevens, who guided the astonishing Horizon League Bulldogs to back-to-back championship games of the NCAA Basketball Tournament, the first of which came within a half-court heave by an Indiana kid, Gordon Hayward, of being one of the great sports stories of all time. The only thing that might have matched it would have been if the Hick From French Lick, Larry Bird, had been able to get Indiana State past Michigan State in 1979. Bird went onto to have a pretty fair professional career before returning home to coach and lead the Pacers.

Bird's on the short list of any Greatest of All Time discussion. So is Oscar Robertson, who led Crispus Attucks to a groundbreaking championship that forever altered our view on race. We saw the Big O so dominate the NBA that he averaged for a season what players today hope to get in a single game: a triple double.

We saw a fellow Hoosier, John Wooden, hie off to UCLA and win 10 national championships in 12 years. We saw another Hoosier, Damon Bailey, win a state basketball championship in front of 41,000. Think about that for a moment. Still another Hoosier, Stephanie White, led Purdue to the national title. And an adopted Hoosier, Tamika Catchings, guided the Indiana Fever to the WNBA title.

The Bob Knight Era came – and went – at IU, adding three national championships but a divided legacy. At Purdue, Gene Keady went toe-to-toe with Knight and elevated the Boilermaker-Hoosier rivalry to unprecedented and heated heights. In football, first Jack Mollenkopf with Bob Griese, and then Joe Tiller with "basketball on grass" and Drew Brees got the Boilers to the promised land in Pasadena. John Pont did likewise with Indiana in a giddy season not since matched. Under Bill Mallory, Indiana gained a semblance of football respectability and Terre Haute's Anthony Thompson almost won the Heisman.

Notre Dame football tallied more national championships under Ara Parseghian, Dan Devine and Lou Holtz and (Joe) Theisman did indeed rhyme with Heisman. A pretty good quarterback named Joe Montana also found his way to South Bend. Irish basketball beat unbeatable UCLA.

An eighth alternate came out of nowhere – ok, Arkansas – to win the 1991 PGA Championship at Crooked Stick. Hello, John Daly.

So. Many. Incredible. Moments. Twenty-five isn't nearly a big enough number.

Again, I don't know what's to come. All I'm saying is that the last 60 years have been more than a golden era in Indiana sports. They've been platinum. The next 60 years have their work cut out for them.

In all that time, we really only screwed up one thing and yes, you knew I would get around to it eventually.

Single-class basketball.

– Bill Benner

The Greatest Sports Stories in the History of Indiana™ is a thoughtful collection of reflections on why we are and always will be loyal sports fans in Indiana. These compelling stories will entice readers to learn just how sports have become a defining feature of our state.

Sports have shaped the lives of Hoosiers both young and old, regardless of sex and race. The values sports teach participants and spectators alike, the lessons they impart, the bonds they form, the memories they make—all contribute to the value we find on sports fields of every sort. All of us are touched in some way.

What has made Indiana sports so endearing and enduring is a special brand of loyalty that exists between the people of Indiana and the sports they love. Telling the stories of this love affair with sports is what makes this collection special.

How did we come up with the top 25?

Over the course of many months during 2015-16, sports journalists all over the state were invited to submit nominations for *The Greatest Sports Stories in the History of Indiana*™. A second ballot allowed for ranking of these stories, which is the final order in the book. There is little surprise that the top three stories were very close in voting and there are dozens of stories you might think are missing. Although it would have been wonderful to include 50 stories, 25 stories had a ring to it, and is easier to digest. It should also be noted that 20 out of the top 25 stories are amateur related, which bodes well for the purists.

Working with the Indiana Sportswriters and Sportscasters Association, the compilers of this collection have tapped a vast reservoir of experiences by a great group of journalists who have followed Indiana sports for decades. The contributors of the stories in this book are among the most distinguished writers in the state of Indiana. Many observers consider Indiana sports journalism the best in the country. These writers will take you on an inspiring journey. Come along and celebrate some of our state's greatest sports treasures.

I encourage you to read these great sports stories, reminisce from your own perspective, and share with our younger generation why we revere and celebrate sports in Indiana. These stories recall lessons of determination, perseverance, teamwork, discipline, and courage that should never be forgotten.

With that being said, we bring to you…

– Brent Slinkard

25 Greatest Sports Stories
in the History of Indiana™

Nominating, voting on and documenting *The 25 Greatest Sports Stories in the History of Indiana*™ was a difficult and challenging experience. But, above all, it was extremely rewarding for those of us in the Indiana Sportswriters and Sportscasters Association.

When our association was approached about the possibility of being heavily involved in this project _ helping to organize the nominating and voting process and then writing the stories for this documentary – it was a no-brainer for our board of directors.

The sentiment was unanimous. No discussion was needed. No motions. No seconds.

It was just a very enthusiastic, "Let's do it."

If there was any doubt at that time, it was the tremendous scope of the project. Was it going to be possible to pull it off?

But the presentation was so complete, the vision so clear, our board knew we wanted to do our part.

After all, many of our ISSA members, including our Hall of Fame members, were directly involved in many of the elements of these top sports stories in our state's history, either writing about them or broadcasting them.

We had witnessed first-hand many of the events, and we had interviewed many of the athletes and coaches involved.

It was only natural for ISSA members to write the essays about the people and events voted as the Top 25 in Indiana sports history for this documentary.

The Indiana Sportswriters and Sportscasters Association, founded in 1946, is a proud organization.

Our Hall of Fame is now 100-plus members strong. They are a Who's Who of Indiana sportswriters and sportscasters.

That being said, our task of trimming the 63 nominated stories, plus write-in possibilities, down to a Top 25 was a daunting task.

Personally, after coming up with a Top 25, I agonized over my list _ making changes for more than a week – before I finally pulled the trigger and sent in my vote.

As a side note, I must add that I am not a native Hoosier. I spent the first 18 years of my life in Michigan, before leaving in the mid-1960s to study journalism at Indiana University.

I had to learn about this state's rich sports history and traditions.

At first, I remember being disappointed that Indiana's major city didn't have any major professional sports teams. While I quickly latched on to the excitement of the state's collegiate sports action, I didn't initially understand Hoosier Hysteria – the fascination with Indiana high school basketball.

But I steadily began to learn about, and appreciate, the many outstanding teams, coaches and players _ and historically relevant games and events – this state has produced.

And I now totally understand what Indiana high school basketball is all about. Since I retired in 2008, after a 40-year career as a sports writer, one of my "hobbies" is to travel around the state to take in some of the top games, watch some of the star players and visit some of the cathedrals of the sport.

I think it is kind of a badge of honor that the story voted No. 1 of our Top 25 is a high school basketball story.

How many other states, if they selected their Greatest Sports Stories of All Time, would end up with a high school basketball story at the top of the list?

I'd venture to say none of them.

It was largely these sports stories, and many others, of course, that transformed me into a Hoosier. I may be an adopted Hoosier, but in my mind I am definitely a Hoosier.

Whenever a Top 25 or Top 50 list about anything is published, whether by Sports Illustrated, ESPN, Time Magazine, etc., there are bound to be disagreements Controversy, if you will.

Why wasn't this higher, or lower, on the list? How come this didn't make the list?

In a way, that's the beauty of these things _ to inspire reflection, to create discussion and, yes, in some cases a cause for serious debate.

It truly has been an honor for the ISSA to have played a vital part in this very special project.

And, again, on a personal note, it has been a privilege, indeed a once-in-a-lifetime opportunity, to be so directly involved.

It has been a true labor of love, especially to have been one of the authors involved with the task of trying to bring these Top 25 stories back to life.

We hope reading about *The 25 Greatest Sports Stories in the History of Indiana*™ rekindles many thrilling and emotional memories that are so special to us Hoosiers.

–**Tom Kubat**
President
Indiana Sportswriters and Sportscasters Association

"Psychologist and sociologists would study us and conclude Indiana and sports are about pride and tribal togetherness. We'll buy that. We connect through our teams and our sports, and we love them, win or lose."

– Angelo Pizzo

"And without being able to foresee what will evolve after I check out for the final time, I nonetheless declare that as a Hoosier and both follower and chronicler of sports for the past half-century plus, there is little doubt I have lived in our state's grandest era."

– Bill Benner

"The 25 Greatest Sports Stories in the History of Indiana™ rekindles many thrilling and emotional memories that are so special to us Hoosiers."

–Tom Kubat

"To Hoosiers, these stories represent who we are. It is undeniable that when growing up in Indiana, our hearts; if not our souls are forever connected to sports."

– Doug DeFord

"As Hoosiers we have been bountifully blessed with sports people and events and achievements and performances. In Indiana, The Golden Era of Sports began early and seems to be unending."

– Bob Hammel

"Sports have shaped the lives of Hoosiers both young and old, regardless of sex and race. The values sports teach participants and spectators alike, the lessons they impart, the bonds they form, the memories they make all contribute to the value we find on sports fields of every sort. All of us are touched in some way."

– Brent Slinkard

#1 The Miracle of Milan

By Bob Hammel

Bob Hammel spent his 52-year newspaper career in Indiana, the last 40 in Bloomington. A Huntington native, his career began there (at 17) with nine years as sports editor of the Huntington Herald-Press. He worked at four other Indiana papers before starting at the Bloomington Herald-Telephone Oct. 24, 1966. There he covered Bob Knight and 3 IU NCAA basketball champions, Mark Spitz and 6 NCAA swimming champions, IU's 1967 Rose Bowl team, 5 Olympics, 23 Final Fours, 29 state high school finals, and 17 times was named Indiana Sportswriter of the Year.

The first clue that you weren't there, that you weren't within Indiana's borders, that you weren't lucky enough to have Hoosier blood flowing through your veins that immemorial night, is if you call it an upset.

A dream come true, for hundreds, thousands, millions – just about every Hoosier not from Muncie Central? Yes, it was.

But Milan 32, Muncie Central 30, for the 1954 state high school basketball championship – an upset?

You weren't there …

You weren't anywhere in Indiana when the tiny high school from Ripley County, tucked just inside the Ohio border near Cincinnati, introduced itself to Indiana by winning the Indianapolis Semistate in nineteen-fifty-three. So there Milan was, in the Final Four that year – a full season before 1954.

The week leading up to the 1953 finals was when we Hoosiers learned this wasn't muh-LAHN, as in Italy, but MY-lun, as in Indiana. That was the week when we learned they got there under a first-year coach named Marvin Wood, who had been there before – not in the Final Four but at Butler Fieldhouse, because he had been an unheralded player at Butler for the coaching legend whose name wasn't on the building yet, Tony Hinkle, before young, prematurely balding Marvin Wood began a legend-producing coaching career of his own.

We were introduced then to a spunky guard who was their best player, Bobby Plump. This was the time when, if Marvin Wood were to act like Gene Hackman/Norman Dale, that movie Hoosiers scene would have happened: he'd have brought out a ladder and tape measurer to show his wide-eyed players that, yes, it sure is a big place, but the baskets are 10 feet high, just like the ones back home …

> Milan's coach, Marvin Wood, was only 26 when Milan won the state championship title.

But Wood didn't, because Milan's kids had already beaten Attica and Shelbyville there the week before to earn the trip back up there for the 1953 State. So that Muncie Central game was actually Milan's seventh game on that shiny Fieldhouse floor, and each Bearcat's second.

We watched Plump play in that 1953 State as we expected – impressively, in scoring 19 points – but his team look a little bit wowed, as we expected, in losing 56-37 in the afternoon semifinals

Milan 1954 Champions - Front row: Fred Bushing, Manager; Roger Schroder and Oliver Jones, manager. Second Row: Kenny Wendelman, Bob Wichmann, Ronnie Truitt, Glen Butte, Bob Engel, Rollin Cutter. Back Row: Assistant Coach Clarence Kelly, Jr., Ray Craft, Bill Jordan, Gene White, Bob Plump, Principal Cale Hudson and Coach Marvin Wood. Photo courtesy of the Indiana Basketball Hall of Fame.

Milan 1954 Champions. Photo courtesy of the Indiana Basketball Hall of Fame.

to the South Bend Central team that went on to win the State Championship game that night.

So Milan had an identity and was on all Indiana's radar screen the next season before going into the sectional 18-2 and standing 24-2 when it was back in the Indianapolis Semistate again. Just another nice, feel-good, small-school Hoosier Hysteria story, we all felt – till Plump and the Indians didn't just win their way back to the State, did it by clouting renowned major-school power Indianapolis Crispus Attucks, 65-52, for their second straight Indianapolis Semistate championship. History made that win even bigger than we thought at the time: it turned out to be the only high school tournament loss ever for the great sophomore star of that Attucks team, Oscar Robertson.

So now in 1954 Milan was back in the State as more than a little-town wonder. And when the Indians whipped another big-time power, Terre Haute Gerstmeyer, 60-48, in the afternoon semifinals, there wasn't a basketball fan in all Indiana who at dusk on that electric 20th day of March wasn't awake to the fact that that – Hey! This little school that is in the State for the second time and has just run up double-figure victories over Attucks and Gerstmeyer …

Hey!

This could be the night!

This could be the little school that wins it all!

By tip-off time for Muncie Central and Milan, no one was looking at enrollment sizes. We were looking for a ball game.

With the best chance for a small-school champion in a long, long time.

The whole country knows that it happened. And how it happened, at the end, anyway.

In full context and real life: Milan, with its best front-court man limited by a back injury, went to the cat-and-mouse game that Hinkle always had ready at Butler, and that he taught well. In the fourth quarter, down 28-26 with four minutes to play, Milan put the ball in the hands of Plump, who defied convention – his team was behind – and stood ball-in-hand for more than a minute, two minutes, as precious State Championship Game seconds ticked off the clock. After a time out, Milan came out of the delay game, Plump missed an open shot, and the Bearcats had the ball and the lead. Shouldn't have wasted all that time, Coach. Ah, well …

But, a Muncie Central turnover gave the Indians another chance and Ray Craft's jump shot tied the game. Milan got the ball back, Plump hit two free throws and Milan led 30-28 entering the last 90 seconds. And the Indians got the ball back, with less than a minute left, that dream small-school championship no longer fantasy.

They could have killed vital seconds with a stall, but – with less than a minute and all Indiana breathless – Craft went for a knockout punch, cut to the basket for a driving layup … that teased in, then rolled out. Muncie Central's Gene Flowers tied the game 30-30 with a close-in shot, and – as Jimmy Chitwood did for Hickory in *Hoosiers* – Plump, with all his teammates off to the side in a cluster that took their men with them and cleared the court for him and defender Jimmy Barnes, held the ball till the clock was well under 10 seconds, made a subtle fake left, cut to his right and freed himself for the short jump shot that won everything.

Oh, sure, the ancient Fieldhouse exploded. The movie captured that.

What even the movie couldn't convey was that this new wonderbox called television had explosions like that happening in living rooms all over Indiana … couldn't begin to duplicate the feel, the golden glow that, once the screaming and celebrating ended, almost palpably settled over the whole state of Indiana that night, and was still there the next morning. When the team finally made its way back to its hometown on Sunday, estimates were that 20,000, some say 40,000, people had found Milan, lining the one road in from 11 miles out, to help celebrate the 160-student high school's day of unimagined glory.

32-30.

Numbers that yawn.

Unless you were there … within Indiana's borders … with Hoosier blood flowing through your veins. That immemorial night.

Plump wasn't even Milan's leading scorer that game. Craft was, with 14 points, to Plump's 10. The basket Flowers hit to tie the game made him Muncie Central's leader with 11.

But Plump hit The Shot.

And it was on Plump that everlasting statewide fame settled that night.

Funny how those things work. The Milan combination that went to the State twice in a row was nothing close to a one-man team. There was no star system. And – you think Milan is small; Pierceville doesn't even show up on a map nor on a modern census list but four players from that crossroads hamlet three minutes outside Milan, population

Before winning the state championship title, Milan won seven of its first eight tournament games by double-digit margins.

maybe 50, were on that 1954 championship team – Plump, Gene White, Glen Butte and Roger Schroder, whose Dad's general store had a lot out back and a backboard with a one-lightbulb court. A lot of dreams started right there. Plump, White and Schroder were in the same class, Butte a couple of years younger but big and skilled enough that he's the one who wound up winning a letter at big-league Indiana University.

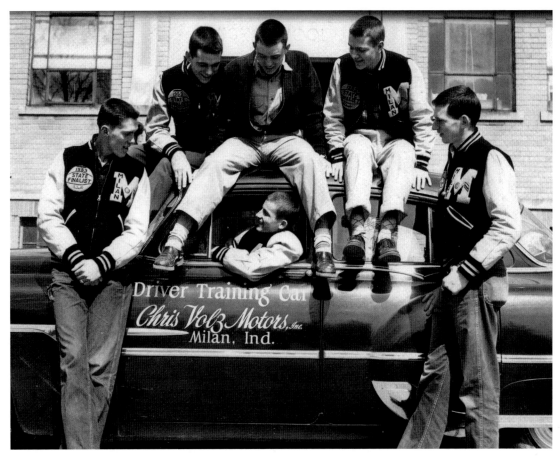

Bobby Plump was named one of the most noteworthy Hoosiers of the 20th century by Indianapolis Monthly Magazine.

At Milan High, the Pierceville nucleus met up with the other parts that fit together to pull off The Ultimate Dream. Bob Engel was bigger and in some ways better than Plump – at 6-1 and strong the other starting guard with Plump on the 1953 Finalists. His all-round skills excited some big interest: Cincinnati, Xavier. Two things happened before the '54 Finals: Wood moved Engel to forward (opening a spot at guard for the fiery Craft), and in December a practice-floor scrimmage bump that didn't seem like much caused a back injury that sharply curtailed Engel's contributions the rest of the year. Still he was outstanding, and vital at times – in the Regional, when Milan avenged one of its two regular-season losses and got by what might really have been a better team, Aurora from neighboring Dearborn County, Engel led everyone with his season high, 17 points. But that was atypical, though a teasing show of how good a player he was, how valuable he could have been in, say, the Muncie Central game when he was able to – in what had settled into almost a routine – start, play just a few minutes before the back pains forced him to the bench, and on this night of nights watch with an understandable blend of wonder and thrill and envy the last three quarters while the team on which

Milan 1954 Champions. Photo courtesy of the Indiana Basketball Hall of Fame.

he should have been starring was winning the state championship game without him. That's a part of the "Miracle of Milan" rarely noted: the 32-30 cat-and-mouse game might never have happened, or been needed, if the Milan that scored in the 60s in double-figure victories over powers Attucks and Gerstmeyer had been at full strength with a hardy Engel that night.

Or, if Plump had been the Plump who scored 28 against Attucks and 26 against Gerstmeyer, All-Star performances against strong opponents, not the Plump who couldn't get shots to go in for 31.9 minutes against Muncie Central and Jimmy Barnes.

But –

There was Craft with 10 first-half points to steady the ship.

And center Gene White, the team's best defensive player and rebounder, who neutralized Muncie Central's advantage inside.

And Rollin Cutter, one of three non-seniors dressed for Milan that game, who delivered a scoreless but aggressive relief performance.

And starting forward Ron Truitt, who scored 5 points in mixing it up well with the bigger, stronger Bearcats inside – then went on to an immortality of his own. Guy Lewis

then was a young coach just getting a program going at Houston, and he talked Truitt into taking the biggest collegiate jump of any of those Milan heroes. Ron Truitt wasn't a star at Houston, but he played; then he coached a high school team there to a state championship; then he left coaching to become a beloved principal out there. And when cancer took his life first of all the champion Indians, they named a school for him in Houston.

Front-line sub Bill Jordan didn't score but played some key minutes in the championship game, his common role. The next time you heard about Bill Jordan he was making a name for himself on Broadway as an actor.

And Ken Wendelman, who had a baseball shot with the Cincinnati Reds organization, was another senior contributor with semifinal and final-game minutes.

Bobby Plump is quick to tell about each of them, to underline their individual importance in a team's grand achievement – and, always, to mention the monumental coaching achievement of young Marvin Wood, who is in the Indiana Basketball Hall of Fame along with Plump, and Craft, and Schroder, who went from his Milan start to an exceptional coaching career himself, mostly at Indianapolis Marshall.

In Hoosiers, Jimmy Chitwood, who is loosely based on Plump, makes his last-second shot in the championship game from exactly the same spot as Plump in the 1954 state final.

Four Hall of Famers … a man with a school named after him … a player a back injury away from possible national collegiate notability – a whole complement of contributors.

But Bobby Plump is Mr. Milan. More than 60 years have passed, and in every one of them he has been Mr. Milan. He didn't follow Jordan to Broadway but he excelled in delivering his lines, time after time, day after day, patiently and pleasantly telling the story of Milan to anyone and everyone, only if they ask. Which they unceasingly do.

"We don't need a publicity agent – we've got Bob," Rollin Cutter told author Greg Guffey for the magnificent 1993 book *The Greatest Basketball Story Ever Told*, which Guffey, not even born when The Milan Miracle happened, pieced together interview by interview, conversation by conversation, question after question after answer after question, then stitched together very well.

It is Plump, Cutter told Guffey, who "has continued the legend for so long by his personality. He will talk to you at the drop of a hat. He's just that kind of guy."

Plump wasn't miscast for the hero role that he has taken on. He was an outstanding player. They had been giving a Mental Attitude Award to a senior player on a State Tournament team for 37 years and Bobby Plump was the first player from a championship team to win it. Then he was named Indiana's 1954 "Mr. Basketball," and his last-minute rebound basket gave Indiana a 75-74 win over the Kentucky All-Stars. Indiana University had won the NCAA championship in 1953 and spent much of that 1953-54 season No. 1-ranked while winning a second straight Big Ten title, but that was a glamour that eluded Plump. On a recruiting visit to the campus, IU senior star Bobby Leonard mentioned that national title and "That was the first I'd even heard about it," Plump recalls.

He passed up IU for his coach's school, Butler, and became one of the school's all-time greats – became what a healthy Engel might have been but Plump instead was: by far the most successful collegiate player of the group. He had 41 points in a game against Evansville to set a school record, and set another with his 1,437 career points. Both have been surpassed since, but he set them in the 1950s and they lasted until the '70s. Twice he was team MVP and all-conference. He was a standout guard in a three-year career with the Phillips 66 team in the National Industrial Basketball League, though just 6-1 and 150 pounds. Long after his retirement as a player, Indianapolis Monthly magazine named him one of the most noteworthy Hoosiers of the 20th century, and Sports Illustrated magazine named him one of the 50 greatest sports figures from Indiana in the 1900s.

In 2014, six decades after his Milan shot, Butler modernized its 86-year-old fieldhouse, a group of donors gave $50,000 in Plump's name, and the building's south concourse ramp now carries his name.

In his Butler playing years and for almost 60 years since, rarely does a day pass without someone bringing up to him that Milan championship, and his shot.

Other shots have won state championships, even national championships in basketball-bewitched Indiana, but there remains only one Bobby Plump … only one Milan.

They said in the '70s when other states all around were going to separate championships for varying enrollment groups that Milan's 1954 championship was the one reason why Indiana bucked the trend and continued to crown just one winner.

In 1998 when that finally changed they said the reason was because there hadn't been another small-school champion since Milan and there never would be one again.

But they played 87 tournaments like that in Indiana before tradition died.

And did anyone notice the perfect symmetry?

They played 43 one-champion tournaments before Milan, and 43 after.

If you were there to feel that golden glow that March night in 1954, you'll see that as the perfect zenith.

★ ★ ★

But … if you weren't there …

Angelo Pizzo and David Anspaugh, who weren't either, supplied you and all America with the next-best thing to being there.

Those two native Hoosiers, tykes when Milan was happening, grew up with that glow still alive as a growing legend in the state and in the sport that were passionate parts of their DNA.

Through their Indiana University student days and into their early careers in different phases of the movie business – Bloomington native Pizzo as a blossoming screenwriter, Decatur native Anspaugh as a developing director – they kept in the back of their minds and the forefront of occasional conversations what a feat it would be, bordering on a mission, to take the essential Milan story to movie audiences across a land that, to its great loss, was nowhere nearly so enamored with high school tournament basketball as they and their state were.

And so 32 years after the fact, Milan begat "Hoosiers," always a contender, frequently the choice, for Best Sports Movie Ever.

Of course it was fictionalized. Elementary to successful let alone great movie making is an interwoven element of conflict within the story. Pizzo probed for some, found none. So Milan became "Hickory" and Bobby Plump's shot was launched by "Jimmy Chitwood" – and "Hickory" did on the screen what Milan did in Butler Fieldhouse: did indeed win the Indiana state championship game "for all the small schools that never had a chance to get here."

And audiences have been cheering and smiling and crying just a little bit at every showing since.

Pizzo and Anspaugh are in the Indiana Basketball Hall of Fame, too.

The Miracle of Milan will never die.

There is a restaurant called "Plump's Last Shot" in the Broad Ripple neighborhood of Indianapolis that honors Bobby Plump and is currently run by his son, Jonathan.

#2 Indiana University's Men's Basketball: 1976 National Champs

By Bob Hammel

The Hoosiers of '76. National Collegiate Champions (32-0) - Indiana Classic Champions - Holiday Festival Champions - Big Ten Champions – First row (left to right): Bobby Wilkerson, Jim Crews, Scott May, Quinn Buckner, Tom Abernethy, Kent Benson; Second row: manager Tim Walker, Rich Valavicius, Mark Haymore, Scott Eells, Wayne Radford, Bob Bender, manager Chuck Swenson; Third row: head coach Bob Knight, assistant coach Harold Andreas, Jim Roberson, Jim Wisman, assistant coach Bob Donewald, assistant coach Bob Weltlich. Photo courtesy of Indiana University archives.

The 1976 National Championship win was the third National Championship title for IU Basketball.

The team was led by Bob Knight who was in his fifth year of coaching "at" IU.

It certainly didn't feel like the dawning of an atomic age.

On the night of March 18, 1974, the old but venerable St. Louis Arena, where 12 months before the Bob Knight Era in Indiana University basketball had popped eyes with its frisky run at an upset of imperial and imperious UCLA, was so vacant and quiet its creaks could almost be heard as IU was walloping Southern Cal for something called the Collegiate Commissioners Association championship.

Whoopee!

Knight himself wasn't even cajoling from courtside. Ejected after drawing three technical fouls in the first half, he had chosen as his place of isolated confinement a spot high in the empty bleacher seats still in Missouri but a long, long way from where IU was finishing its 85-60 rout of a USC team that in March had been seventh-ranked in the country – probably a 4 or 5-seed if the NCAA tournament field had been filled then as it is today.

Instead, only one team could go from each conference then, and USC was in UCLA's league, nominally, so the Trojans were in the CCA. There, too, was Big Ten co-champion Indiana, which almost felt sentenced to serve time there for losing a playoff game to Michigan.

So 3,000 or so people live and maybe a dozen TV sets outside Hoosier-crazy Indiana joined the high-roosting Knight in watching something click on the court that night.

Most obvious was how much better, how much more collegiate, heralded freshman center Kent Benson was at season's end than at its start, or even its midpoint. The star of Knight's 1973 Final Four team, center Steve Downing, was gone, so the 6-10 Benson, Indiana's "Mr. Basketball" that year at New Castle, stepped right in as a starter – and struggled. Knight was so unimpressed he didn't play him a second in the Hoosiers' Big Ten opener at Michigan, when Benson-less IU ran out to a 15-point halftime lead but, just as Benson-less, watched it disappear into a 73-71 loss. He returned to the starting lineup and got better, and better. That last night he bullied USC for 17 points and a game-high 7 rebounds and earned the CCA's Most Valuable Player Award.

Sophomore forward Scott May had emerged by then as something special: good-on-the-way-to-great as a scorer, a rebounder, and a defender, a Knight ideal. Junior forward Steve Green could shoot, really shoot; sophomore guard Quinn Buckner already was close to peerless at running a team. Junior guard John Laskowski had NBA potential as a tall and lean backcourt scorer.

But from that high perch that night in St. Louis, Knight saw, as he had seen all along, the future of a sophomore who didn't fit into positional norms. Bobby Wilkerson was 6-6, and long-armed, and lithe, strong, cat-quick.

All-American and College Player of the Year Scott May.
Photo courtesy of Indiana University archives.

16

Quinn Buckner pushes ball during a game in 1975. Photo courtesy of Indiana University archives.

and cuts and screens and fakes based on reading what the defense was doing and capitalizing – making whatever it chose to do wrong.

It took on a shorthand tag of "motion" – "Knight's motion offense." It already had been tried and eventually adopted as IU's "regular" offense by the end of that 1973-74 season and overnight jumped in scoring from 70 points a game to almost 85.

The wave of IU's basketball future was in "motion."

Tennessee Tech was the first to feel it: 113-60 in the highest-scoring opener IU ever had as the launching point for 1974-75.

Tests came fast – at No. 7 Kansas, where Scott May first flashed his All-America emergence by taking over in overtime for a 74-70 escape; against No. 15 Kentucky at Assembly Hall, where the Hoosiers opened a shocking 88-54 edge before sitting down to watch things end 98-74; at No. 11 Notre Dame, where All-American Adrian Dantley couldn't withstand a 94-84 Hoosier victory. In the postgame press conference, Irish coach Digger Phelps was the first to throw the No. 1 tag at his longtime buddy. The polls were still saying what they had from the start: No. 3, which turned out to be as low as Indiana was to get for the next two years.

After the win at Notre Dame, IU moved into No. 2, passing UCLA. Reigning national champion North Carolina State was No. 1, but when the 'Pack fell Jan. 3 and IU still was unbeaten, Indiana became No. 1 – for the first time under Knight, the first time since the McCracken-Schlundt-Leonard days of the early '50s.

It was the start of a long run. Not another regular-season poll ranked Indiana anything but No. 1 till that May-Buckner-Wilkerson-Abernethy-Crews group had graduated.

The '75 Hoosiers, with seniors Steve Green and John Laskowski playing key scoring roles, might be the best Big Ten team in history.

And the '76 Hoosiers, already proclaimed by national fans' poll the all-time best NCAA tournament champion, may have been the best college team in history.

It's not a contradictory possibility.

When May – named a consensus first-team All-American at the end of the season – went out of a game at Purdue with a broken arm Feb. 22, Indiana was standing 25-0 – and 14-0 in the Big Ten. The Hoosiers had topped 100 five times and won those 14 games in its ultra-competitive league by an average score of 85-59.

There is nothing in Big Ten record books to even approach that.

Starting with an 83-82 escape on "May Day" at Purdue, the Hoosiers won their last four Big Ten games to complete the first 18-0 season in league history, but their average score those last four games was 94-82, a clear indication that the vaunted defense keyed by the Buckner-Wilkerson linkup at guard slipped

A good-to-fair, not a great shooter, but an excellent passer. And jumper. And rebounder. And defender. The wheels long before St. Louis had begun to spin for Knight. What if … Wilkerson was made a full-time guard, alongside the strong, quick-handed, ballhawking Buckner? And May and Green were scorers at both forwards, and Benson kept coming on as a center, and Laskowski's savvy and instant-scorer mentality gave nightly "Super-Sub" boosts?

What if … happened!

A mushroom cloud came out of Knight's Assembly Hall laboratory, center of college basketball's world for the next two years.

The atom split had come in the summer of 1973 when – his roots implanted in both the teaching and the recruiting aspects of his IU coaching job, those roots richly nourished by a surprise Big Ten championship and Final Four trip just weeks before – Knight set out to devise the most defense-defeating offense possible. He started with the thought that the hardest offensive approach to defense was free-lance, though its very nature implied a minimum of organization – i.e., "coaching." He began amassing a stack of 3x5 cards with diagrams of what each player could be doing as each pass is made: a myriad of passes

The 1976 IU Hoosier team included three All-Americans.

The captains of the team were Quinn Buckner and Scott May.

Bobby Knight speaking to Quinn Buckner and Scott May in 1974. Photo courtesy of Indiana University archives.

measurably when Wilkerson was shifted to defensive forward as May's replacement and Laskowski joined Buckner at guard. In their third NCAA tournament game, the No. 1-ranked Hoosiers went down 92-90 to the Kentucky team it had walloped three months before.

Knight still counts as his gravest coaching error breaking up that Wilkerson-Buckner tandem, which he calls the best set of defensive guards college basketball has ever seen.

They were back together, with Laskowski's high school teammate Abernethy taking Green's forward spot, when the '76 Hoosiers began a unique quest. Before their practice, Knight said in plain words the only thing that would give them a passing grade from him: not a repeat Big Ten championship, not even an NCAA championship – both of those plus an unbeaten season.

Even that had been done before, though never in the contentious Big Ten. Four UCLA teams, plus San Francisco and Bill Russell in 1956 and North Carolina in 1957 won NCAA titles without losing a game.

None ran the gauntlet Indiana faced, starting with UCLA, the team that had won the 1975 championship Indiana fans will always consider fate-stolen. It was a tall and talented UCLA team, regrouping under coach Gene Bartow, heir to retired 10-time champion John Wooden's program. In a nationally televised season opener on a neutral court at St. Louis, Indiana flashed its readiness: 84-64, with returnee May scoring 33 points.

Unlike the '75 team, remarkably consistent with a trademark fast start and pullaway from there, the '76 Hoosiers seemed a tad less focused in games that didn't seem dangerous. Hence, a couple of near-misses: a 78-69 overtime victory over a graduation-weakened Kentucky team that only a game-tying rebound basket by

Kent Benson subdued; a 72-67 overtime win at Assembly Hall over a Michigan team that came in languishing in the teens in the national rankings but was much better than that – as its eventual NCAA-runnerup finish proved.

But always there was a resolve that the experience of 1974-75 left in the returned Hoosiers. Their league opponents seemed to feel they had seen the best shot from the Indiana team in '75 and now felt better prepared to deal with what – minus Green and Laskowski – they considered a less powerful offensive team. Always, those teams got a season's-peak turnout when Indiana came in, season's-peak volume from their fans. But Indiana won at all nine arenas by an average of 13 points a game, the one squeaker that game with Michigan back in the friendly Hall where their own history gave them every reason to feel unbeatable.

Tournament play was different. That was the challenge, the ultimate test.

There was no seeding in the tournament, no shipping teams into distant regions to spread the power around. Only the champion and one other team could come from any conference. Marquette finished the season No. 2-ranked, beaten only once – by Minnesota, which wasn't the second Big Ten selection. Michigan was.

Only those second teams – "at-large" selections – could move outside the geographical region in which the league sat. In Indiana's case, that was the Mideast, which also got the Southeastern Conference. At-large teams could move only one region away. That meant the second team from the always-strong Atlantic Coast Conference had to go to the Mideast. And that's how the SEC champion, No. 8-ranked Alabama, wound up playing the ACC champion, No. 6-ranked North Carolina (upset in its conference tournament), in the first round of the tournament – the winner moving on to play No. 1 Indiana, which after scrambling to edge out Alabama in that second-round game got to play Marquette – No. 1 in the nation against No. 2 – in the regional championship game, before ever getting to the Final Four.

That entanglement and that too-early 1-2 matchup ultimately led to NCAA tournament seeding, but it didn't change Indiana's 1976 path.

Nor did it deter the Hoosiers. In the Final Four at Philadelphia, they got a semifinal rematch with the No. 5-ranked UCLA team that had gone 27-2 and won the Pac-8 Conference title since the opening-night loss.

And then there was the championship game with the very much unconvinced Michigan team, for the national title.

Memories of the '75 fade after May's loss hit home for Hoosier fans when Wilkerson went out of the championship game barely two minutes in, victim of a severe concussion. Michigan led 35-29 at halftime, but Indiana – with what is still the highest-scoring half in NCAA championship-game history – stormed away to the 86-68 victory that solidified their claim to all-time ranking.

There was championship basketball at Indiana before the '75 and '76 runs – Branch McCracken's 1940 team that won just the second NCAA tournament ever played, and the 1952-53 team that was IU's first to be ranked No. 1, first to win a clear-cut Big Ten championship, first to score 100 points in a game, and second to win the NCAA.

And there was national championship basketball at IU afterward – the 1980-81 team, with Isiah Thomas leading the way and Landon Turner, Ray Tolbert, Randy Wittman, Ted Kitchel and James Thomas playing outstanding roles, and the 1986-87 Hoosiers, led all season by four-year scoring star Steve Alford and propelled down championship-game stretch by game hero Keith Smart.

Well into the 21st century, Tom Crean rebuilt from a historic IU low to two Big Ten champions in four years, joining Basketball Hall of Famers McCracken and Knight as the only IU coaches ever to win outright Big Ten titles.

But the zenith – at IU, in all the Big Ten – came with that overpowering 63-1 two-year run in the mid-1970s.

Maybe there'll be better days or a better team sometime. Not likely.

Indiana is the last team to go unbeaten through the entire season, through pre-conference and conference seasons, and also to finish unbeaten winning the NCAA Tournament.

IU ATHLETICS

The spirit of Indiana in athletics must be the spirit of the team. The team must be competitive in spirit and have the will to win over and above the will to star... Without this spirit of the team and this goal of school above self, we fail miserably--not only here in our sports life, but in the world of business and society after we leave this campus... **With it, we exemplify the true Spirit of Indiana in athletics.**

The 1925 "Indiana Creed of Sportsmanship"
-John S. Hastings, LL.B'24, Former IU Trustee

THE SPIRIT OF INDIANA | 24 sports ONE team
IMPACTING LIVES. CHANGING THE WORLD.

For the last 130 years, Indiana University student-athletes have taken pride in the rich tradition of competing *For Indiana*. We ask IU fans near and far to join us in honoring Indiana's Bicentennial by celebrating the past, present and future accomplishments of IU Athletics, and by enjoying Greatest Sports Stories in the History of Indiana.™ Cheers, Hoosiers, to the next 200 years.

#3

The Indianapolis 500:
"The Greatest Spectacle in Racing"

By Curt Cavin

The field pulls away for the 1983 Indianapolis 500.
Photo courtesy of the Indianapolis Motor Speedway.

Curt Cavin is in his 28th year covering sports for The Indianapolis Star. The Franklin College graduate specializes in motor sports, but he also has covered the Indiana Hoosiers, the Indiana Pacers and the Indianapolis Colts, among other teams.

When Louis Meyer won the race in 1936, he celebrated with a frothy mug of buttermilk. Eighty years later, milk is still the traditional drink of the winner.

Louis Meyer after winning the 1928 Indianapolis 500. Photo courtesy of the Indianapolis Motor Speedway.

One hundred years of the Indianapolis 500 is more than men, machines and the grueling pursuit of victory in what's become the world's most famous race.

At Indianapolis Motor Speedway, family traditions have been made, with generations of parents taking their children, who have passed on their love of the event to their children and their children.

This is an event where people gather in the same parking lots, in the same grandstand sections, in the same seats, for the same reasons for decades. They have developed Memorial Day friendships, met at the yard of bricks for marriages. Ashes have been scattered on the property, symbolic of how much this event is loved.

The 500 is about more than how cars have performed; it's how safety has evolved. From the days of drivers wearing T-shirts, regular pants and not much more than thin-layered leather helmets have emerged space-age technology, with fire-retardant suits and full-faced gear.

This is the event where a rear-view mirror was first used (by Ray Harroun in the inaugural event in 1911 to offset critics who believed driving without a riding mechanic as a spotter would be too dangerous). It's where tire technology went to new heights. How many lives have been saved by Indy's revolutionary fencing and the energy-absorbing barrier installed a decade ago now an industry standard?

People around the globe know the tradition of drinking milk in Victory Lane (done first by Louis Meyer in 1936) and of kissing the bricks (by Dale Jarrett after winning the 1996 Brickyard 400). It's where A.J. Foyt said his career was made. It propelled Mario Andretti to international fame, the Unsers to unprecedented heights, Helio Castroneves up a fence.

This is Indy, and Indy is purely ours.

The event almost wasn't, however. Carl Fisher might not have gone through with a plan to build a testing facility for the then-fledgling automobile industry if not for the numerous tire troubles he'd had on bumpy, inadequate roads. One day in 1908, on a drive back from Dayton, Ohio, yet another tire failure sent Fisher into a tirade, leading friend and passenger Lem Trotter to go searching for appropriate farmland to fulfill

Fisher's dream. Four 80-acre plots were discovered northwest of Indianapolis along the train tracks heading to Crawfordsville. The rest is Indiana history.

Fisher had envisioned a five-mile circuit, but the property couldn't accommodate that. So a plan was laid out; Hoosiers today know the layout because it's the same that exists today.

Imagine how much the world has changed since Fisher's track took shape in 1909. But almost everything about this racetrack remains the same, including the shape, the radius of the corners, even the banking. The initial surface was crushed rock and tar, but it proved to be inconsistent, dusty and dangerous. So, 3.2 million Indiana paving bricks were laid on their side, an installation that took just 63 days. Later, asphalt was poured on top of them, but the Brickyard, as the facility is known, is still true to its name.

The earliest 500-mile races were a collection of small car companies, many based in Indiana. But the momentum of the event was derailed by the closing of the track for World War I. That stoppage was for three years, and there would be another for World War II. There would be cries that the action was too dangerous, but management stood fast that the daredevils were too much of an attraction, the progress of speed and safety were too important to discontinue.

Harroun won the first 500 with an average speed of 74.602 mph, which equated to traveling the distance in 6 hours, 42 minutes and 8.03 seconds. Today, the race can be won in as little as 2 hours, 40 minutes so long as there aren't many stoppages for wrecks or weather.

The first race at the Indianapolis Motor Speedway didn't involve cars. Instead, helium balloons took off from the track in June 1909, hence the pre-race release of thousands of helium balloons.

Cars drive into turn one during the inaugural Indianapolis 500 in 1911. Photo courtesy of the Indianapolis Motor Speedway.

Starting positions in the first race were assigned by date of entry, but qualifications, as they're known today, illustrate the progress made. The fastest qualifier in 1912 was David Bruce-Brown at 88.45 mph, with the field in that race averaging 81.76 mph. By 1925, the field average was 104.488 mph, and by 1938 it was over 120 mph. Of course, that seems slow by today's standards. The highest in history came in 2014 with 33 car-and-driver combinations averaging 229.698 mph.

Speed barriers have fallen in step. Parnelli Jones broke the once-unthinkable 150 mph in 1962, Tom Sneva topped 200 mph in 1977, and Roberto Guerrera blew past 230 mph in 1992. The one-lap record stands at 237.498 mph, set by Arie Luyendyk in 1996.

The amount of money paid to 500 participants also reflected growth in the event. Harroun won $14,250 for that first victory, but it took until 1957 before the winner (Sam Hanks) collected more than $100,000. In 1989, Emerson Fittipaldi was the first to garner $1 million for the win. The record is $3,048,005 received by Helio Castroneves in 2009.

We watched the competitiveness of the race improve over the years, too. Ray Harroun won by 1 minute, 43 seconds, and Jules Goux won the third race by 13 minutes, 8.4 seconds. It wasn't until 1961 that the margin of victory was under 10 seconds (that was A.J. Foyt by 8.28 seconds over Eddie Sachs), and the record was still 5.18 seconds when Gordon Johncock and Rick Mears staged that epic late-race battle in 1982 that saw Johncock win by 0.16 seconds. Today, such close finishes are the norm.

As much as families have supported the event from a spectator standpoint, families have participated as drivers. The most successful has been the Unsers, with three different winners (Bobby, Al and Al Jr.), but family success started with the three Chevrolet brothers: Arthur, Louis and Gaston, the last winning the 500 in 1920. Five members of the Andretti family have raced at IMS, four Bettenhausens, three Foyts, three Laziers, three Mears, three Snevas, three Vukoviches, three Whittingtons and now three Brabhams.

Specifically, the biggest names in 500 history are A.J. Foyt, Al Unser and Rick Mears – the only four-time winners. But the list of heroes is much longer, with Ralph DePalma, who still ranks second in laps led in a career, among the first (he won in 1915). From Louis Meyer to Wilbur Shaw to Rex Mays to Mauri Rose, the 500 established names most of the country knew.

The race's heydays were the 1950s and '60s, with such stars as Bill Vukovich, Johnnie Parsons, Tony Bettenhausen, Jimmy Bryan, Bob Sweikert, Pat Flaherty, Rodger Ward, Jim Rathmann, A.J. Foyt, Eddie Sachs, Lloyd Ruby, Parnelli Jones, the Unsers, Mario Andretti, Jim Hurtubise, Joe Leonard, Dan Gurney and Gary Bettenhausen attracting eyes. But it was the European invasion of Jim Clark, Graham Hill and Jackie Stewart that forever changed the event.

Louis Strang looks at the vision of the Indianapolis Motor Speedway in 1909. Photo courtesy of the Indianapolis Motor Speedway.

The Indianapolis Motor Speedway is 107 years old

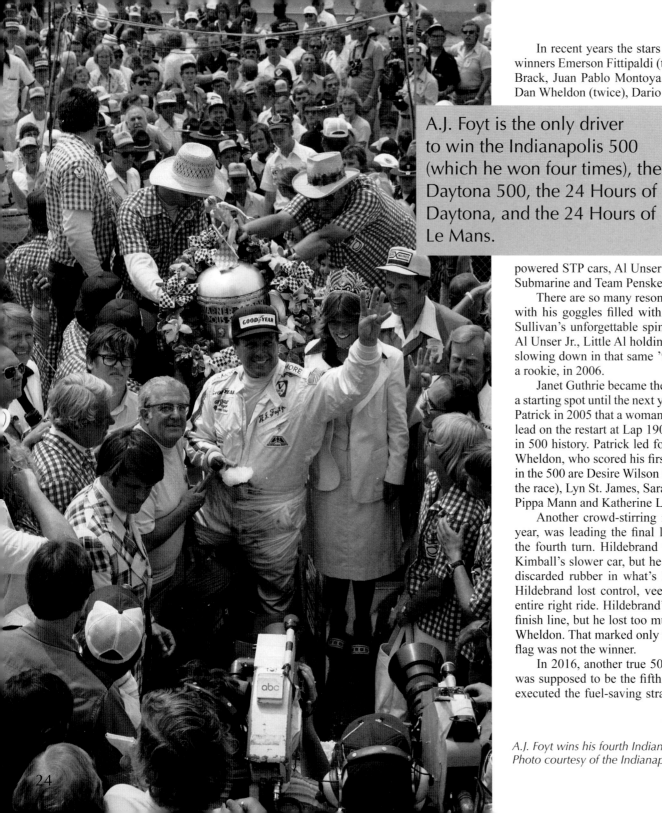

A.J. Foyt is the only driver to win the Indianapolis 500 (which he won four times), the Daytona 500, the 24 Hours of Daytona, and the 24 Hours of Le Mans.

In recent years the stars of the event have been distinctly international, including winners Emerson Fittipaldi (twice), Arie Luyendyk (twice), Jacques Villeneuve, Kenny Brack, Juan Pablo Montoya (twice), Helio Castroneves (three times), Gil de Ferran, Dan Wheldon (twice), Dario Franchitti (three times), Scott Dixon and Tony Kanaan.

The cars of this generation haven't been distinctive, but the 500's history is decorated with showstoppers, including the first champion, the No. 32 Marmon Wasp that Harroun drove (it occupies a prominent spot in the IMS Museum). The No. 8 National that Joe Dawson drove to victory in 1912 is another of the race's early stars, and the Maserati that Shaw won twice with – 1939 and '40 – is another of the all-time greats. Jones drove Ol' Calhoun in '63, Foyt drove the Sheraton-Thompson Special in '64, Jim Clark's Lotus in '65, Andy Granatelli's turbine-powered STP cars, Al Unser's Johnny Lightning Special, Johnny Rutherford's Yellow Submarine and Team Penske's Mercedes with a pushrod engine.

There are so many resonating moments, such as Parnelli Jones driving as a rookie with his goggles filled with blood after he was struck by debris. There was Danny Sullivan's unforgettable spin and win, the Lap 1989 clash of Emerson Fittipaldi and Al Unser Jr., Little Al holding off Scott Goodyear in 1992, Michael Andretti famously slowing down in that same '92 race, Sam Hornish Jr. overtaking Marco Andretti, then a rookie, in 2006.

Janet Guthrie became the first woman competitor in 1976, although she didn't earn a starting spot until the next year. A few women tried after her, but it wasn't until Danica Patrick in 2005 that a woman led a lap. Patrick was a rookie that year and her taking the lead on the restart at Lap 190 (of 200) created one of the biggest roars from the crowd in 500 history. Patrick led four laps in that sequence before being overhauled by Dan Wheldon, who scored his first victory at the track. The other women to have competed in the 500 are Desire Wilson (she passed her rookie test in 1982 but failed to qualify for the race), Lyn St. James, Sarah Fisher, Milka Duno, Ana Beatriz, Simona De Silvestro, Pippa Mann and Katherine Legge.

Another crowd-stirring moment occurred in 2011. JR Hildebrand, a rookie that year, was leading the final lap when he came upon Charlie Kimball's lapped car in the fourth turn. Hildebrand tried to give himself cautionary room on the outside of Kimball's slower car, but he gave too much and his right-side tires rolled through the discarded rubber in what's known as outside the groove. In that slippery moment, Hildebrand lost control, veered toward the wall and hit hard enough to damage the entire right ride. Hildebrand's wheels kept rolling and his car was pointed toward the finish line, but he lost too much momentum to get to the checkered flag ahead of Dan Wheldon. That marked only the second time in race history that the leader at the white flag was not the winner.

In 2016, another true 500 rookie was able to reach victory lane. Alexander Rossi was supposed to be the fifth of Andretti Autosport's talented drivers, but he perfectly executed the fuel-saving strategy of his team to win. Rossi had planned to spend the

A.J. Foyt wins his fourth Indianapolis 500 in 1977 becoming the first four-time winner. Photo courtesy of the Indianapolis Motor Speedway.

season in Formula One, but he lost a chance at one of those rides to a driver bringing more money. Without a job in Europe, Rossi signed with Michael Andretti's team just three months before the 500. He hadn't even seen IMS until an Easter Sunday visit with track president Doug Boles.

Michael Andretti never won the 500 as a driver, but he sure has had success as a team owner. Through the first 100 years, an Andretti Autosport car has won four times with four different drivers (Dan Wheldon, Dario Franchitti, Ryan Hunter-Reay and Alexander Rossi). Marco Andretti and Carlos Munoz have finished second for the Indianapolis-based team.

For all of Michael Andretti's success, he still lags 14 car owner victories behind Roger Penske, who won his first in 1972 with the late Mark Donohue. Penske's wins have come with Rick Mears (four times), Bobby Unser, Danny Sullivan, Al Unser, Emerson Fittipaldi, Al Unser Jr., Helio Castroneves (three times), Gil de Ferran, Sam Hornish Jr. and Juan Pablo Montoya. Penske cars also have won the 500's pole a record 17 times, including a record six by Mears.

As late-race duels go, the longtime standard was in 1960 when Jim Rathmann and Rodger Ward exchanged the lead as late as Lap 197. But even that doesn't compare to the 2014 race when Ryan Hunter-Reay and Helio Castroneves were effectively side-by-side at the yard of bricks on each of the final four laps. Hunter-Reay led each time, so there was no official lead change, and their margin at the checkers was a scant 0.0600 seconds. That ranks second in event history only to Al Unser Jr.'s 1992 win over Scott Goodyear.

Care for some other cool Indy statistics/facts?

Al Unser led a record 644 laps in his career, the equivalent of nearly three and a half races.

Mario Andretti actually led one more lap in his Indy career than his rival, A.J. Foyt.

Today's 500s are scheduled for Sundays. The first was on a Tuesday because it fell on May 30, which was tradition through 1974.

A.J. Foyt and Johnny Parsons on pit road in 1973.
Photo courtesy of the Indianapolis Motor Speedway.

Al Unser, Sr. is the only person to have both a sibling (Bobby) and child (Al Jr.) as fellow Indy 500 winners.

1977 Second row of A.J. Foyt, Gordon Johncock and Mario Andretti.
(All previous winners.) Photo courtesy of the Indianapolis Motor Speedway.

Rick Mears has the top six Indianapolis 500 ten-year qualifying streaks in the 200 mph (320 km/h) era.

Front-engine cars won every 500 through 1964. Rear-engine cars have won every race since.

Troy Ruttman became the first teenager to start the 500. He's also the youngest winner at 22 years, 80 days (in 1952). A.J. Foyt IV is now the youngest competitor on record, competing in the 2003 race on his 19th birthday.

Helio Castroneves might have become the first to win in his first three starts had he not been overly cautious lapping Foyt IV on Lap 170. Gil de Ferran blew past both of them and held off for his first and only victory. Castroneves finished second.

Al Unser and his son, Al Jr., were not only the only father-son combination to start the same 500 (in 1983), they became the first (and only) to each win the race. Big Al became the oldest winner (47 years, 360 days) in 1987.

Bill and Harry Endicott were brothers in the first 500.

A Stoddard-Dayton was the first pace car, used in 1911. Track founder Carl Fisher drove it.

Harry Hartz finished second three times without winning.

Yes, A.J. Foyt won four times, but he finished with a record 35 starts. He ran his last, in 1992, at age 57 years, 128 days.

Jean Alesi became the oldest rookie in 2012 (47 years, 128 days). Lyn St. James was the oldest Rookie of the Year in 1992 (45 years, 72 days).

Nineteen drivers have won the 500 more than once. Tommy Milton was the first to do so.

Parnelli Jones breaks the 150+MPH barrier, thought to be unbreakable, in 1962. Photo courtesy of the Indianapolis Motor Speedway.

U.S.-born drivers have won 74 of the 100 races.

Among car numbers, three is the record holder with 11 wins. No. 2 is second with nine, No. 1 third with seven. Maybe there's something to have a single digit: 62 winners have had one.

Twice there have been co-winning drivers (in 1924 and '41). In '41, Mauri Rose won the pole in one car (the Maserati) and went to victory lane in relief of Floyd Davis (in the Noc-Out Hose Clamp Special, a Wetteroth/Offenhauser).

Easily, Offenshausers powered the most winners (27), with Millers second with 12. Fifty-six winning engines were eight cylinders.

Equipment reliability has improved dramatically over the years. Fifty years ago, the number of cars running at the finish 11.9. In the 2010s it's 23.2.

Billy Arnold led 198 of the 200 laps, a record, in winning the 1930 race. Ralph DePalma led 196 laps in 1912 but didn't win.

Rex Mays, who won four poles, led nine races without winning any of them, which remains a record.

Indiana leads all states with seven winning drivers. They came from Odon, Crawfordsville, Jonesville (south of Columbus), Lafayette, Indianapolis and Shelbyville. It's our race, after all.

Alexander Rossi in Victory Circle after winning the 100th running of the Indianapolis 500. Photo courtesy of the Indianapolis Motor Speedway.

#4 High School Basketball is King in Indiana

By Mike Lopresti

Mike Lopresti is a Richmond, Ind. native who spent his entire career in the Hoosier state, even while working for 31 years for USA Today and Gannett newspapers as a sports columnist. He has covered 37 NCAA Final Fours, 32 World Series, 31 Super Bowls and 16 Olympics. He has been inducted into the U.S. Basketball Writers Association Hall of Fame, Indiana Sportswriters and Sportscasters Hall of Fame and Ball State journalism Hall of Fame. He and his wife of 40 years, Kris, have three children and still live in Richmond.

There is an early scene in the movie *Hoosiers* where the Gene Hackman character – coach Norman Dale –is ready to open the door and walk onto the court for his first game. "Welcome," he says softly to himself, "to Indiana basketball."

What a remarkable world there was, and still is, through that door.

Through that door was a state with hoops on the barns, and dreams of kids that began to grow from the time they shoot a small ball through a father's circled arms. "I think every youngster growing up in Indiana wants to be a basketball player," said Sam Alford, who played and coached, and also fathered future Indiana University All-American Steve Alford. "It's something they'll have the rest of their lives."

Through that door were Friday nights, when all roads led to the high school gym. And months of March, where an entire state gathered around the tournament as if it were a campfire – in a frenzy that burned long before the NCAA ever dreamed of, or marketed, its madness. Starting in the 1920s, the state finals were sold out more than 60 consecutive years.

Through that door were rivalries between towns that grew so intense, they raged beyond death itself. A legendary coach from Vincennes, Gunner Wyman, is buried in Kentucky. On the back of his tombstone are these words: "I had rather be here than in Jasper, Ind." Jasper and Vincennes, separated by 38 uneasy miles, might as well have been North and South Korea during basketball season.

Through that door was a place where high school gyms were routinely built large enough to accommodate every man, woman and child in town. Plus visitors. Where even now, 13 of the 14 largest prep gymnasiums in America stand. And it is not just the yawning expanse of 9,000 seats at New Castle – the king of them all – but so many hoop homes spread across the farmland. A high school arena with a capacity of 3,000 would be extraordinarily large in most states. There are 157 of them in Indiana.

"It was a way of life," Jim Jones said. "It was a religion. Friday night, Saturday nights, Tuesday nights, you went to the games. Wednesday nights and Sundays, you went to church. You go into the

Butler Fieldhouse, 1954.
Photo courtesy of the Indiana Basketball Hall of Fame.

In 1925, James Naismith (the inventor of basketball) visited an Indiana basketball state finals game and wrote that though the sport was invented in Massachusetts, "basketball really had its origin in Indiana, which remains the center of the sport."

restaurants of a morning, they're talking basketball. They're either talking about the game you just played or the game you were going to play."

Jim Jones? He once coached at a southern Indiana school, Springs Valley. Among his players was a tall, gangly blond named Larry Bird.

"People in general, and I think rural areas in particular, needed something to do in the wintertime," Jack Butcher said. "People didn't ask, 'Are you going to the game?' They asked, 'What time are you going to the game?' It was a source of entertainment and pride in your community."

Jack Butcher? He won 806 games, the most of any coach in Indiana history, and every last one of them came at a dot on the map named Loogootee – population of 2,701, gym size of 4,571 (and pronounced la-GOAT-ee; Hoosiers pronounce things their way).

"I think the best way to describe it was very similar to *Friday Night Lights*, about Texas football," Lyndon Jones said. "During those winters they would roll up the sidewalks in Marion and everybody would attend the games on Friday and Saturday. The kids were almost like rock stars in the town of Marion."

Lyndon Jones? He was a co-Mr. Basketball and three-year star for Marion in the 1980s, when the Giants under Bill Green became the first three-peat state champions in more than 60 years, playing in front of 7,000 nearly every home game.

"It could be something that was overwhelming, and at some point get out of control, depending on how you take it and your support system, who you have around you," Lyndon said. "We had a coach and we had support systems that kept us level-headed, and that's how we were able to accomplish the things we were able to accomplish. At one point, we knew this was all going to be over."

Through that door was one magical Saturday in 1990, when the Final Four was played at the Hoosier Dome in Indianapolis, and 41,000 people showed up to watch. A national record then, a national record now, probably a national record forever.

Dan Bush coached the Bedford North Lawrence Stars that day, and was led to the championship by state folk hero Damon Bailey, who scored his team's last 11 points in the title game, then raced up into the stands to embrace his parents. "I remember walking on the floor prior to the game, right before the national anthem was played, and looking into the stands, and there were people as far as the eye could see," Bush said. "And thinking to myself, 'This will probably never happen again.'"

Through that door is the love for a game that runs so deeply and so pure, that the father of basketball himself was moved. Invited once to hand out awards at the state championship game, James Naismith later wrote, "The possibilities of basketball as seen here were a revelation to me. Basketball may have been invented in Massachusetts, but it was made for Indiana."

The game at the high school level, has been played in a thousand places in Indiana. At schools named Greenfield, Greencastle, Greentown and Greens Fork. Amboy and Amo and Ambia. Marengo and Freedom and Deputy and Napoleon.

The first week of the tournament – the sectional – is a prize that every community has coveted for a century. Through 2016, there had been 755 different schools win a sectional, from Kokomo with its massive collection of 74 trophies, to the endless small burgs that had but one moment in the sun.

Damon Bailey at Bedford North Lawrence.
Photo courtesy of the Indiana Basketball Hall of Fame.

29

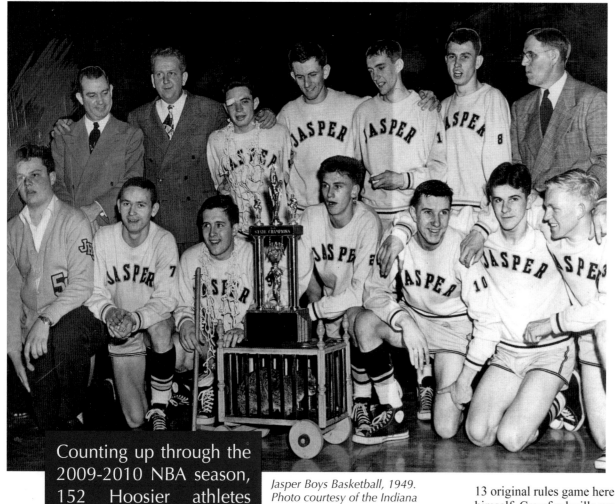

by far the state's biggest city, did not produce a winner until the wondrous Oscar Robertson and Crispus Attucks in 1955 – 44 years after the tournament began. And the small towns around Indiana rather liked that Indianapolis drought.

The Attucks Tigers, who repeated in 1956 and produced the state's first perfect championship season, were not only testaments to the skill and will of Robertson and his teammates, but also changing times. They came from the first all-black school to ever win an open state tournament in the nation. Between Indiana's regard for basketball and Attucks' enormous feats, the Tigers pushed a lumbering state forward in race relations – no matter how unwilling parts of Indiana (where the KKK thrived) might have been. If you wanted to make the most conspicuous noise about anything in the Hoosier state, even social issues, do it on a basketball court.

"By us winning, it sped up integration," Robertson once told the Indianapolis *Star*. "I truly believe that us winning the state championship brought Indianapolis together."

High school basketball in Indiana, then, has been entertainment, and a catalyst. It has been a local pastime, a state symbol, and a national sensation. It has been a story book that never runs out of chapters.

So many pages from the past spotlight what the game has meant to the 19th state in the Union. To understand, a few should be shared. This, too, is Indiana basketball …

It is an unimposing sign in a parking lot on Main Street in Crawfordsville. "Cradle of Basketball," the landmark proclaims. It was here on March 18, 1894, on the second floor above a tavern that is now a bank, the game first came to Indiana. It was introduced by the Rev. Nicholas McKay, a YMCA emissary who brought basketball and its 13 original rules game here from the East, having studied at the right hand of Naismith himself. Crawfordsville won the first high school state title in 1911, and the next seven champions would all come from within 30 miles of that sign. The cradle, indeed.

It is a tiny hamlet in south central Indiana called Hall; a hard-to-find crossroads with no stoplights and no sign of commerce. John Wooden came into the world there in 1910. Later, he would help win the state title for Martinsville in 1927, and then help lose it in 1928, with a missed late free throw.

It is the Jefferson City Tigers of 1955, who won the Whitley County tournament with 10 players coached by Doc Holycross, a local physician. He delivered all 10 as babies.

It is a picture of Vice President Dan Quayle dribbling, as he helped to dedicate the Indiana Basketball Hall of Fame in New Castle. Not that he would be mentioned inside the shrine much. He was cut from his high school team in Huntington.

It is James Dean, playing guard for the Fairmount Quakers, before heading for Hollywood and star-crossed fame …

… and Edwin Hubble coaching the New Albany Bulldogs to a sectional

Counting up through the 2009-2010 NBA season, 152 Hoosier athletes have played professional basketball in the world's top league.

Jasper Boys Basketball, 1949. Photo courtesy of the Indiana Basketball Hall of Fame.

Indiana and its tournament formed a love affair that quickly blossomed. There were a dozen schools in the inaugural event in 1911. By 1924, just 13 years later, there were 665. It was that torrid romance each spring, many believe, which made Indiana a basketball hotbed. "We were one of the first states to have a state finals," Alford said. "We kind of got in on the ground floor, and it just grew and grew. Indiana was kind of the groundbreaker for all the tournaments and all the state champions."

The passion, and the success, were concentrated early in the endless tiny communities of Indiana, where there was little else to do, except hope for rain for the crops. Indianapolis, championship, before a noted astronomy career that would one day put his name on a telescope …

…and Lee Hamilton winning the Mental Attitude Award for state runnerup Evansville Central, on his way to a 17-term, impactful career in Congress.

> Today there are 22 Hoosiers in the NBA, which is more than one for every 150,000 male residents.

It is Rick Mount, the shooter from Lebanon who knew no limit to his range, as the first high schooler on the cover of Sports Illustrated. But also unable to get his team to the Final Four, when his legs cramped up during the one-point loss in the semistate championship game.

It is a stone monument in Heltonville, honoring native son Damon Bailey. "From your hometown fans in recognition of all you have achieved, with great pride and much love."

It is a sign at the edge of Wingate, reminding all passersby that yes, this speck in western Indiana was home to the 1913 and '14 state champions.

It is another highway sign not far from Wingate: "Welcome to New Richmond. AKA Hickory." New Richmond was used as downtown Hickory in *Hoosiers*. The Hickory Café is still open in town.

It is Hinkle Fieldhouse on the Butler campus, built in 1928 to hold 15,000 people, not because college basketball was that hot, but because the Indiana High School Athletic Association had pleaded for more room to cram in the crowds for its state finals. The next unsold seat for the finals would not come until the 1990s, when the event was moved to the Hoosier Dome.

It is Jasper going 11-9 in 1949, losing four of its last five regular season games, yet somehow winning the state championship. Strange forces seemed at work. There is one story of how Jasper had provided space for students from a local Catholic school that had been damaged by lightning, and a Sister from the school had predicted good things would happen in the tournament as repayment. There is also the story that one of the team's key players, Bob White, had been going to Communion every day, and by the week of the state finals, half the town was headed for Mass, Catholic or not. Could that explain what happened? "It's the only thing that makes sense," longtime Jasper journalist Jerry Birge said.

It is the magical year of 1969, when Hoosier Hysteria burned brightly. The Evansville *Courier* ran an 18-page special section that March on the sectional. The Final Four at Butler brought together Indianapolis Washington, Gary Tolleston, Marion and Vincennes Lincoln – four schools with a combined record of 110-1. Only Tolleston had lost – to a Chicago team, when some starters were out with flu. Washington, with towers George McGinnis and Steve Downing, beat Marion by one point and Tolleston by three to survive possibly the most power-packed day in the history of the tournament.

It is that rare group of threepeat state champions, spread across time. Franklin in the 1920s, Marion in the 1980s, and Lawrence North with Greg Oden and Mike Conley in the 2000s. "I really think it is going to take some time before we get put in the 'great' category," Oden said then. No, it wouldn't.

Jones remembers the pressure of the Marion chase. After a loss to North Central his junior season, "I called a team meeting and I just kind of ripped into everybody, including I gave myself some criticisms as well. We got it turned around."

He and Marion would lose only one more game his high school career. "When I was a senior, everybody in the community thought we were favorites. Everybody in the state thought we were favorites, so we just tried to take one game at a time and go at it that way."

It is East Chicago Washington, not only going unbeaten and winning the state in 1971, but producing three players who would play in the NCAA Final Four – UCLA's Pete Trgovich, Louisville's Junior Bridgeman and North Carolina State's Tim Stoddard (who also pitched in the major leagues).

"I think there were colleges offering all five starters scholarships, and I thought we can't compete as a team on the next level," Trgovich said. "But looking back on that I really believe our high school team would have been a Final Four team in the NCAA two or three years later."

That was the last state finals at Hinkle Fieldhouse, and 45 years later, Trgovich still cherished the fact that he had scored the last basket.

Indiana basketball is the North

George McGinnis of Indianapolis Washington High School. Photo courtesy of the Indiana Basketball Hall of Fame.

Central Conference, for decades the epicenter of power. The league produced 28 state champions as of 2016, and eight times put both teams in the title game. From 1927 to '92, 34.1 percent of the berths in the state championship game – 45 of them – went to this 10-team conference. One year, 1952, the 10 teams went unbeaten in the tournament, none losing to an outsider, Muncie Central beating Indianapolis Tech in the final game.

The NCC is where the truly mammoth gyms were built, from New Castle to Anderson to Richmond to Muncie Central to Kokomo. The NCC is where some of the classic stories of community fervor were born.

Norm Held coached the Anderson Indians at the famed Wigwam, where there was a time the school sold twice as many season tickets as the Indiana Pacers. "Sanity probably wasn't part of it," he said. "It was crazy. People lined up at 4:30 outside in the morning to get a stub for a chance to get a sectional ticket that night at a drawing. We'd have 5,000 at a pep assembly. This is a story we can tell, but nobody is going to believe it, because it just doesn't exist today. But it was all true.

"It was the heartbeat of the city, no question about it. Friday night or Saturday night is what Anderson looked forward to. I mean doctors, lawyers and Indian chiefs were there. Everybody in town was there – if they could get a ticket. I can't validate this story but I'm pretty sure it's true, people actually willed their tickets to their offspring, from one generation to the next. Can you imagine that? We're talking about high school, this isn't the University of Kentucky."

Jack Colescott, longtime Marion coach who led the Giants to the glittering 1969 Final Four:

"They asked me when I was making a talk one day, 'When did you feel the most pressure in your years at Marion?' I said no doubt about it, going into the sectional, because there were eight teams in the sectional that hated Marion and they were all against Marion. A coach realizes a good way to lose your job is lose the sectional. Yet that was the spirit of basketball.

"We got 3,500 tickets for the sectional and we probably sold 5,000 season tickets. I felt so bad for some of the season ticket holders. We had some tough situations. For the 1969 finals, we had a parent of one of our basketball players, he hadn't been to a game all year. Don't ask me why. He came in and said, `This is the last chance we'll ever have to see our boy play basketball.' We couldn't get him two tickets. We had four or five thousand others who weren't going to get tickets. It was sad, but it shows how much basketball meant to communities in those days."

Listen to Frank Kovaleski, athletic director during the Kent Benson and Steve Alford years in New Castle, where one weekend during the Alford era, the 9,000-seat arena would sell out on both Friday and Saturday nights:

"We had season ticket holders in Ohio, we had some from Illinois. They were coming from southern Indiana and northern Indiana. The impact financially on the program is tremendous. When I left New Castle we had $350,000 in the athletic account and it was directly connected to basketball. It not only puts you on the map, but it helps you financially. I was doing things like repaving tennis courts, putting in a new track, buying buses."

Marty Echelbarger, member of the 1963 Muncie Central team that gave the Bearcats a then-unprecedented fifth state title:

"Muncie was just eaten up with basketball. They loved it. It was an honor if you got a chance to play. Our gym held 7,000 people and I never saw it not packed. I did see it when you couldn't find an aisle, with all the people sitting.

"I remember when I was younger, they had only seven season tickets left to sell. I got in line at about 7 o'clock the night before and stayed there all night, until my mother took my place in the morning, so I could go to school. We got two of the seven tickets."

Muncie Central is the program shut down for a year by the IHSAA in 1964, for various rule violations. Also the place, so the story goes in the book *Hoosiers* by Phillip Hoose, that at the same City Council meeting in the 1920s, a motion was voted down to spend $300 for a school library, while a motion was passed to spend $100,000 on a new gymnasium. Muncie Fieldhouse still stands today.

As of 2016, Muncie Central and Marion share the state record with eight state titles each. "It means a great deal to me and it means a great deal to everyone who lives in Marion," Jones said. "We know we'll always be in the history books in terms of what we did. We'll always be known as one of the best towns in Indiana for basketball."

Muncie Central's history not only includes shining glory but also immortal defeat. The Bearcats were on the wrong end of the Milan Miracle. They were the team Bobby Plump gunned down in 1954.

"When Milan beat us, I'll never forget being home," Echelbarger said. "My parents went out to some friends' house, so they could watch it on television. When it happened – I was stupid enough, I was so young – I was excited because it was a great game. I

called out there to them, and everybody was crying. The adults were all crying. It was beyond comprehension."

Ah, Milan. The mother of all underdog tales in Indiana. Plump's last-second shot and the deeds of a school of 161 kids in 1954 echoed all the way to the nation's cineplexes. No Milan, no *Hoosiers*. How often has he been asked to relive that moment in the decades that followed? "Thousands of times," Plump said.

Yes, Indiana basketball is certainly about Milan. But also – and this is what makes it even more special – all the almost-Milans.

It is the Montezuma Aztecs of 1954. Senior class of 14, seven boys and seven girls. No place to play home games. The Gymless Wonders, people called them. They shared their practice area – 60 feet by 27 – in the school basement with the band and an home economics class, and couldn't put much air under their shots because of the low ceiling. The coach's wife had to wash the uniforms, hanging them on her clothes line to dry. They went all the way to the Sweet 16, before running into ... Milan. "For our 15 minutes of fame," team member Ron Baumann said, "it's went on for quite a while."

It is Odon of 1959, a Milan-size Cinderella going all the way to the semistate championship game, on the cusp of the Final Four. Then the Bulldogs lost to New Albany 70-68 in the last sudden death overtime in the history of the tournament. It would be the only sectional Odon ever won. The *Hoosiers* that could have been.

"I can remember the war coming to an end. I was a young lad and I remember being on my dad's shoulders," said Norm Beasley, a player on the team. "It was raining and they were celebrating victory…shooting guns in the air…people honking their horns. That was big. But the people that had seen both say the celebration in 1959 outdid the war. I don't know, I don't think that's fair. But I do know the caravan was something like five miles coming back into town."

Along the tournament path, Odon had to knock off Huntingburg in a two-pointer that included Beasley saving a ball from going out of bounds in the last minute.

"Every Huntingburg fan swears he was out of bounds," said Buddy Graham, another Odon starter. "At least 15 years later, we go to the Indiana-Kentucky All-Star Game. We stop in Huntingburg (at a pub) on the way home. I walk in and after a couple of beers, they knew who I was. This old guy in bib overalls comes up and says, `Beasley was out of bounds.' Fifteen years later."

Graham missed a shot early in the sudden death semistate overtime that could have ended the game and sent his team to the Final Four. New Albany scored the winner soon after. Beasley still claims Graham was fouled, Graham still is not so sure. But that moment has never gone away.

"I still get up at night sometimes. It gets in my head," Beasley said.

"I don't even think about it. I don't want to think about or talk about it," Graham said. "It's still hard for me to do that. I couldn't drive through New Albany. Four years ago was the first time."

Indiana basketball is also the Ireland Spuds, a school of 146 kids, making it to the 1963 Sweet 16 with no starter over 5-10.

"The town of Ireland had about 500 people. That Saturday night they said somewhere between four and five thousand people were partying," Dave Small, a player on the team, said of the sectional championship celebration. "They had green

The Indiana High School Boys Basketball Tournament, is one of the oldest and most prestigious state high school basketball tournaments in America.

beer on every corner. We had a state trooper who lived here. He was directing traffic, because we didn't have a stoplight.

"It gave you the feeling anything is possible. It carried me all through my life."

Ireland's history includes the Great Egg War in 1962. Ireland is only six miles from much larger Jasper, and relations were always a bit strained.

"They came down after they beat us in the sectional finals of '62," Small said. "They come down blowing their horn and strolling through town like a parade. And one of our cheerleaders said, `You ain't coming to our town and parading,' and threw an egg at them. They turn around and go back to Jasper and buy eggs.

"They picked the wrong community to come down with eggs. We lived on a farm of about 600 acres, we had about 20,000 laying hens. Another teammate of mine had about 10 or 15,000 laying hens down the road. They came down there in a convertible throwing eggs at us out of a damn store in Jasper. We went down to the farm and got cases of eggs and brought them back."

Indiana basketball is a man staying in his small hometown, called by the love of the game and his roots, and building a legend. Butcher mentioned the day his graduating class marched into the gym at Loogootee High School.

"As I walked through the big doors, when I got to the free throw line at the east end, I decided I'd like to be a coach. I think that's the first time I ever contemplated that."

So he was, for 806 wins and two Final Four trips, all at Loogootee, deciding home was always better than anywhere else.

"At some point, I think it became my destiny."

So it has gone in high school basketball, year after year, from Ireland to Indianapolis. The universe changed in Indiana in 1998 when the state tournament went to four classes. No more Milans, or Odons, or Montezumas.

Many blame the attendance drop which followed on the switch; divine retribution for giving a cold shoulder to tradition.

"Today's philosophy is everybody wins, everybody's got to get a trophy," Held said. "Nobody loses. I just don't think that's very realistic. It's great to learn how to win, but you also have to learn how to lose. Which we did a couple of times.

"They kind of ripped the heart out of Indiana basketball."

Indeed, there is no denying some of the magic and mystique have vanished. The unmatchable aura of the Cinderella story are gone. The NCAA Tournament became March Madness when the bracket went to 64 teams, smaller fry were invited, and the underdog tales commenced. First-week upsets are now the lifeblood of college basketball.

Indiana was onto that idea decades earlier, but legislated it away. Still, even today there are sometimes full arenas, and unforgettable moments, and stories that will be retold for generations.

"It's still there," said Tim Grove, a member of the IHSAA board, who helps dispense awards at the tournament. "You watch the faces of the kids playing. I've been fortunate to hand out some rings, the kids today still love it the way we did."

Grove was such a kid in 1978 when the energy crunch from a prolonged coal miners' strike threatened to darken the Midwest. Some thought the state high school tournament in Indiana might be scrubbed. The governor himself told the IHSAA to find a way.

"I think if they would have canceled the tournament," Grove said, "the governor might have been lynched."

So Indiana simply outwaited the crisis. The state champion, Muncie Central again, was crowned on April 15.

Bristol High School, 1946. Photo courtesy of the Indiana Basketball Hall of Fame.

The stories of the game never end, to be retold by fathers to children. Lyndon Jones mentioned his daughter Lark, a volleyball player whose Hamilton Southeastern team was beaten in the semistate.

"We were riding in the car one day," Jones said, "and she said, `Dad, I see what you're talking about now. It's just so hard getting to the state championship, let alone you guys winning it three times in a row.'"

The roars of the crowd, the symbols of the past, the memories of an old coach, the admiration of a young daughter. All part of a game that is still a treasure in Indiana, and always will be.

"Hoosier Hysteria" is the nickname given to describe the state of excitement surrounding basketball in Indiana, specifically the Indiana high school basketball tournament.

#5 The Indianapolis Colts

By Mike Chappell

Mike Chappell is a member of the Indiana Sportswriters and Sportscasters Association Hall of Fame and was named 2014 Indiana Sportswriter of the Year by the National Association of Sportswriters and Sportscasters. He is a long-time member of the Pro Football Hall of Fame Selection Committee and has covered the Colts since their relocation to Indianapolis in 1984. He currently does so for CBS4, Fox59 and Indy Sports Central.

To provide proper context to the Colts transforming themselves from nomadic franchise and early afterthought in their new environs to one of the NFL's most successful, consider their lineage.

They have called Indianapolis home longer than they did Baltimore.

"That's hard to believe for those of us who lived through (the move) and remember it," offered long-time Colts executive and Pro Football Hall of Fame inductee Bill Polian.

"Pretty crazy," added veteran placekicker Adam Vinatieri, whose bronze bust one day will join Polian's in Canton, Ohio.

Crazy, but true.

Baltimore embraced the Colts and their legendary icons – Johnny Unitas, Raymond Berry, John Mackey, Gino Marchetti, Art Donovan, Lenny Moore, Jim Parker and so many others – from 1953 until March 1984 when cantankerous owner Robert Irsay uprooted the franchise and dispatched a fleet of Mayflower vans to Indianapolis.

That 31-year relationship consisted of 438 games and produced 230 wins, including the playoffs. The Baltimore Colts reached the postseason 10 times and won three world championships. They were featured performers in the "Greatest Game Ever Played," the 23-17 overtime victory over the New York Giants for the 1958 NFL championship.

The 2016 season marked the Colts' 33rd season in Indy. It's been a stretch that featured Hall of Fame-level luminaries – Peyton Manning, Marvin Harrison, Edgerrin James, Reggie Wayne, Dwight Freeney, Robert Mathis, Eric Dickerson and Marshall Faulk among them – and similar success. As Hoosiers, there have been 541 games and 286 victories overall. There have been 15 trips to the postseason, two to the Super Bowl, and a world title after the '06 season.

What once was so revered but ripped out of Baltimore has gained a serious foothold in the Midwest.

Who can forget the decade of the 2000s, when the Manning-led Colts won 115 regular-season games, the most by a team in any decade in NFL history?

Or the scintillating comeback at the expense of the New England Patriots in the 2006 AFC Championship game? Next stop: Super Bowl XLI. Bad news comin', Bears.

Or Manning becoming the NFL's first four-time MVP? Or No. 18 breaking Dan Marino's single-season touchdown record with No. 49 finding its way to Brandon Stokley against San Diego Dec. 26, 2004?

Or the Colts doing the impossible at Tampa in '03, winning in overtime after trailing 35-14 with five minutes to play?

Or Manning and Green Bay's Brett Favre combining for 753 yards and nine touchdowns in a '04 shootout?

Or Aaron Bailey coming oh-so-close to securing Jim Harbaugh's Hail Mary on the final play of the '95 AFC Championship game in Pittsburgh?

Or Dickerson running through Denver's defense for 159 yards and four touchdowns in a '88 Monday Night Football masterpiece despite being pulled one series into the third quarter?

"The memories are endless," said Jim Irsay, who assumed ownership of the Colts following his father's passing in 1997.

And to think it all began with the new kids on the block stumbling so often in front of their new fans.

Step one on Hoosier soil came Sept. 2, 1984 in downtown Indianapolis' heretofore vacant palace, the 60,000-seat Hoosier Dome. The Colts' first official venture was a losing one, 23-14 to Pat Ryan – yes, Pat Ryan – and the New York Jets.

Ben Utt, a veteran guard whose career spanned Baltimore and Indianapolis, recalled a rockin' Hoosier Dome.

"The place was just packed. It was packed for every game," he said. "We just didn't get it done.

"Shoot, that whole season wasn't very good."

Shoot, those early years weren't very good and tested the patience of Robert Irsay. In the first nine seasons, there were twice as many head coaches/interim coaches (six) as winning records (three).

It didn't take long for the novelty to wear off. The image of Robert Irsay and Mayor William Hudnut walking – hands joined, arms raised – into the Hoosier Dome April 2, 1984 for a welcome-to-Indy ceremony quickly faded.

Rick Venturi experienced the eroding relationship in Baltimore that led to the messy, public divorce and those infant steps in Indy. His 12-year association with the Colts included stints as linebackers coach, defensive coordinator and interim head coach when Robert Irsay jettisoned Ron Meyer with 11 games remaining in what would be a 1-15 1991.

"I can remember everything about the move like it was yesterday," Venturi said. "But those early seasons, and I kind of hate to admit it, they're sort of blank to me.

"I have no recollections of them. Maybe getting drilled has a lot to do with that."

The Colts were 12-36 in their first three seasons and reached the playoffs once in their first 11 years in Indianapolis. That lone postseason appearance came during the strike-shortened '87 season, when the front office was better than most at building a viable replacement roster for three games.

Other than that, the first dozen seasons were a collection of catchy snapshots rather than the sustained excellence that would follow.

> Late one night in 1984, without any kind of announcement, Bob Irsay (the previous owner of the Colts) hired movers to pack up the team's offices in Owings Mills, Maryland, while the city of Baltimore slept.

Upon the Colts' arrival in Indianapolis, over 143,000 requests for season tickets were received in just two weeks.

There was Ray Butler's version of the Immaculate Reception in that inaugural season that turned away, ironically enough, the Pittsburgh Steelers; the blockbuster '87 trade that delivered Dickerson to the roster and gave the Colts the national credibility that had been missing; Dickerson running roughshod over the Broncos on the one-year anniversary of the trade; and the team following Harbaugh – aka Captain Comeback – on a captivating march through the '95 postseason that fell a Hail Mary short of the Super Bowl.

"The sad thing about it is '87 was our break-through year," Venturi said. "We had won those last three with Ron in '86, then we had a strong '87 and went to the playoffs for the first time.

"I absolutely believe we were on the cusp, maybe not of a Super Bowl, but on the cusp of being a pretty good team. You know, a team that goes 9-7, 10-6, maybe gets 11 wins.

"Then we started dismantling it."

The regression was accelerated by the failed attempt at handing the reins of the offense to hometown hero Jeff George, the first overall pick in the 1990 draft, and sending Pro Bowl left tackle Chris Hinton and promising receiver Andre Rison to Atlanta to get into position to select George. As he did with the Los Angeles Rams, Dickerson once again wore out his welcome. Another significant personnel misstep involved acquiring linebacker Fredd Young from Seattle for a pair of first-round draft picks and getting very little in return.

"For a lot of reasons, things just didn't work," Venturi said. "Even though there was great interest when we got to Indianapolis, we didn't have the type of football team that was good enough to capture that.

"Even in '87, it was like 'Good job.' But (the support) wasn't over the top at all.

"Obviously Manning changed all of that."

Obviously.

The seismic shift occurred April 18, 1998. It revitalized a team and a city, and would reshape the NFL landscape.

Welcome to Indy, Peyton Manning. The first overall pick in the draft represented the latest lifeline for a drifting franchise.

"When you have that guy, you have a chance all the time in the National Football League," Venturi said. "You make the right choice on Manning, so you have the first piece in place."

Credit the stars aligning for Manning's arrival. The Colts secured the first overall pick in the draft on the final day of the '97 regular season, and only after losing at Minnesota 39-28 and waiting for Arizona to mount a fourth-quarter comeback and overtake Atlanta 29-26. That left the Colts with a league-worst 3-13 record. The Cardinals were one of four teams to finish at 4-12.

"So many things have to happen to have greatness," Jim Irsay said. "It's not as if you can ever have one decision go your way."

Manning was the first significant decision by Polian, who had been hired four months earlier to run the Colts' on-field operations.

"The best move Jimmy made was to bring Bill in," Venturi said. "He basically gave him the keys to the kingdom.

"Bill was really a top guy. People liked him and didn't like him, but he's in the Hall of Fame for a reason. They were on the right track with him."

Manning was the first pillar put in place, but others soon followed. First-round picks included James ('99), Wayne ('01), Freeney ('02), Dallas Clark ('03), Marlin Jackson ('05) and Joseph Addai ('06). Safety Bob Sanders was a second-round pick in '04 and the NFL's Defensive Player of the Year in '07. Robert Mathis was a fifth-round pick in '03 who would become the franchise's career sack leader. Antoine Bethea blossomed from sixth-round pick in '06 to a two-time Pro Bowl selection.

That collection of elite talent buttressed the existing personnel that included Harrison, Faulk, Tarik Glenn, Adam Meadows, Marcus Pollard, Ken Dilger and Jason Belser.

"Of course 18 made it all come true, along with Tony (Dungy) and a lot of other great players as well," Polian said.

The byproduct was an unprecedented run of success. No longer did the Colts reside on the periphery. They generally maxed out their prime-time TV opportunities and always were considered championship contenders.

During Manning's 14-year career – he missed his final season in '11 after undergoing four procedures on his neck – the Colts reached the playoffs 11 times. They advanced to the Super Bowl twice and hoisted the Lombardi Trophy on a rainy Feb. 4, 2007 evening in South Florida.

In a league whose rules are aimed at creating parity, the Colts were an outlier. Beginning with Dungy's arrival as head coach in '02, they won at least 10 games in nine consecutive seasons and set an NFL record by winning at least 12 games in seven straight seasons.

The Manning era ended March 7, 2012 when Jim Irsay, faced with having to pay his still-rehabbing QB a $28 million bonus, terminated Manning's contract. The press conference offered a side of Manning seldom seen. He was emotional, reflective.

Super Bowl XLI was the first to be played in rainy conditions.

"This town and this team mean so much to me," Manning said, frequently pausing to fight back tears. "It truly has been an honor to play in Indianapolis. I do love it here. I love the fans and I will always enjoy having played for such a great team. I will leave the Colts with nothing but good thoughts and gratitude, to Jim, the organization, my teammates, the media and especially the fans.

"Thank you very much from the bottom of my heart. I truly have enjoyed being your quarterback."

Incredibly, lightning struck twice.

It took a confluence of events for the Colts to be in position to hitch their fortunes to Manning in 1998. Similarly, things had to fall into place for the franchise to adequately deal with life after 18.

With Manning on the sidelines, the Colts first turned to 38-year-old Kerry Collins, then Curtis Painter and finally Dan Orlovsky. They opened 2011 with 13 losses, finished with a league-worst 2-14 record – remember the *Suck for Luck* chatter? – and most believed a better mark was obtainable had the coaching staff not stuck with Painter as long as it did. He replaced Collins as the starter in week 4 and lost eight straight before Orlovsky stepped in and ended the maddening skid by leading the Colts to a 27-13 win over the Tennessee Titans.

The damage had been done, which in this case was a good thing. The reward for a forgettable season was yet another franchise QB.

"My gosh, I've been with franchises that were decent that couldn't get a quarterback in 30 years," said Venturi, whose NFL coaching career spanned 27 years and five teams. "That's what is so unbelievable. To have that one anomaly season and have that next guy right there waiting for you . . . you just shake your head."

In '98, Polian chose Manning over Ryan Leaf.

In '12, first-year general manager Ryan Grigson opted for Andrew Luck over Robert Griffin III.

"I feel like the luckiest man in the world right now," said first-year head coach Chuck Pagano. "It's obviously a great time, an exciting time."

Added Grigson: "It is a new era, a new beginning. We got our guy and he's the one we feel is going to take us to where we want to go in this thing."

While Irsay lauded Manning for having lifted his franchise to such heights, he lamented the lack of multiple world championships.

"The only regret I have is winning only one," he said. "That's something all of us feel the sting of, not winning more than one. The seven 12-win seasons, the nine straight playoff berths and many other great things, but in the end it's about championships.

"We'd like to be able to win multiple championships in the new era. I think multiple championships are critical when you want to be measured with the greatest of all time in terms of teams."

With those increased expectations came increased pressure. Luck wasn't just becoming the newest face and driving force for an NFL franchise, he was replacing that franchise's most compelling figure, a no-doubt first-ballot Hall of Famer.

Luck's resume was fat. He was an all-America QB at Stanford and twice finished runner-up in the Heisman Trophy voting. He posted a 31-7 record as a starter and was recipient of the 2011 Johnny Unitas Golden Arm Award, presented annually to college football's top quarterback.

But now, he was replacing Peyton Manning.

"I think big shoes may be an understatement," Luck said. "What he did is, obviously, legendary for this city and for the state. I know that if I woke up every morning trying to compare myself to Peyton, I think I would go crazy. It's impossible.

"I am going to go out there and do the best I can. If one day I can be mentioned alongside Peyton in quarterback lore, it would be a football dream come true."

Until Luck endured an injury-plagued 2015 – injuries to his right shoulder, ribs and kidneys limited him to seven games – the Colts quickly put the humbling '11 campaign behind them.

They reached the playoffs in each of Luck's first three seasons with identical 11-5 records, and advanced one step further into the postseason each year. That culminated with a trip to the AFC Championship game after '14, where they were dismantled by the New England Patriots 45-7.

Individually, Luck appeared in three Pro Bowls; became the fifth quarterback since 1970 to lead his team to at least 30 wins in his first three seasons; passed for 12,957 yards, the most by a quarterback in his first three seasons; and led the league with 40 touchdown passes in '14.

For so long, Wayne had been the unquestioned leader of the team. He had been targeted by Pagano as a must-retain free agent during the 2012 offseason.

That leadership role gradually but undeniably shifted to Luck.

"I'm just keeping the seat warm for him," Wayne said. "At the end of the day, he's our leader. I'm the vice-president, I'm not the president.

"It's his team. He sets the tone. He sets the pace, especially for the offense and whenever he has another mission to take care of, that's when I step in. That's what vice-presidents do."

The arc during the early phases of the Luck era included more than a few storylines.

Pagano's initial venture as an NFL head coach was interrupted Sept. 26, 2012 when he was diagnosed with leukemia. He went on indefinite leave and turned the team over to long-time friend and offensive coordinator Bruce Arians, who was named NFL Coach of the Year for directing the Colts to a 9-2 record and the playoffs in Pagano's absence.

It was announced Pagano went into remission Nov. 2, and he has championed the battle against the disease.

The team's attempt at surrounding Luck with a strong supporting cast had mixed results. The notable misses included linebacker Bjoern Werner, the 2013 first-round pick who was released after three lackluster seasons; running back Trent Richardson, acquired in a much-hyped trade in '13 and released 17 months later after averaging 33.7 yards per game and 3.1 yards per attempt in 29 appearances; and safety LaRon Landry, an expensive and massive free-agent bust.

And who can forget the manner with which the '15 season unfolded? While Luck was missing extended time and the Colts were missing the playoffs, it was reported on many fronts that Grigson and Pagano were at odds.

With the opportunity to push the reset button after his team finished 8-8, Jim Irsay opted for continuity. He signed Pagano, whose contract was due to expire, to a four-year deal. He signed Grigson to a three-year extension.

It remains to be seen if the Luck-led Colts are able to rival the Manning-led Colts. But his mere presence provides the franchise long-term stability at the most influential position.

On June 29, Jim Irsay signed Luck to the richest contract in NFL history. The five-year, $123 million extension keeps him under contract through the 2021 season and will pay him nearly $140 million. It included a record $87 million in guarantees.

"He deserves it," Irsay said. "Look at the total body of work."

Exhibit A: four seasons, three trips to the playoffs, an overall record of 38-23, 14,838 passing yards in 55 regular-season games along with 101 touchdowns and 55 interceptions.

Tony Dungy (the Colts coach who led them to victory in Super Bowl XLI) was the first African-American coach, along with Bears coach Lovie Smith, to become an African-American head coach in the Super Bowl.

"There's no question in our minds that he's going to return and do the things that he's done," Irsay said. "Look, he's been ahead of the curve, going back into the Peyton and Edgerrin James and Marvin Harrison and all those great players' era after four years.

"We hadn't won a playoff game and we hadn't done the things that we've done with Andrew. He is healthy. I've never seen him more motivated to have a great season in terms of taking care of himself and just working out.

"We're blessed to have him and he's very excited to be a Colt."

In a deal estimated at $122 million, Lucas Oil Products won the naming rights for 20 years to the stadium where the Colts play, hence the name, "Lucas Oil Stadium."

Lucas Oil Stadium. Josh Hallett from Winter Haven, FL, USA. This file is licensed under the Creative Commons Attribution-Share-Alike 2.0 Generic license.

In Memoriam
Those Lost Along The Way

By Rex Kirts

The bottom line of athletics is victory or defeat, win or lose. It is the essence of competition.

Seldom is tragedy an intruder in the games we play. Seldom does tragedy infringe on the act of having fun while enjoying the spirit of competition. But sometimes tragedy intervenes, and victory or defeat is eliminated from the equation. Then it's all about life and death.

In the history of sports in Indiana there have been notable occasions when tragedy became the big news, when people lost their lives doing what they loved.

The Indianapolis 500 auto race has lost numerous competitors and several crew members, track workers and spectators. Many of these came in the early days and up through the 1950s at "The Greatest Spectacle in Racing."

In 1903 the Purdue football team was involved in a train wreck in Indianapolis that took several lives.

Legendary Notre Dame football coach Knute Rockne died at age 43 in a plane crash in Kansas in 1931.

In 1977 a plane crash in Evansville wiped out the University of Evansville basketball team and others involved in the program.

Lawrence North High School senior basketball player John Stewart, a 7-foot Kentucky recruit, died of heart trouble in 1999 during a regional game at the Columbus North High School gym.

Purdue's football program suffered again in 1936 when a water heater in a shower room exploded, killing two players.

Two members of the Notre Dame women's swimming team were killed in a bus crash near the campus in South Bend in 1992. They were returning from a meet near Chicago.

The biggest problem, obviously, has been crashes of various sorts.

Seventy-three lives have been lost at the Indianapolis track during the race, qualifications and practice. In the race itself there have been 21 fatalities, 15 drivers and six riding mechanics.

The drivers who died in the race were Wilford Bourque (1909), Arthur Thurman and Louis LeCocq (1919), Bill Spence (1929), Mark Billman and Lester Spangler (1933), Clay Weatherby (1935), Floyd Roberts (1939), Shorty Cantion (1947), Carl Scarborough (1953), Bill Vukovich (1955), Pat O'Connor (1958), Eddie Sachs and Dave McDonald (1964) and Swede Savage (1973).

Bad crashes still occur at the 500 oval. But many improvements in the cars in recent years have made them safer as well as faster.

Riding mechanics were used in the race cars of the early 1900s. Those killed in the race were Claude Kellum and Harry Holcomb (1909), Sam Dickson (1911), Robert Bandini (1919), Paul Marshall (1930) and G.L. "Monk" Jordan (1933).

There have been seven killed at Indy during qualifications. Drivers were Herbert Jones (1926), Bill Denver (1933), Stubby Stubblefield (1935), Chuck Rodee (1966) and Gordon Smiley (1982). Bob Hurst (1933) and Leo Whitaker (1935) were riding mechanics.

Practice for the Indy 500 has claimed 21 drivers and five riding mechanics.

The drivers killed in practice were Tom Kincaid (1910), Harry Martin (1913), Albert Johnson (1915), Joe Caccia (1931), Milton Jones (1932), Peter Kreis (1934), Johnny Hannon (1935), George Bailey (1940), Ralph Hepburn (1948), Chet Miller (1953), Manuel Ayulo (1955), Keith Andrews (1957), Jerry Unser (1959), Bob Cortner (1959), Tony Bettenhausen (1961), Mike Spence (1968), Jim Malloy (1972), Art Pollard (1973), Jovy Marcelo (1992), Scott Brayton (1996) and Tony Renna (2003).

The five riding mechanics who died in practice accidents were Clarence Grove (1931), Harry Cox (1932), Bob Hahn (1934), Albert Opalko (1937) and Lawson Harris (1939).

In 1903 there was not yet an Old Oaken Bucket eagerly carted home by the winner of the Purdue-Indiana football game. There was already a rivalry, however, as the in-state schools had played 10 times, Purdue winning eight. The 1903 game was scheduled for Oct. 31 at a neutral site, Washington Park in Indianapolis. Purdue arranged for its team and about 1,500 fans to travel from West Lafayette on two trains.

In central Indianapolis, the Purdue train carrying the team collided with a coal train. Fourteen players, an assistant coach, a trainer and a fan were killed and about 30 others injured. The game and the rest of Purdue's season was canceled.

The Purdue assistant coach killed was Edward Robertson and the trainer Patrick McClaire. Purdue's players who died in the crash were Thomas Bailey, Joseph Coates, Gabriel Drollinger, Charles Furr, Charles Grube, Jay Hamilton, Walter Hamilton, Roswell Powell, Wilbert Price, Walter Roush, George Shaw, Samuel Squibb, Samuel Truitt and Harry Wright.

The fan who died was businessman Newton Howard.

Among the injured was head coach Oliver Cutts and player-manager Harry Leslie. Leslie later served as governor of Indiana from 1929-33.

Knute Rockne is probably the most famous football name in the history of Indiana and one of the most famous in the nation.

In 13 years as coach of the Irish in South Bend, Rockne had a record of 105-12-5. Included in this was five unbeaten seasons and three national championships (1924, 1929, 1930). His 1924 team, featuring the Four Horsemen backfield, was 10-0 and beat Stanford in the Rose Bowl.

Rockne's career and life ended during his prime, though, in the plane crash on March 31, 1931 near Bazaar, Kansas. The nation's all-time winningest coach when he died, Rockne was on his way to Los Angeles, California to help in the movie "The Spirit of Notre Dame," which was about him.

Rockne's death triggered a national outpouring of grief. King Haakon of Norway, Rockne's birthplace, knighted him posthumously. The crash spurred manufacturers to begin constructing safer planes.

In the college football Hall of Fame as a coach, Rockne played end at Notre Dame.

On Dec. 13, 1977, Indiana Air Flight took off from Dress Regional Airport, headed for Nashville, Tenn. The plane carried the Evansville basketball team, which was scheduled to play Middle Tennessee.

The plane crashed shortly after takeoff, at 7:22 p.m. There were no survivors among the 29 people on board the DC-3.

The crash was determined to be pilot error for failing to remove gust locks on the right aileron and the rudder before takeoff, as well as an overloaded baggage compartment. Aces players killed were seniors Kevin Kingston, John Washington and Marion "Tony" Winburn, juniors Stephen Miller and Bryan Taylor, sophomore Keith Moon and freshmen Warren Alston, Ray Comandella, Mike Duff, Kraig Heckendorn, Michael Joyner, Barney Lewis, Greg Smith and Mark Siegel. Also killed in the crash were student managers Jeff Bohnert and Mark Kniese, head coach Bobby Watson, UE business manager Bob Hudson, UE comptroller Charles Shike, sports information director Greg Knipping, radio announcer Marv Bates, pilot Ty Van Pham, co-pilot Gaston Ruiz, flight attendant Pam Smith, Air Indiana company owner Jim Stewart and company CEO Bill Hartford.

Player David Furr did not make the trip, but two weeks after the crash he and his brother were killed in an auto accident.

The Aces had been a national power under coach Arad McCutchan, who had won five national Division II championships. Watson was in his first year succeeding McCutchan. The Aces, in Division I for the first time, were 1-3 at the time of the crash.

Dick Walters succeeded Watson, and in four years the Aces went 23-6 and made the NCAA tourney.

With 3:58 left in the third quarter of the 1999 basketball game, John Stewart came to the sideline. In a dominating performance the 7-0, 275-pound big man had scored 22 of Lawrence North's 33 points and had 13 rebounds and two blocked shots. But he would forever score no more points or get any more rebounds. Stewart was hurried to the hospital by paramedics but died from a condition known as idiopathic hypertrophic cardiomyapathy. A heart problem.

Lawrence people at the gym thought Stewart had recovered after being taken away, so the game continued. It was the biggest matchup in the state, South being ranked No. 1 and Lawrence North No. 2. South won in overtime, 55-50.

One good thing came out of the tragedy. It gave publicity to a screening echocardiogram, a test that would have caught the congenital structural abnormality in Stewart.

The echocardiogram was in use by some schools then, but after Stewart's death more schools began using it.

The water heater incident involving the Purdue football team occurred on Sept. 12 in '36 at the Ross training facility 10 miles west of campus.

In those days gasoline was used to remove adhesive tape from the players' bodies, and some of the gas came into contact with the heater and ignited. Six players were severely burned, and ultimately two of them died. The two who died were Carl Dahlbeck and Tom McGannon.

On Jan. 24, 1992, Notre Dame suffered the loss of two women swimmers, Margaret Beeler and Colleen Hipp, in a bus crash four miles from campus. Rev. Edward Malloy, the university president, rushed home from a conference out of town to preside at a memorial mass.

The team bus crashed shortly after midnight during a snowstorm on the Indiana Toll Road. State police said the bus rolled over after hitting a patch of heavy snow. There were 35 others on board.

Editor's Note:
This book is dedicated to all that may have lost their life doing what they loved; participating in Indiana sports. You are not forgotten no matter how young or old, in route, or at practice or games. Your spirit is with us all.

#6

Bob Knight

By Bob Hammel

Photo courtesy of the Indiana Press Review.

Indiana basketball fans had no idea what was dawning when in late March of 1971, as UCLA was closing in on yet another national championship, the young coach at Army was announced as the new man at IU.

At Army?

The coach at never-in-the-NCAA-tournament Army?

Not Norm Sloan, the native Hoosier who was building bona fides as the coach at North Carolina State in basketball's big leagues at the ACC. Not Bobby Leonard, a darling from IU's own glory years around the 1953 NCAA championship who had built a colorful coaching resume with the pro Indiana Pacers. Not …

Bobby Knight?

From Hoosier arch-enemy Fred Taylor's IU-antithesis Ohio State program? Yes, he's won some games but … with guys who meet West Point's 6-6 maximum limit … playing slowball, scoring 50 to 60 points a game … and winning with … *defense?*

There was also advance word of this young coach's quick-to-heat temper. "Bobby T," a New York writer had called him, after a technical foul or two. He was to get his share of those as a Hoosier, too, expelled for two or more several times over the years — most notoriously after throwing a chair onto the court against Purdue in 1985. If he had been paid residuals for every time that scene has run on national TV, his net worth might be a digit wider.

But it was in what he was paid to do — coach basketball, in its purest, prettiest, winningest form, while following every NCAA rule and turning out All-Americans and high draft picks and enough college graduates to form a long parade — that the young Bob Knight of advance unfamiliarity in Bloomington delivered the grandest surprise.

Officially, the 30-year-old Knight (the Bobby bobtailed to Bob rather quickly in Bloomington) was replacing Lou Watson, heir to the Branch McCracken legacy in IU's coaching chair. But in a pragmatic assessment, it was Knight coming in and George McGinnis going out — after a one-season college playing career that in sheer production might be the best in IU's now 117 college basketball seasons. As a sophomore, the muscular 6-7 McGinnis — prototype of a basketball species never seen again until LeBron James came along a generation later — was the primary reason IU shed a stretch of four Big Ten cellar finishes in five years to finish third in 1970-71. And that one season (an IU-record 29.9 points a game, a Big Ten-leading 14.7 rebounds) was it for collegian McGinnis, who quite legitimately filed for hardship inclusion in the pro drafts and went to his hometown Pacers, and Leonard, and pro greatness.

Meanwhile, back in Bloomington …

Knight changed everything.

Maybe the most incongruous part of IU basketball's new look was the flashy, Globetrotter-like red-and-white candy-striped warm-up pants, introduced Knight's first

Robert Montgomery Knight was born in Massillon, Ohio on October 25, 1940.

season. They were on the first Hoosier team that came out to play the first game in expansive, expensive Assembly Hall, introducing something that close to half-a-century later is iconic. Striped pants and IU weren't, before Knight.

This, by a young coach who — except for his own eye-catching sport coats in those early years — labored at being almost Amish in his basketball, fundamental the byword. Where points once were a premium, the term "good shot" was introduced. The "Hurryin' Hoosiers" became the "Harryin' Hoosiers," devils to deal with at their defensive end and efficient-over-proficient at the other.

Even with the spectacular McGinnis delivering a show every night in a 17-7 season, the 1971-72 Hoosiers had averaged about 6,600 fans a game at their temporary "New Fieldhouse" home. Now, without McGinnis they were heading into a 17,000-seat arena. If there were administrative worries about filling enough seats not to be embarrassed, they were about to be eased.

Knight played basketball for Ohio State from 1959-1962 as a forward.

Oh, yes, there were early moans and screams in the new arena's stands. As the score read something like 52-47 and the Hoosiers were stalling out the final seconds in one of those early Knight games, the relative quiet of the night was penetrated by a mathematical comedian's shout:

"We want a hundred!"

But in his fourth game, after a 3-0 takeoff in baptizing Assembly Hall, the young coach's restyled team beat Adolph Rupp and Kentucky, 90-89, in double overtime on a December Saturday night at Freedom Hall in Louisville, and Knightball was over the hump in Bloomington. Assembly Hall became the toughest ticket in the Big Ten, its sidelines taking on a national TV identity for their unending sweep of red from floor level all the way up-up-up to the highest balcony seats.

And Knightball itself?

It wasn't *that* bad, even the holdover fans quickly conceded. That first new-era team, when freshmen were ineligible for varsity play so every player was a returnee from the Hurryin' days, did score at least in the 60s in all but two games and averaged over 73 in going 17-8 and, for the first time in school history, making the NIT.

When not coaching on-court, Knight and his young staff were recruiting: their focus regional, border-to-border throughout Indiana and outside only as far as neighboring Illinois and Ohio. Working those limited but lush fields that first full year Knight brought in a bonanza of talent:

from Ohio, forward Scott May, a two-time All-American and 1976 College Player of the Year;

from Illinois, guards Quinn Buckner, a two-time state champion in high school and perennial captain and winner at every level he played, and Jim Crews, starter as a freshman on a Final Four team and a brainy, savvy future coach, and from Indiana, guard Bobby Wilkerson, a 6-7 "Spiderman" who jumped center, led the team in assists as a senior, and guarded anyone – quick, small guard up to tall, rangy center, and forward Tom Abernethy, who rebounded and defended and passed and screened and, when he shot, scored.

That five, augmented a year later by the one still-needed piece, center Kent Benson, finished with a four-year record of 112-8 (exactly .900), four Big Ten championships (three outright), the only two 18-0 finishes in Big Ten history, two unbeaten regular seasons that kept them No. 1-ranked for more than 20 straight regular-season polls, and – in 1975-76 – major college men's basketball's last perfect season/national championship.

Knight's coaching hallmark was his defense, which he taught with an almost preaching effect at an annual clinic of his own and as the featured speaker at other clinics across the nation and around the globe. Man-to-man, half-court only, almost never a press, always alert to where the ball was, passing lanes cut off, firm rules dictating every position and every reaction, it became the standard for the way defense was taught in high schools and in college.

Almost unnoticed was the way his innovations restyled offense around the nation as well. The "we-want-a-hundred" wails in Bloomington gave way to a fast-paced "motion" game that Knight – with some spacing help from his close friend and coaching guru, Hall-of-Famer Pete Newell – drew up with movement diagrams on hundreds of 3x5 cards the summer of '73 in his Bloomington home. The intent was to make a disciplined offense as free-lance as possible, to make every defensive counter-move wrong. He didn't fully employ it until the latter part of the 1973-74 season, but once in and mastered, it revolutionized the game.

With it, the Indiana teams of reputedly methodical, defense-minded, shot-conservative Bob Knight led the Big Ten in scoring in the decades of the '70s, the '80s and the '90s. Forty times the horde at The Hall saw Knight's IU teams score 100 or more. Never did they see an opponent do it there.

And, above or below 100, Knight's teams were winning everything there was to win.

The Hoosiers followed the perfect season in 1975-76 with NCAA championships in 1981 and 1987. They won 11 Big Ten championships. Six different Knight teams were No. 1-ranked, a list that didn't include the '81 and '87 teams that never were No. 1 until the NCAA tournament was over.

It did include his last great team – the one in 1992-93 that had the national Player of the Year in Calbert Cheaney, who still, more than 20 years later, has the Big Ten career scoring record, and another all-time Hoosier great in high school superhero Damon Bailey. That one just missed joining the 18-0 Big Ten list, finishing 17-1 – the only loss in overtime at Ohio State a game after losing rebounding leader Alan Henderson to a knee injury.

Bobby Knight and Isiah Thomas during a game in 1980.
Photo courtesy of Indiana University archives.

Knight perfected and popularized the motion offense.

In addition to coaching the IU Hoosiers, Knight also coached for U.S. Military Academy and Texas Tech.

Bobby Knight and Dan Rather during an interview in 1980. Photo courtesy of Indiana University Archives.

That team was sill No. 1 when it lost to Kansas in the NCAA regional finals. The year before, the Cheaney-led Hoosiers made the Final Four and had defending champion Duke on the ropes before falling to foul trouble and the Blue Devils.

Those were two of many near-misses by strong teams that almost added to Knight and IU's NCAA championship banners. Primary among the others:

Knight's second team, in 1972-73, won a surprise Big Ten championship and kept going in NCAA tournament play to reach the Final Four. There, against prohibitive favorite UCLA and All-America center Bill Walton, the Hoosiers shocked the unbeaten Bruins by coming from 22 points down to get within 3, only to have their charge stymied by a late-game charge-blocking foul call that would have been Walton's fifth but instead went against Downing, who outscored Walton that day 26-14 but fouled out seconds after the controversial call in UCLA's ultimate 70-59 victory.

The '74-75 Hoosiers were No. 1 and 31-0 when, after All-American May broke his arm with a month left in the season, they lost 92-90 in the regional final to a Kentucky team it had trounced in regular-season play.

The '81 champions lost sophomore star Isiah Thomas to the NBA but figured to make another run with a 6-10 All-American center, Landon Turner, before a summertime auto accident left Turner paralyzed for life – and immortalized in Indiana lore for the inspiring way he turned his plight into a forum for leading the disabled.

In 2000, the year he was fired at Indiana, he was named the Big Ten's basketball Coach of the Century.

How long he would have gone at Indiana if university President Myles Brand had not fired him Sept. 10, 2000, for insubordination is open to guesswork, indeterminable. Clearly, he was planning another run or two. He had stockpiled an unusual collection of inside-outside 6-9-and-up talents – holdovers Kirk Haston and Jeff Newton and homegrown Indiana "Mr. Basketball" Jared Jeffries – plus two other big traditional post players, 6-10 George Leach and 6-8 Jarred Odle. His X's and O's had as many as four of them playing at one time, occasionally in an un-Knightlike 1-3-1 zone with the long-armed Leach out front against point guards. The guard corps around them was deep with shooters – Kyle Hornsby, Tom Coverdale, Dan Fife – and freshman A.J. Moye offered a different dimension. The group's strength wasn't illusory; with a totally different battle plan that capitalized on the guards' 3-point skills, the Hoosiers one year later played in the national championship game for Knight successor Mike Davis. It amounted to the last what-if from the Knight era, and a year or two beyond.

Photo courtesy of the Indiana Press Review.

During his coaching years, Knight was praised for running clean programs (none of his teams were ever sanctioned by the NCAA for recruiting violations.)

It was a 29-year run that rewrote IU and Big Ten records and – until the next perfect-record champion comes along – stands unmatched nationally.

After his firing, Knight was out of basketball for a year before taking over at Texas Tech. His first year there *Basketball Times* named him National Coach of the Year. His best of five Tech seasons was a Big Eight Tournament runnerup finish in 2005, when his team reached the Sweet 16.

And, at Texas Tech, on Jan. 1, 2007, his Red Raiders beat New Mexico, 70-68 – his 880th career coaching victory, giving him the NCAA major-college men's record. The next year, days after becoming the first coach to reach 900 career victories, he retired in late-season and turned the job over to son Patrick.

He won at least one major National Coach of the Year award in five different seasons – 1975, '76, '87, '89 and 2005. He retired with 902 victories, the only coach to win the amateur Grand Slam – the NCAA (1976, '81 and '87), the NIT (1979), the Pan American Games (1979) and Olympic Games (1984). When his NCAA career victories record fell, it was to his former West Point captain, Mike Krzyzewski of Duke.

Knight followed his coaching years with a long career as an ESPN analyst. He retired from that after the 2014-15 season.

In 1991, at 49 he became one of the youngest coaches to be inducted into the Naismith Basketball Hall of Fame. When the College Basketball Hall of Fame opened in Kansas City, he was a charter inductee. Knight and another charter inductee and close friend, Dean Smith, are the only men to both play on and coach NCAA championship teams – Knight as a player at Ohio State in 1960 before his three IU championships, Smith as a player at Kansas in 1952 before winning twice with his North Carolina teams.

#7 The Big "O"- Oscar Robertson

By Bob Hammel

Robertson was ranked as the 36th best American athlete of the 20th century by ESPN.

Oscar Robertson.
Photo courtesy of the Indiana Basketball Hall of Fame.

O as in Oscar

Looking back, it's inconceivable that until the night of March 3, 1951, outside its immediate environs not one ardent Indiana high school basketball fan in 100 had ever heard of Crispus Attucks or of the downtown Indianapolis high school named for him.

By the end of that decade, all Hoosierland danced to its theme song.

And then from the Indiana high school basketball skies the comet was gone, as quickly as it came.

But it will never be forgotten. Or eclipsed. Or its place in history lessened.

Or its brightest star ever dimmed.

Call that decade of the 1950s Hoosier basketball's Era of Oscar. The schoolboy sport that was Indiana's trademark was great before and great after, but never, ever greater than in that Attucks-dominated decade.

Oh, yes, in there was Milan. And Muncie Central, and South Bend Central, and some great though never-champion Terre Haute Gerstmeyer teams.

But the strongest thread that ran through those fabulous '50s was Crispus Attucks.

And of course he played in less than a third of it, but still Oscar Robertson towered over that Decade of Hoosier Decades.

There's no real parallel for the lasting effect one high school's basketball program had in enlightening a whole state, or one player had in setting a standard of excellence that discouraged even comparisons.

Oscar Robertson.

Indianapolis Crispus Attucks Flying Tigers.

Names and memories for Indiana high school basketball's ages.

There had been an Attucks High School in Indianapolis since the 1920s, but it was a school put together in hatred: to keep other public high schools in the city all-white or nearly so and confine all African Americans to one "separate-but-equal" – a term that took on its own deserved scorn in later generations – high school. As Gary grew, it built one, too, named Roosevelt; Evansville led everyone in irony, naming its segregated school Lincoln. And until 1943, those three – along with Catholic and a few other parochial, church-financed high schools – couldn't even play in the state's pride and joy, its open-to-everyone(?) boys' basketball tournament.

Even that didn't open all doors. Most public-school neighbors declined to schedule Attucks, or Roosevelt, or Lincoln, so they went to schools that would play them, sometimes out of state. This at a time when the national pastime, baseball, had its own racial barriers in place, and so did the United States army.

But Joe Louis was the heavyweight boxing champion of the world, and Jackie Robinson came along in baseball, and first Johnny Wilson, then Bill Garrett gave Indiana popular "Mr. Basketballs" who led first Anderson, then Shelbyville to state championships, and Garrett went on to end forever the vaunted Big Ten's "gentlemen's agreement" by enrolling at, then playing for, then starring for Indiana University – all that in the late 1940s.

And then there was that night of March 3, 1951, when all Indiana was attuned to what was going on at 16 regional sites around the state, and out of Indianapolis came a thunderbolt of a news flash: mighty Anderson, always a tournament favorite, had fallen – by the stunning score of 81-80. And the morning papers on Sunday told the story of how that had happened, and introduced to the state a basketball name it never was to forget: Robertson.

This was a sophomore, Bailey Robertson, who nailed a deep shot – didn't really swish it; the ball swirled within the rim, bounced off the backboard and banked in – just ahead of the buzzer and that shocking score forwarded on to the Indianapolis semistate the school with that unusual name: Crispus Attucks High School.

Now it had identity, and when it followed its first sectional championship and first regional championship by walloping Covington and Batesville it had its first trip to the Final Four. And that's when we all learned not what but who Crispus Attucks was, that as hard as the Ku Klux Klan had pushed to get a white name like Jefferson on their forced creation,

Oscar Palmer Robertson was born in Charlotte, Tennessee on November 24, 1938.

proud Indianapolis African Americans won out and got a black name on their reluctantly accepted segregated school: the name of Crispus Attucks, the first-generation son of a slave, whose mother was Native American – Crispus himself a career sailor who stepped up at Lexington-Concord and was the first American to die in the Boston Massacre that launched the Revolutionary War.

Attucks High School in 1951 had a great sophomore named Willie Gardner who scored 22 points and a scholarly center named Bob Jewell who took home the tournament's hallowed Trester Award, but the Tigers lost at the State that time to Evansville Reitz.

But the rocket was launched. All Indiana knew about Attucks, and Indianapolis – not overnight, but noticeably – was shamed into opening its own scheduling so a school in the state's biggest "neighborhood" didn't have to go on bus trips to Sheridan, Otterbein, Rensselaer, Hope, Pine Village, Rossville, Monrovia and New Winchester to fill out its schedule.

Attucks lost in the sectional in 1952 but didn't lose another one the rest of the decade. In 1953, it had the state's "Mr. Basketball" in Hallie Bryant.

And in 1955, it had Oscar.

Through the magic Milan year of 1954, Indianapolis – the whole city, with all its big schools – had never won a state championship. That ended in 1955 when Attucks, with junior Robertson scoring 30 points in the championship game, won it 97-74. The opponent in the game that seemed to propel the Hoosier game forward into another century was Gary Roosevelt, the nation's first all-black champion in an integrated state tournament winning out over one of the two other all-black schools in that state.

There were stars all over the court that night. Willie Merriweather, on his way to an all-Big Ten career at Purdue, had 21 points for Attucks. Wilson "Jake" Eison, the

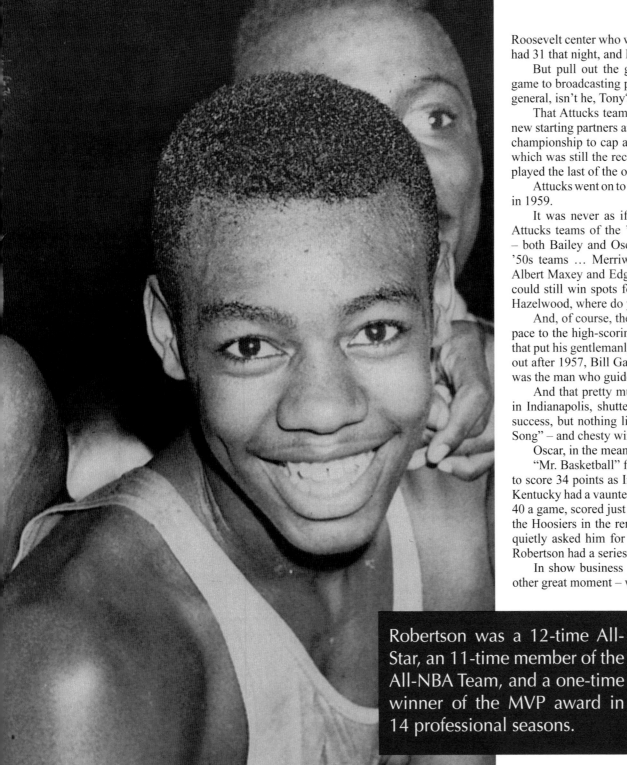

Roosevelt center who was the year's "Mr. Basketball" because only seniors could win it, had 31 that night, and Dick Barnett, later legendary with the New York Knicks, had 18.

But pull out the game film and hear broadcaster Tom Carnegie remark in late-game to broadcasting partner/Butler coach Tony Hinkle, "That Robertson is some floor general, isn't he, Tony?" Some indeed.

That Attucks team had lost just once all year. Back Oscar came in 1956 with four new starting partners and Attucks did what no one ever had done – won an Indiana state championship to cap an undefeated season. Oscar went out with 39 in that title game, which was still the record for a winning champion when more than 40 years later they played the last of the one-class open state high school tournaments.

Attucks went on to reach the finals again in 1957, and win its third State championship in 1959.

It was never as if Oscar didn't have talent around him. Ten players from those Attucks teams of the '50s are in the Indiana Basketball Hall of Fame at New Castle – both Bailey and Oscar Robertson … Jewell, Gardner and Bryant from those early '50s teams … Merriweather and Bill Scott have rings from the '55 championship, Albert Maxey and Edgar Searcy from '56, and Larry McIntyre from '59. Strong cases could still win spots for more – LaVern Benson, Stan Patton, Bobby Edmonds, Jerry Hazelwood, where do you stop?

And, of course, the coaches: starting with Ray Crowe, the man who stepped up the pace to the high-scoring teams that won the championship but maintained a discipline that put his gentlemanly stamp on the entire, remarkable program. When Crowe stepped out after 1957, Bill Garrett, the barrier-breaker from Shelbyville and IU, moved in. He was the man who guided the '59 Tigers to their title.

And that pretty much was it. For a long while, there was no Attucks High School in Indianapolis, shuttered for cost reasons. It has reopened and had some basketball success, but nothing like the '50s when all the state knew the school's jaunty "Crazy Song" – and chesty windup: You can beat everybody … but you can't beat us!

Oscar, in the meantime, by 1960 was just getting started.

"Mr. Basketball" for 1956 came to him in a shoo-in vote. He wore the No. 1 jersey to score 34 points as Indiana crunched the Kentucky All-Stars at Indianapolis in June. Kentucky had a vaunted star of its own, "King Kelly" Coleman, who had averaged about 40 a game, scored just 16 in the first game, but vowed to get revenge against Oscar and the Hoosiers in the rematch at Louisville. Coach Angus Nicoson said later Robertson quietly asked him for the defensive assignment against Coleman. That second night, Robertson had a series-record 41 points, Coleman 4.

In show business parlance, all of that – state championships, All-Stars and every other great moment – was just a sneak preview.

What Indiana had learned, the basketball world was about to.

Oscar Robertson had no peers.

The numbers numb, the honors crowd each other for attention, but settle for one:

In the year 2000, the National Association of Basketball Coaches, 26 years after he played his last game, named him Player of the Century.

Oscar Robertson.
Photo courtesy of the Indiana Basketball Hall of Fame.

Robertson was a 12-time All-Star, an 11-time member of the All-NBA Team, and a one-time winner of the MVP award in 14 professional seasons.

By then they had seen Bill Russell and Wilt Chamberlain, Kareem Abdul Jabbar and Michael Jordan, Jerry West and Elgin Baylor, Magic Johnson and Larry Bird – they had seen them all.

And they gave No. 1 to the kid from Crispus Attucks. The Big O.

He said in a bylined New York Times story in 2008 that he "had always hoped to play for Indiana University" but racial attitudes redirected him to the University of Cincinnati. As a sophomore, he was leading the nation with a 30-point average for a team ranked in the Top 3 nationally but a pretty much unproved hotshot from the hinterlands when he and Cincinnati played in Madison Square Garden for his first time. He scored a Garden-record 56 points and was never doubted again. In his three college seasons, he was three-time national scoring champion, three-time All-American, three-time College Player of the Year. His college scoring averages were 35.1, 32.6 and 33.7, and at 6-5 he averaged 15 rebounds a game for his college career. The Bearcats went 79-9 his three years.

He spent the summer of 1960 winning the Olympic gold medal with the greatest amateur team ever, then took on the NBA as no one ever has done – before or since.

Much is made that in his second pro season, he averaged a triple double – 30.8 points, 12.5 rebounds, 11.4 assists per game. And much should be made of that; no one else has come close.

But look closer. After five years, his career averages were 30.1, 10.4, 10.6 – a five-year NBA triple-double.

He won every individual award the league could give, but its biggest prize kept eluding him. Finally, in 1971 at age 32, a trade united him with young Abdul-Jabbar at Milwaukee and he won an NBA championship ring.

He is the only Hoosier ever to be "Mr. Basketball" on a state champion and add an Olympic and NBA title. He just missed adding a fourth item; twice he led Cincinnati to the NCAA Final Four but the Bearcats lost out to California and his Olympic coach, Pete Newell, both times.

And sure he's in the Hall of Fame – every basketball Hall of Fame, including of course Indiana's. The United States Basketball Writers Association gave him its Player of the Year award twice and later named the annual award for him. The University of Cincinnati, the Milwaukee Bucks, the Sacramento Kings (where the Cincinnati Royals wound up) all retired his number – three different numbers: 12 with the Cincinnati Bearcats, 1 with the Bucks, 14 with the Kings. And surely no one dares wear 43 at Attucks.

The Big O.

Oscar.

In Indiana basketball, certainly not a story untold.

But, untopped.

Oscar Robertson and Ray Crowe. Photo courtesy of the Indiana Basketball Hall of Fame.

The United States Basketball Writers Association renamed their College Player of the Year Award the Oscar Robertson Trophy in his honor in 1998.

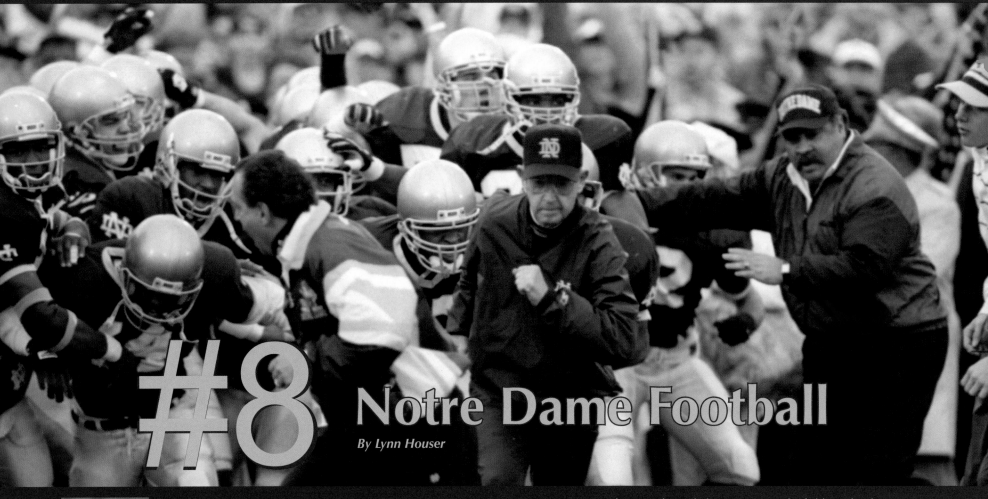

#8 Notre Dame Football

By Lynn Houser

Coach Lou Holtz and players run onto the field vs. Florida State in 1993.
Photo courtesy of the Notre Dame Archives.

Lynn Houser is a native of Fort Wayne, a graduate of Indiana University and a U.S. Navy veteran. He began his writing career in 1976 for the Kendallville News-Sun. In 1984 he began writing for the Bloomington Herald-Times. His 28 years in Bloomington included IU's 1987 NCAA championship, IU's 2002 Final Four run and the 2007 Super Bowl between the Colts and Bears. Houser was elected to the Indiana Sportswriters and Sportscasters Association Hall of Fame in 2010. He is now retired and living in Florida with his wife, Patricia.

Notre Dame: The Home of Legends

When trying to discuss the phenomenon that is Notre Dame football, where do you begin?

With Knute Rockne? Hollywood made a movie about him.

The Gipper? Featured in that same movie and played by a future president, Ronald Reagan.

The Four Horsemen? Immortalized by Grantland Rice.

Frank Leahy? All he did was coach the Irish to six undefeated seasons and four national championships.

How about 11 national championships altogether, second only to Alabama?

How about seven Heisman Trophy winners, more than any other school?

How about those golden helmets, fashioned after the Golden Dome, the iconic landmark?

And, for the love of Touchdown Jesus, who else has its own television network?

It feels like an absurdity to even attempt to describe Notre Dame football, but we are going to give it the old college try.

A good starting point is to go directly to a couple of living Notre Dame legends, Ara Parseghian and Lou Holtz. Parseghian coached the Irish to two national championships in his 11-year coaching career from 1964-74. Holtz also coached the Irish for 11 seasons, 1986-96, and guided them to their last national championship in 1988.

Holtz still talks about the "spirit" of Notre Dame.

"You can't explain it, but there's a spirit there," he says. "If you open up your heart to that spirit, it will reach you."

Parseghian felt it the day he took the job in 1964.

"When I first drove up Notre Dame Avenue, I felt a surge go up my back," he says. "All of a sudden I realized I was responsible for what happened to the football program, a huge tradition to uphold."

Notre Dame first caught the nation's attention in 1913, when it stunned mighty Army, 35-13, thanks to a newly discovered passing game featuring quarterback Charles "Gus" Dorais and a receiver named Knute Rockne.

If that didn't introduce the little school from South Bend to the world, Grantland Rice did. Following Notre Dame's 13-7 win over Army in 1924, Rice delivered a rhetorical lead for the ages:

"Outlined against a blue-gray October sky, the Four Horsemen rode again. In dramatic lore they are known as Famine, Pestilence, Destruction and Death. These are only aliases. Their real names are Stuhldreher, Miller, Crowley and Layden. They formed the crest of the South Bend cyclone before which another fighting Army football team was swept over the precipice at the Polo Grounds ... A cyclone can't be snared. It may be surrounded, but somewhere it breaks through to keep on going. When the cyclone starts from South Bend, where the candle lights still gleam through the Indiana sycamores, those in the way must take to storm cellars at top speed ..."

There are Irish fans out there who can recite the entire story word for word.

Knute Rockne at practice with players, c.1920s. Photo courtesy of the Notre Dame Archives.

Notre Dame is one of three schools that compete as an Independent at the National Collegiate Athletic Association (NCAA) Football Bowl Subdivision level, however they play five games a year against opponents from the Atlantic Coast Conference.

Notre Dame is the only individual school to have its own national television contract, with all of its home games televised on NBC since 1991.

GAME DAY AT NOTRE DAME

Notre Dame is known for its game day traditions. No visit is complete without the following stops:

The Grotto: Behind the Basilica of the Sacred Heart is Our Lady of Lourdes Grotto, fashioned after the famous grotto in Lourdes, France, where it is said the Blessed Mother Mary visited St. Bernadette 18 times in the 1800s. At Notre Dame, you will find visitors there at all hours, lighting candles and offering prayers. The Rosary is said daily at 6:45 p.m., rain or shine (and especially if the Irish are trailing at halftime).

The Golden Dome: The iconic landmark at the top of the Administration Building is painted a brilliant gold to reflect the gold helmets the Irish wear. Looks good on your Facebook page with you standing in front.

The Band of Fighting Irish/Irish Guard: The Notre Dame Band of Fighting Irish performs a free concert on the steps of Bond Hall, with the grand finale always being the "greatest of all victory marches," the Notre Dame Victory March. Around the corner, you might catch the Irish Guard going through their pre-game inspection. Tradition has it that the most impeccably dressed guardsmen gets to lead the band into the stadium with cheerleaders and Leprechaun in tow. As the band marches across campus to its destination, fans fall in by the hundreds. Hundreds more already are in the stadium, having made "The Walk" through campus with the football team. By kickoff, all seats are filled.

Patriotic pieces: Make sure you are in your seat for "America the Beautiful," followed by the "National Anthem," as the Irish Guard raise the Stars and Stripes. It is often accompanied by a flyover of some kind. Nobody does it better.

"Here Come the Irish:" The standing-only, loud reception as the team comes charging out of the north tunnel. Game on!

Mid-game: When the band cranks up the 1812 Overture, the students chop their arms in unison. Perfectly acceptable for alums and visitors, too.

Post-game: Stick around as the players gather in front of the student section, raise their helmets and sing "Alma Mater, Notre Dame." Then it's the Irish Clog high-stepping to "Hike, Notre Dame," usually a victory

Famed Notre Dame Stadium in October, 1999. Photo courtesy of the Notre Dame Archives.

"If you are a part of Notre Dame, no explanation is necessary," Holtz says. "You have to look at the mystique of Notre Dame, which goes back to the days of Knute Rockne, Gus Dorais and the forward pass on the shores of Lake Erie. I remember watching Notre Dame highlights on Sunday mornings, with Lindsey Nelson saying, "Moving on to further action ..."

With its national appeal, Notre Dame was made for television. Is it any surprise that one day a network would partner up? That's what NBC did in 1991, when it purchased the rights to Notre Dame home games. Talk about a long-running show: NBC is celebrating a quarter century of Notre Dame football this season and is on board for another nine years, through 2025.

At a lot of schools, such exposure might hurt home attendance, but not Notre Dame, which boasts 249 consecutive sellouts. In fact, it is not uncommon for Notre Dame fans to show up with no tickets in hand, just to enjoy the atmosphere.

As Holtz notes, "How many come in a mobile home, park there, go to the luncheon, the pep rally – everything – then go back into their mobile home to watch the game because they don't have tickets? They just want to be a part of the atmosphere, to visit the Golden Dome, the Grotto (to the Blessed Mother) and Touchdown Jesus (the large mural on the library facade north of the stadium)."

"You must spend a weekend at a Notre Dame home game and enjoy all the activities," Parseghian says. "It should be on your bucket list. I thought I knew all about Notre Dame when I came here, but the thing that struck me is the universal interest. It wasn't just a small school in a little town called South Bend. It was recognized by the world."

Proof of Notre Dame's international appeal is its "Global Gateways" program, with academic hubs in London, Dublin, Rome, Jerusalem and Beijing. The university is just as proud of its academic excellence as it is of its football success. For nine consecutive years, the Notre Dame athletic program has boasted the nation's top graduation rate. The football team's most recent graduation rate was 93 percent, good for fifth, trailing only Stanford, Northwestern, Rice and Duke.

"Notre Dame has done all this without sacrificing its commitment to academic excellence," Holtz says. "They want to set the standard for everybody else."

While those standards make it difficult to keep up with powerhouses having lower academic requirements, it is the expectations that make coaching at Notre Dame such a weighty proposition, Parseghian says. He stepped down at the height of his success because the job became too burdensome.

"At Notre Dame you become a victim of your own success," he says. "You don't dare go 8-2 when there are expectations of winning a national championship. I remember telling Lou Holtz, 'You'll find a lot of demands from that chair as head coach. If you are conscientious, it is hard to say 'no' when so many people are looking for a 'yes.' The need to accommodate all those people becomes grinding. And, if you go undefeated, the best you can do is repeat, and that's very difficult. You can't do any better."

"Boy, was Ara ever right," Holtz says. "Once you win a national championship, they expect you to be perfect."

Despite those challenges, both Holtz and Parseghian are Notre Dame men for life. Parseghian, now 93, still lives in South Bend and serves as the chairman for the Ara Parseghian Medical Research Foundation, an organization founded in 1994 to find a cure for Niemann-Pick Type C, a neurodegenerative disorder that affected three of his grandchildren. The organization has raised almost $45 million toward that goal.

"It is certainly my biggest challenge," Parseghian says. "National championships pale in comparison."

The Fighting Irish hold the highest winning percentage among college football programs, and have 13 national championships recognized by the NCAA.

Ara Parseghian.
Photo courtesy of the Notre Dame Archives.

Holtz, 79, retired as an ESPN commentator in 2015 but can still be heard on radio from his home in Orlando, Fla. Although he also had successful coaching stops at Arkansas, Minnesota and South Carolina, Notre Dame holds a special place in his heart.

"I have been to a lot of great schools and loved every one, but Notre Dame ... Three of my children graduated from Notre Dame ... my wife and I will be buried there. The religious atmosphere, the campus, the loyalty the students have – there is something magical about it."

NOTRE DAME'S WINNINGEST COACHES
(Ranked by winning percentage)

	W-L-T	Pct.	Titles
Knute Rockne, 1918-30	105-12-5	.881	3
Frank Leahy, 1941-43/1946-53	87-11-9	.855	4
Ara Parseghian, 1964-74	85-17-2	.836	2
Lou Holtz, 1986-96	100-30-2	.765	1

PERSONAL FAVORITES: PARSEGHIAN, HOLTZ

It is hard for any successful coach to single out a favorite moment, but here are a couple that came to mind quickly for Ara Parseghian and Lou Holtz.

Ara Parseghian: "Catholics vs. Baptists," Dec. 31, 1973. In a battle of unbeatens, No. 3 Notre Dame went deep into the heart of Dixie to take on No. 1 Alabama. After six lead-changes, the Irish were clinging to a 24-23 lead and facing 3rd-and-9 from their own three in the final minute. In one of Parseghian's boldest calls, the Irish went to the air, with quarterback Tom Clements completing a 35-yard pass to reserve tight end Robin Weber for the first down that allowed them to run out the clock. The next day they were voted national champions.

Pareseghian: "It was the first time Notre Dame had ever faced Alabama, and they were calling it 'Catholics vs. Baptists.' It was also the first time I had ever coached against Bear Bryant. Both teams were unbeaten, and the fact we won it in a dramatic way in the fourth quarter is a fond remembrance."

Lou Holtz: "Catholics vs. Convicts," Oct. 15, 1988. The Miami Hurricanes, college football's Bad Boys, stormed into South Bend with a 36-game regular season win streak. The Irish never trailed but had to foil a two-point conversion attempt by the Hurricanes in the final seconds to escape with a 31-30 victory. The Irish never looked back after that, surging to a perfect season and national title.

A record seven Notre Dame players have won the Heisman Trophy, and the program has produced 97 consensus All-Americans.

Players about to run on the field against USC in 1993. Photo courtesy of the Notre Dame Archives.

Holtz: "I think back to the team Mass before the game. I told every young man I recruited that 'You don't have to participate in the Mass, but you will go to it and respect it.' At this Mass, when they called for sharing the 'Sign of Peace,' the players and coaches hugged each other for 20 minutes. I had never seen anything like it. It was such a spirit of togetherness. In the interview after the game I said, 'The spirit of Notre Dame won this game,' and I truly believed it."

GAMES OF THE CENTURY (And more)

No team has been involved in more "Games of the Century" than Notre Dame, five to be precise:

1935: Notre Dame-Ohio State: Irish rally for 18 points in final minutes to overtake Buckeyes, 18-13.

1946: Notre Dame-Army: Irish and Cadets play to 0-0 tie in Yankee Stadium.

1966: Notre Dame-Michigan State: Another tie among unbeatens, 10-10.

1988: Notre Dame-Miami: Irish hang on to win "Catholics vs. Convicts" battle, 31-30.

1993: Notre Dame-Florida State: Irish win late-season battle of No. 1 vs. No. 2, 31-24.

And then there were these historic contests:

1957: Notre Dame 7, Oklahoma 0: Irish end Sooners' 47-game win streak.

1970: Texas 21, Notre Dame 17: In the Cotton Bowl, the Longhorns spoil ND's first bowl game since 1925.

1971: Notre Dame 24, Texas 11; Irish return to Cotton Bowl to end Longhorns' 30-game win streak.

1973: Notre Dame 24, Alabama 23: In the Sugar Bowl, Ara Parseghian's Irish beat Bear Bryant's Crimson Tide in a showdown for national championship.

1977: Notre Dame 49, Southern Cal 19: Notre Dame comes out in green jerseys for the first time in 14 years and blasts the Trojans.

1978: Notre Dame 38, Texas 10: A Cotton Bowl win so dominating the Irish vault from fifth in polls to claim national championship.

1979: Notre Dame 35, Houston 34: in the worst ice storm in 30 years, Irish rally from 22-point deficit to win Cotton Bowl on game's final play, a TD pass from Joe Montana to Kris Haines.

Notre Dame has one of the most financially valuable football programs in the country, allowing them to remain independent of a conference.

#9 Peyton Manning

By Zak Keefer

Zak Keefer, an Indiana native, has written for The Indianapolis Star since 2011. He currently covers the Indianapolis Colts and also serves as a sports enterprise writer. His work has been honored by The Best American Sports Writing, the Associated Press Sports Editors and The U.S. Basketball Writers Association.

A franchise's fate, a city's future, the eventual landing spot for the 22-year-old once-in-a-generation prodigy who'll transform a state's sporting conscious, all resting on the right arms of two forgettable quarterbacks playing in two forgettable football games a thousand miles apart.

Then and now, Kelly Holcomb and Jake Plummer share no conceivable thread save the moribund football teams they led onto the field on Dec. 21, 1997, and the ripples of that fateful afternoon, ripples that are still felt two decades later.

★★★★

Holcomb was first up. He was summoned into a game against the Minnesota Vikings in the second quarter, called upon in relief of the Indianapolis Colts' bruised and battered starter, Jim Harbaugh. It went awry. Quickly.

In what must be some sort of record, Holcomb coughed up the football five times in just 15 snaps — three interceptions and two fumbles. The Colts lost 39-28. Their season was over. Their record was 3-13. "This one's on me," Holcomb grumbled after the loss. "Holcomb Provides Nails for Coffin," blared the headline in the following day's *Indianapolis Star*.

Yet in many ways that Sunday was the Colts' 1997 season — if that team was anything, it was a fantastic loser. They fought; they made you believe; they blew it. Rinse and repeat, Sunday after Sunday. No one knew it at the time, but that day, Dec. 21, 1997, Kelly Holcomb and his five turnovers secured the most important loss in the Colts' 64 years of existence.

Then Plummer lent a helping hand. Later that afternoon, the rookie gunslinger rallied his Arizona Cardinals from 12 down in the fourth quarter to a 29-26 win over the Atlanta Falcons. It clinched the Cards' fourth win of the season. No matter, right? Wrong.

Plummer's heroics left Indianapolis as the league's only three-win team. The order for the following spring's NFL Draft was thus decided. The Colts would pick first. The mockery ensued. "The Colts have already found their team MVP for 1998: Jake Plummer," quipped the lead of a story in the following day's *Star*.

From there the dominoes fell. The Colts and their new team president, Bill Polian, wrestled with the decision for months before finally landing on Tennessee's Peyton Manning.

Thing was: No one saw Manning as a once-in-a-generation prodigy. Certainly not then. Polian, one of the greatest talent evaluators in football history, envisioned Manning as the next Bernie Kosar and little more. "Can you live with Bernie Kosar?" he shouted at his boss, team owner Jim Irsay, while slamming his fists on Irsay's desk in the tense days leading up to the draft.

Irsay could. Manning was the pick and the future.

The San Diego Chargers mortgaged their future on the tantalizing talent of Washington State's Ryan Leaf, unloading three draft picks and a Pro Bowl running back to Arizona in exchange for the second pick. Aided by the benefit of hindsight, we now know this: Never in NFL history has a draft-day decision made one team look so brilliant and another so foolish.

Peyton Manning attended Isidore Newman High School in New Orleans, and led its football team to a 34–5 record during his three seasons as starter.

Manning was among the most sought after high school players in the country and was recruited by about 60 colleges.

Manning lasted 18 seasons and redefined the position. Leaf washed out in San Diego after three years. "I always joke," Polian says now, "that if I'd have taken Ryan first, I'd be parking cars at Lucas Oil Stadium right now."

What Polian forgets to mention: If he'd passed on Manning, there wouldn't be a Lucas Oil Stadium.

To think: Two forgettable quarterbacks, two forgettable football games, one serendipitous December afternoon camouflaged in an otherwise lost season that would come to transform a city, a state, a franchise, a league.

What if Holcomb had rallied the Colts to victory that afternoon?

What if Plummer and the Cardinals had come up short?

What if the Colts had to settle for the second pick, took Leaf and watched him implode?

What if the dominoes hadn't fallen the way they fell?

But they did. The Colts owned the first pick. And Manning, being the control freak he is, wanted to make certain they didn't blow it. He sat during lunch with Irsay at the swanky Surf Club restaurant in Miami a month before the draft, looked the owner straight in the eyes and said this: "You know, Mr. Irsay, I'll win for you."

Irsay would admit years later those eight words sent shivers down his spine.

But that didn't decide it. Sitting in Polian's office in the days before the draft, Manning grew irritated that Polian refused to spill if he was going first or second. So Manning got up to leave, only to turn around at the last moment.

"If you draft me, I promise we'll win a championship," he said. "If you don't, I promise to come back and kick your ass."

Polian was left speechless.

Fate. Kelly Holcomb coughs up the football five times on Dec. 21, 1997.

Fate. Jake Plummer rallies the Cardinals to a fourth-quarter win later that afternoon.

Fate. Peyton Manning lands in Indianapolis. Throws 114 touchdowns to Marvin Harrison. Meshes with Edgerrin James. Hits Marcus Pollard and Reggie Wayne and Dallas Clark over the middle. Again. And again. And Again.

Engineers the biggest one-year turnaround in NFL history, lifting the Colts from 3-13 his rookie season to 13-3 a year later. Makes the RCA Dome roar so much it shakes.

Wins.

Argues with Jeff Saturday and Tarik Glenn on the sideline. Zings one over the middle to Brandon Stokley for touchdown No. 49. Slumps on the bench, head down and heart racing, praying for one … last … stop … in the gut- wrenching final moments of the biggest game of his life — the 2006 AFC Championship. Gets up and smiles ear-to-ear when his defense delivers.

Hoists the Lombardi Trophy in the rain in Miami two weeks later, proud as hell of what his team accomplished – proud, too, because he knows he shut up the "Peyton Manning Can't Win The Big One" chorus once and for all.

Wins.

Wins some more.

Shows Indianapolis how to fall in love with football. Begs them to keep quiet while he's changing the play at the line of scrimmage. Silences the Colts-to-Los Angeles rumors. Inspires hundreds of football fans in the Hoosier state to name their newborn boy or girl "Peyton." Never shows up on the police blotter. Never runs from the pressure. Never hides from his shortcomings. Never takes the game for granted. Lends his name, his time and his money to a local children's hospital.

Cries the day it ends. Retires on top in 2016 with a statue on the way, one that'll stand right outside the $720-million football palace that wouldn't exist without him.

The day Peyton Manning was drafted, he spent the flight to Indianapolis memorizing the names of everyone who worked in the Colts' front office. He learned his first pro offense inside a hotel room at the now-defunct Signature Inn off 38th Street, where he spent three days waiting for NFL rules to allow him to join his teammates at minicamp.

He came in on his off days as a rookie to throw out-routes to an equipment manager. He used to call the front desk of the team facility just so he'd get put on hold and get to listen to radio highlights from the previous season.

If there was ever a football nerd, it was Peyton Williams Manning.

He was different from the start, the wunderkind quarterback armed with a veteran's mind but blessed with a rookie's body. Even a young Peyton Manning never felt all that young. He missed the first few days of training camp his rookie year while he and his agent negotiated a $48-million contract.

Meanwhile Holcomb, still on the roster, ran the offense. One afternoon he forgot the play and ran straight into Pro Bowl running back Marshall Faulk. "Get that rookie quarterback in here!" Faulk barked.

Manning arrived shortly thereafter. Ten minutes into his first practice everyone on the field realized he had the entire playbook memorized. Watching from the sideline, offensive coordinator Tom Moore turned to Holcomb. "You come over here and stand by me now," Moore told him.

Manning missed one snap over the next 13 years. His backups couldn't even get a snap in practice.

Not long after the ink dried, Manning was asked by a reporter what he planned on doing with all that money. Buy a new house? A fancy car? The rookie millionaire didn't hesitate. "Earn it," Manning deadpanned.

So he did.

That he lived alone in a nondescript two-bedroom apartment his first few years in Indianapolis was by design: Manning wanted nothing to go home to. He spent his days and nights at the Colts' West 56th Street facility, poring over film, trying to win his eternal chess match against the defense.

He'd stay until 10 p.m. most nights during the season, sometimes falling asleep with the remote in hand. His teammates saw it early. "Oh, shit!" Marvin Harrison shouted the first time he saw Manning practice. "He wants to be good!"

Photo courtesy of the Indianapolis Colts.

In those early years, he'd volunteer to help out on special teams coverage during practice, figuring he needed the extra conditioning. He refused a separate workout in the weight room simply because he was a quarterback. If a defensive back danced after breaking up one of his passes, Manning went right after him the next play.

His very first throw in a Colts' uniform, during a preseason game in August 1998? A slant to Harrison that ended as a 48-yard touchdown. "This NFL's easy," he told himself as he ran down the field, celebrating. He just never treated it like it was.

The MVPs piled up. The first one in 2003. Another in 2004. Another in 2008. Another in 2009. Another in 2013.

Manning worked like he was a scout team quarterback trying to make the 53-man roster. He'd regularly call the team's video coordinators at 9:30 p.m. on weeknights. "Hey, do we have a copy of that Tampa game from five years ago against the Cowboys?" He'd force the team's weight coach, Rich Howell, to come early and stay late so he could get in extra snaps. They did it so often Howell developed carpel tunnel syndrome and nearly needed surgery.

"You play the game," says Edgerrin James, "but you've never seen someone that gave their all to the game until you've met Peyton Manning."

He lost the big ones. He won the big ones. He grew from prodigy to Pro Bowler to first-ballot Hall of Famer. He became one of the most dependable athletes in history. He made the ridiculous the routine.

In the 14 years before he arrived, the Colts made the playoffs just three times; in the 13 seasons he suited up, they missed it only twice. They became one of the league's most consistent winners. They became world champions.

The cocky college quarterback who arrived 18 years ago with that awww-shucks smile and slow-roasted Louisiana drawl, the kid bursting with ambition and the work ethic to match? He changed everything.

★★★★

Not bad for a guy Bill Polian tagged as the next Bernie Kosar.

"The word GOAT (greatest of all time) got popular real quick," offers Cardinals coach Bruce Arians, who spent 1998 as Manning's first position coach in the NFL. "To me, he is. I think he's arguably the best that's ever played."

The man who picked him first in the draft? Bill Polian is in the Hall of Fame. The receiver who caught more passes from him than anyone else? Marvin Harrison is in the Hall of Fame. His coach for the bulk of his time in Indianapolis? You guessed it. Tony Dungy is in the Hall of Fame. Above all, Manning did what every quarterback is asked to do — he made those around him better.

He forever altered the way the position is played, prepared for and perceived. "You inspired me to work hard. To be disciplined. To take notes," Seattle's Russell Wilson has said of Manning.

There aren't many players in NFL history of which this can be stated, but Manning is one of them: He changed the way the game is played. The NFL he entered as a rookie in 1998 — a league that still included John Elway, Dan Marino and Troy Aikman and was largely dominated by run-first offensive schemes — is now a relic of the past.

Manning was the first quarterback to perfect the no-huddle offense; now it's everywhere. He ignited an offensive explosion; now teams are throwing the football — and scoring — more than ever.

He leaves with the most passing yards and passing touchdowns in league history. As the only quarterback to win 200 games. And as the only to win two Super Bowls with two different franchises.

Photo courtesy of the Indianapolis Colts.

Manning chose to play college football for the University of Tennessee, leading the Volunteers to the 1997 SEC Championship in his senior season.

Manning completed his degree in three years, a Bachelor of Arts in speech communication.

No. 18 was never just one of 53. He was the quarterback all others were measured against. And he will be for a long time.

Yet Manning's largest footprint remains on the city where he spent the first 14 seasons of his career. Just as the NFL was a different place in 1998, so was Indianapolis.

The city formerly mocked as "Naptown" was largely ambivalent toward its professional football franchise, one that migrated west from Baltimore on a snowy March night in 1984. Who could blame them?

Save a miracle run to the 1995 AFC Championship Game, the Colts stunk. They were a loser, a laughingstock, so perpetually lousy that fans regularly turned down free tickets. Go see the Colts lose? No thanks. I've got better things to do.

Five winning seasons in 14 years. One AFC East title. Three playoff appearances. In the city's sporting conscious, the Colts sat somewhere near the bottom, buried beneath the NBA's Pacers, the Indianapolis 500, their beloved high school hoops, Indiana University basketball and Purdue University basketball. No more. Winning changed all that. Manning changed all that.

Eleven trips to the playoffs changed that. He led them to an NFL-record seven straight 12-win seasons, to two Super Bowls and one world championship. Nothing has been the same since.

"It was basketball, basketball, basketball, and it was car racing, car racing, car racing," Manning says now. "Football was probably in that third priority. That's simply no longer the case. This is a football town, and it's as good a football town as any."

His mark is indelible and immeasurable, felt in the bustling metropolis Indianapolis has become. A city's urban awakening was sparked by sports, and no athlete played a larger role. Blue jerseys started popping up everywhere. Rivalries *(see: the New England Patriots)* blossomed. Ratings soared. Ticket prices skyrocketed.

Civic pride swelled. Downtown boomed. Restaurants opened. Bars opened. Hotels opened. Peyton Manning's Children's Hospital opened. It employs 50 pediatric specialists and treats thousands of patients every year.

Lucas Oil Stadium opened. And in its first eight years of existence, the world-class venue has hosted a Super Bowl and two NCAA Final Fours. It remains a fitting memorial to one man's influence, The House That Manning Built.

Slowly and steadily, a basketball state, and car racing state, became a football state. In Indianapolis these days, the Colts are king, easily the hottest ticket in town. It started with one draft pick, with a lunch at the Surf Club in Miami, with a promise of a championship. Manning kept his word.

"I can't say enough for what he has meant to this franchise, to this city and state," Irsay said the day he announced no Colt will ever again wear Manning's iconic No. 18. "You just simply run out of words thinking about how much he means to us."

The statue is coming in the fall of 2017, just outside the stadium that wouldn't exist without Peyton Manning. It will serve as a fitting tribute to the greatest athlete Indianapolis has ever seen, and may ever see. The player who saved a franchise, transformed a city, and showed Indianapolis what winning football looks like.

And to think: Without Kelly Holcomb, Jake Plummer and the afternoon of Dec. 21, 1997, it might never have happened.

From 1998 to 2010, Manning improved the fortunes of the struggling Colts franchise, leading them to several division and AFC championships, and one Super Bowl, the franchise's first since 1971.

#10

Larry Bird –
"The Hick from French Lick"

By Dave Krider

Dave Krider is a life-long Hoosier, raised in Elkhart and has spent most of his adult life in La Porte. When he was 11 years old he accepted Jesus Christ as his Lord and Savior and his life has been one gigantic blessing ever since. A high school sportswriter for 55 years, he is a member of the Indiana basketball, baseball and sportswriters and sportscasters halls of fame. First newspaperman to make the National High School Hall of Fame (1997). He and his wife, Lois, sponsor the Fellowship of Christian Athletes huddle at La Porte High School.

Indiana has produced many legendary high school basketball players over the years. Some of them – like Oscar or Damon – even are recognized strictly by their first names.

Larry Bird is another Indiana legend, but he had to wait for a brilliant college and professional career to rightfully earn the title of Larry Legend.

A native of tiny West Baden, Ind., Larry already was immersed in basketball at age four. He credited "my older brothers" as the biggest influence. "It was my brother Mark early on. He was a good high school player.

"Basketball was very important. I can't remember missing too many days on the basketball court. I was blessed. We had a JV and varsity coach (Gary Holland and Jim Jones) who spent a lot of time with us in the summer. We also fished together."

From a large family, Larry developed a strong work ethic at a young age – once working 100 hours for a new bicycle – and it carried over into basketball.

Possessing great hand-eye coordination, he developed an uncanny shooting touch "just through practice and repetition. The coaches taught us (well). We always had great coaches." (It didn't hurt that he also had 20-20 vision.)

★★★★

His legendary passing ability was honed during his sophomore year at consolidated Springs Valley High School (French Lick) after he broke his ankle and didn't get to play until the state tournament sectional.

"I couldn't move very well," he admitted. "So I just tried to pass the ball. I always had a great feel."

Dave Bliss, then an assistant coach at Indiana University, recalled that Larry "had the best set of hands I had seen since Bill Bradley. They were strong, big and like magnets. He would go where the basketball was going – like he knew the answers to everything that was going to happen. He was a 20 (on a scale of 1 to 10 for intelligence). As time goes on the one thing people forget the most is how TOUGH Larry Bird was."

Larry pointed out that his great hands came "from throwing rubber balls against a wall, probably in fourth or fifth grade. I would throw from right to left. I played a lot of baseball as a kid. I always worked on my wrists."

During his prep career he was plagued by talent evaluators who claimed he couldn't run or jump and played against average competition.

"If I was in the 100-yard dash (yes)," Larry conceded when asked about his lack of speed. "As far as jumping (he actually had a pretty decent 31-inch vertical) I got position and boxed out. I was not a great individual defender, but I learned the team aspect."

Concerning his prep competition, the Springs Valley star conceded, "I was from a small town, small school. I understood it. I never played against big schools."

Larry Bird at Indiana State University. Photo courtesy of the Indiana Basketball Hall of Fame.

Max Rein, who originated the Derby Festival All-American Game in Louisville, scouted Larry during his senior year. He recalled, "He had 50 points and 25 rebounds that night and as I walked out of the gym I still didn't know if he could play or not.

"It was because of his build (6-7, 185), because he was so slight. I could tell he was not fast. It (his opponent) was a small team. Maybe the tallest kid they had was six-feet tall. He really wasn't even considered (for his game)."

Drafted into the NBA sixth overall by the Boston Celtics in 1978, Larry Bird started at small forward and power forward for 13 seasons.

Even after dominating constant double- and triple-teaming with outstanding senior averages of 30.6 points and 20.6 rebounds (school record games of 55 points and 38 rebounds), Larry made only third-team All-State. Being named Mr. Basketball, of course, was out of the question.

Seemingly surprised, the 59-year-old celebrity quipped, "I didn't even realize I was third-team All-State. We don't get much news down here in southern Indiana."

Even getting the talented teenager on the Indiana All-Star team, which played Kentucky every summer, was a stretch, according to Jim Jones, who coached him until his final year.

"We were just fortunate to get him on the team," Jones confided.

He did have 12 points and seven rebounds as Indiana beat Kentucky 92-81 in the first game, but he collected just six points in the second game, a 110-95 Hoosier victory, in very limited playing time.

It would not be incorrect to call Larry Bird the "Rodney Dangerfield of Indiana High School Basketball," because outside of the French Lick area he never got the full respect he deserved.

Despite the ever-present naysayers, Larry insists that he never developed a chip on his shoulder.

Coach Joe B Hall watched his final prep game and declared he was too slow for the University of Kentucky. Denny Crum wanted him to visit Louisville, but Larry beat him in a game of H-O-R-S-E to avoid taking a visit.

Larry signed with nearby Indiana University, but left school and hitch-hiked home before the first practice.

"It was sad I had to leave, just because of the money situation," Larry said apologetically. "I didn't have extra money for things like clothes. I hate having that on my resume – that I dropped out at IU."

Quite frankly, the only thing Larry Bird lacked at the time he left IU probably was physical strength – and possibly a little confidence. He graduated from high school at age 17 as the youngest student in the class of 1974.

"I had self doubt," he confided, "because that was what people were telling me."

Well, a year working for the City of French Lick, which included collecting garbage one day a week, did wonders for his strength – and probably his outlook on life, too.

Larry corrected one old story when he noted, "I wasn't good enough to drive. I had to pick up the trash. I was the guy on the back of the truck. That was me," he laughed.

He definitely got stronger and headed to Indiana State University, which he said "really was my second choice (after IU). It was the right fit. I needed Indiana State more than they needed me."

Larry continued to grow in college (he later played in the pros at 6-9, 220). After sitting out a transfer year at ISU, he exploded for a triple double in his first varsity game. During his three-year career he averaged 30.3 points and 13 rebounds and led the Sycamores to a 81-13 record.

His senior year ISU won 33 straight games before losing the most-watched-ever televised NCAA championship game, 75-64, to Michigan State and its megastar, Earvin Magic Johnson. Larry was named College Player of the Year by at least three organizations.

"The pro game never really was in my mind until I graduated from Indiana State," the rising superstar pointed out.

Some observers believe that the arrival of Magic and Bird saved the NBA, which at the time was plagued by drugs and low attendance. Their rivalry definitely was a league highlight for many years and they remain good friends today.

"In college I never knew if I could play at the next (professional) level," Larry confided. "The same thing (some self doubt) happened when I got to Boston (drafted No. 6 by the Celtics). (He said to himself) I guess I'm going to see how good I am."

After a mere three days of practice, he discovered, "This is not as hard as I thought."

All those years of listening to others tell him what he couldn't do were wiped away forever. He finally realized he could play with anybody on the planet and he was on his way to becoming Larry Legend - a Naismith Hall of Famer and one of the game's Greatest 50 Players.

One of the biggest surprises is that the shy youngster from southern Indiana became one of the premier trash talkers in the NBA.

"I have no clue," he claimed of the rather shocking transformation. " Everybody talked to me. I just talked back. I probably felt more at home on the court."

Over the years, he said that Michael Cooper of the Lakers defended him the best because he "was the most consistent."

Never one to puff himself up, the humble superstar said that his best memory of the Celtics was being "fortunate enough to play with the same guys for a long time. That made the game a lot easier."

Serving as co-captain with the 1992 Gold Medal champion USA Olympic Dream Team "was a great memory because I was playing with guys I competed against during my whole career."

He claims he had a "lot" of worst games, but did mention a 3-for-15 shooting night during a playoff game in Atlanta. "You (most) remember the bad games," he admitted.

As a Celtic, Larry was Rookie of the Year (his five-year contract for $3,250,000 was a record for a rookie), a 12-time All-Star, NBA MVP three times and starred for three NBA champions during a career which lasted from 1979-92. He scored 21,791 points

He played his entire professional career for Boston, winning three NBA championships and two NBA Finals MVP awards.

(24.3 average) with a high game of 60. He led the NBA in free throw shooting three times, once making 71 in a row.

He also made the NBA All-Defensive Second Team three times – a remarkable feat for someone who "can't run or jump." Along the same lines, he set a Celtics career record with 1,556 steals.

He continued to be a winner until a painful back condition forced his retirement. During a 12-year period he teamed with Robert Parish and Kevin McHale on one of the NBA's best-ever frontlines to post 690 victories against 276 losses.

Bird was a 12-time NBA All-Star and was named the league's Most Valuable Player three consecutive times (1984–1986).

His goal in life was "to play the perfect game, but I never got it."

It should be pointed out, though, that his all-around skills and unselfishness always made his teammates better and no one can come closer than that to true perfection.

He was so smart and seemed to always be thinking at least one play ahead that an observer once said he was playing chess while his opponents were just playing checkers.

Asked about pressure, Larry replied, "I never felt pressure in any game. I always felt I was in control."

If playing today, would he prosper in the game's three-point revolution?

"I just never practiced the three-point shot," he pointed out. "If I was playing now I would be practicing a lot."

As far as fans/autographs, etc., were concerned, he said he drew the line "only when they came to my house. That was off limits."

Larry later coached the Indiana Pacers for three years and was named NBA Coach of the Year in 1998. As the Pacers' President of Basketball Operations, he was named NBA Executive of the Year in 2012. He currently is the Pacers president.

Some call Larry the most valuable member of the Pacers' organization, but he quickly says, "I think Bobby Leonard (former player, coach and now radio announcer) is, because I always look up to him. He's always been good to me. He's the Face of the Pacers."

Larry says as a coach, he loved "just being able to coach a group of guys who are professionals." As an executive, he says, "(Seeing the team) do better than what we expected, especially the young players. Watching the young kids develop."

If he could have chosen another sport, Larry said he would have played baseball. He especially liked catching because of the constant action. Major problem – 6-foot-9 catchers aren't in great demand today. He also was a 2-handicap golfer in his younger days.

Over the years, Hoosiers have honored Larry with a song (Indiana's Got a New State Bird) and his old high school is located on Larry Bird Boulevard.

He humbly observes, "It's sort of embarrassing. I understand, but do it for somebody else."

He has been asked why he doesn't move to such a nice climate state as Florida where he wouldn't even have to pay state taxes.

His Hoosier roots run deep, however, emphasizing, "It's where I'm from and I really like it."

Asked how he would like to be remembered, Larry replied, "through my hard work and dedication to the game. Basketball has given me everything I have."

Larry Bird at Springs Valley. Photo courtesy of the Indiana Basketball Hall of Fame.

Bird was a member of the 1992 United States men's Olympic basketball team ("The Dream Team") that won the gold medal at the 1992 Summer Olympics.

Since retiring as a player, Bird has been a mainstay in the Indiana Pacers organization, currently serving as team president.

Larry Bird at Springs Valley. Photo courtesy of the Indiana Basketball Hall of Fame.

INDIANA STATE

Athletics

Indiana State University is grounded in a strong foundation and dedicated to the state of Indiana. As Indiana celebrates its bicentennial, we begin our sesquicentennial celebration.

Reflecting over the past 150 years, some of our stand-out moments include Sycamores like basketball legend Larry Bird and four-time Olympic wrestling medalist Bruce Baumgartner. We're proud of our Sycamore athletes and commend them on making a positive impact on the community, the country, and the world long after their time at State.

We look forward to the years ahead and to creating more great sports stories in the state of Indiana.

Go Sycamores!   **indstate.edu**

15O YEARS

INDIANA STATE UNIVERSITY

SESQUICENTENNIAL ERA
2015-2020

Women's Sports in Indiana By Blake Sebring

One day during the early 2000s, Teri Rosinski, the 1977 Miss Basketball, was asked to address the banquet honoring the all-conference team in one of the state's larger cities. At first, the current athletes listened politely as Rosinski told stories of what it was like during the very early days of organized female school athletics, but then they started talking among themselves and ignoring the speech.

They couldn't relate to what Rosinski was talking about, which was difficult for Rosinski to understand. She and her fellow classmates had to overcome so many roadblocks just to be able to start playing athletics at their schools, but in one way the reaction showed how successful pioneers were. They had advanced their goals so far that today's athletes could actually take all their work for granted.

More than 15 years later, it's very likely none of today's female high school athletes knows the story of how Indiana high school female athletics started or cares about it.

But they should.

In 1969 Johnell Haas of South Bend Riley High School wanted to play golf, except there was no girls team. An Indiana High School Athletic Association rule prohibited girls from competing in boys sports, so Haas sued the organization.

The circuit court in Plymouth ruled in favor of the IHSAA. Proving she was competitive, Haas didn't give up, appealing to the Indiana Supreme Court. On Nov. 27, 1972, the court said it was unconstitutional to take opportunities away from female athletes in non-contact sports.

During the 1972-73 school year, the IHSAA sponsored volleyball and gymnastics, followed by adding golf and track the next year and swimming and tennis in 1974-75. Basketball was added in 1975-76.

"I can't attribute all of that to the lawsuit, but some of it," said former IHSAA Assistant Commissioner Pat Roy, one of those fighting for opportunities at the time. "The girls were already saying to themselves, 'If athletics are good for boys, why can't they be good for girls?' They were beginning to ask some pointed questions that people could not answer."

1902 Attica team. Photo courtesy of the Indiana Basketball Hall of Fame.

Blake Sebring has worked for The News-Sentinel in Fort Wayne for more than 35 years, winning national awards for his coverage of hockey, tennis and volleyball and in 2015 was inducted into the Indiana Sportswriters and Sportscasters Hall of Fame. He is the author of eight books.

The first ever sanctioned IHSAA girls basketball state champions, the 1976 Warsaw Tigers
Photo courtesy of the Indiana Basketball Hall of Fame.

The first Indiana Miss Basketball, Judi Warren being interviewed after
she led Warsaw to the first girls state championship.
Photo courtesy of the Indiana Basketball Hall of Fame.

But 40 years later, the pioneers who fought for girls sports during those early years have been forgotten by today's athletes. Those athletes did not think about the future the way today's athletes don't think about the past. The biggest difference is that the early athletes had no past to build a future on.

"I never felt I was fighting a battle," former Fort Wayne track coach and athletic director Bobbi Widmann-Foust said. "I simply wanted the opportunity to participate in athletic events I felt I had ability in. In Indiana there were not the opportunities for women."

Before the IHSAA started sponsoring sports, girls competed in the Girls Athletic Association, which was a glorified form of intramurals. Those opportunities were limited because there was no organization other than throwing a basketball out for what was essentially open gym.

"I remember there were intramurals with either gymnastics or basketball," recalls former Leo girls basketball star Tonya Burns-Cohrs. "I remember asking if I could play basketball, and the instructor said it was only for boys."

The sports were phased in over a period of four years to allow schools the chance to find coaches and officials and work out schedules. Girls teams were almost always given practice times late at night after the boys had used the gym during prime hours.

Reporters of the time pushed gently for the inclusion of girls sports, but only if it would not offend their friends who were coaches of boys sports.

The crowd at Hinkle after Warsaw won the 1976 state title.
Photo courtesy of the Indiana Basketball Hall of Fame.

A special contribution from Joe E. Kernan
48th Governor of Indiana

The Godfather of Title IX

United States Senator, Birch Bayh, recognized there was flagrant inequality on college campuses for women students and faculty.

As a result, he authored and introduced Title IX of The Higher Education Amendments of 1972, which for the first time, PROHIBITED discrimination on the basis of sex in the classroom and on the athletic field, protecting both students and faculty.

Prior to the Senator's legislation, women were denied equal access to medical, law and other graduate schools. Women student athletes were denied equal participation in sports.

Today's rise of women in all academic disciplines and in sports at every level is a direct result of Title IX legislation. At the time, there were those who were skeptical and said that Title IX would be a disaster for men's sports. Clearly, that was not the case, and Title IX did not affect men's sports.

Before Title IX, women's sports received less than two percent of college athletic budgets. Now, they receive 37 percent.

A 2006 study credited the legislation with a significant increase in physical activity and improvement in weight and body mass among adolescent girls and young women since the 1970s, lowering the risk of medical problems.

Women's participation in college sports has increased more than fivefold since the law's passage. This legacy will continue forever.

TITLE IX
"No person in the United States shall, on the basis of sex, be excluded from participation, be denied the benefits of, or be subjected to discrimination under any education program or activity receiving Federal financial assistance."

It is safe to say that Senator Birch Bayh has had an extraordinary impact on the lives of women in the United States since 1972. And the importance of that impact will continue for generations to come.

We now have women who have made a difference in their own lives, as coaches, teachers, athletic directors, academics, and CEOs. That is not just in Indiana, but across our country. In fact, there are many places where women's sports have become more popular than men's.

Senator Birch Bayh is undoubtedly one of The 25 Greatest Sports Stories in the History of Indiana, and in every other state in our country.

Thank you Birch Bayh!

– Joe E. Kernan

"Now we may not make too many friends among high school athletic directors, but this writer is of the opinion that sports should not be limited to boys," wrote Jim Costin in the Dec. 1, 1972, News-Sentinel. "Thousands of dollars, in fact millions when you consider the cost of gymnasiums, are spent annually for a boys program. Why leave the gals to leading cheers?"

Often the girls were ridiculed.

"It's as if Doris Day were trying to play the part of Dick Butkus," wrote John Peirce in the Auburn Evening Star. "Volleyball has about as big a following in Indiana as property taxes. The day a well-executed spike in volleyball becomes more important to a female volleyball player than whether her blouse is well-pressed is the day volleyball will begin to grow to spectator proportions."

The first female athletes also had to use shoddy equipment, and the uniforms were usually hand-me-downs. Sometimes the socks for the girls basketball team were previously used by the boys baseball team. Rosinski remembers buying boys shorts for the girls team so they didn't have to practice wearing cutoff jean shorts, even though the boys shorts hung past the girls' knees.

Widmann-Foust used to run distance races in Ohio under the name Bobbi instead of Roberta because girls were not permitted to run distances in Indiana, and organizers in Ohio weren't sure if she was a boy. She remembers passing male runners who would spit at her. While she was at Purdue, women were not allowed to run on the track. She ran on the golf courses instead.

For several years Lee Ann Berning of Fort Wayne Concordia was the class of female tennis players in the state. In 1974 she won the GAA state title by beating Shelly Fredlake of South Bend St. Joseph's 6-3, 7-5, but her accomplishment was not recognized by the IHSAA, which began the state tournament the next year. Fredlake won the first "official" state title.

"The year after I graduated, she wins it and gets all the accolades, but I'm not bitter," Berning said, laughing. "I'm over it. It's only been 25 years. I can still beat her today."

Now Berning can laugh about it, but not then.

Coaches at that time worked three or four sports, some in the same season. Referees often called junior varsity and varsity games. Girls basketball teams had one ball, while the boys had 12. The males who coached were often fathers of girls who wanted their children to have more opportunities.

Today women can become head coaches, and athletic directors would like to find more of them. Female athletes can earn college scholarships, and there are plenty of role models for them. They can even earn a living as professionals in soccer, tennis, basketball, golf, volleyball and track and field, and have role models such as Ruth Riley, Stephanie White, Danica Patrick, Serena Williams, Skylar Diggins and dozens of Olympians.

"Now I think the sky is the limit, and kids really can create their own destiny," said Rosinski, who was 13 when Title IX passed in 1972.

They have been given marvelous opportunities, with Title IX as the law and gender equity as the norm. It's all because the pioneers fought and never gave up.

"I think we're all pretty proud of what has happened, but we're all a little bit afraid maybe that girls right now are not very appreciative of what they have and the darn thing will fall through the cracks," Roy said. "I've talked to more than one woman of my vintage that has that fear.

"We almost lost it during the Reagan administration, and politicians can still come along and rip it apart. I'm not sure that the participation means a lot to some of the girls these days. The women that are coming along in leadership positions to take our places do not understand either."

It's understandable why they are so protective, because they fought so hard to get the opportunities in the first place. Today's athletes take their opportunities for granted, which by another measure means the pioneers won their battle against tradition, stereotypes and chauvinism.

They won the first and only competition that truly mattered.

In 1977, Janet Guthrie was the first woman to qualify and compete in Indianapolis 500. She finished 29th with engine troubles. Photo courtesy the Indianapolis Motor Speedway.

Bardach Awards is proud to recognize The 25 Greatest Sports Stories in the History of Indiana™. As a Women's Business Enterprise, we also give thanks to the strong female athletes and role models that were a part of women's sports prior to the implementation of Title Nine, and the progress that occurred afterward regarding equality in the state of Indiana and throughout the nation.

Bardach Awards strongly believes that Success is a derivative of hard work, perseverance, and dedication to our chosen profession. As Hoosiers, we are at our best when we are united in working together toward making our state and nation a better place. Not only is it a great time to be a Women's Business Enterprise, but it is also a great time to celebrate our sports history and Hoosier roots.

– Diane Bardach

#11

The Olympian – Mark Spitz

By Bob Hammel

The 1972 Summer Olympics, where Spitz won seven gold medals, was held in Munich, Germany.

The Rio Olympics of 2016 have passed, American swimmer Michael Phelps has pushed his gold-medal total into the 20s from his five Olympic Games, and even Mark Spitz has proclaimed him not only "the greatest swimmer of all time and the greatest Olympian of all time, he's maybe the greatest athlete of all time … the greatest racer who ever walked the planet."

So what does that make Mark Spitz? What does that say about the polished product of Doc Counsilman's Indiana University swimming program's seven golds, seven world records in Munich in 1972?

Incomparable seems an appropriate word … still.

What Spitz did as an amateur, in training built around full-time university student realities, and the phoenix quality of it – from the ashes of embarrassing failure to very real but very, very brief status as the dominant newsmaker in all the world – should stand forever on its own lofty pedestal. What Phelps has been able to do, staying with his sport, living handsomely off it, and establishing himself as one of America's all-time athletic greats, is as undeniable as it is remarkable.

But The Mark Spitz Story, and its seven gold, seven-world record climax at Munich, remains – is there a better word? – golden.

There's one other aspect of pertinence in recognizing where that tale ranks among all-time Indiana sports stories. For a lifelong Californian, swimmer Mark Spitz's career tale is richly Hoosier, beginning to end.

Spitz's first competitive coach, at Santa Clara Swim Club in California, was George Haines, who developed his own swimming acumen in a 20-yard YMCA pool in Huntington, Indiana, as a discovery and protégé of an unspotlighted master coach named Glen Hummer. From that little bathtub of a pool Hummer produced seven national YMCA team champions, Olympic medalists Gary Dilley (silver, 1964, Tokyo) and Matt Vogel (two golds, 1976, Montreal), somewhere close to 100 collegiate scholarship swimmers – and George Haines, International Swimming Hall of Fame 1977.

Haines caught, maybe even triggered, a new wave in private non-scholastic coaching, founding the Santa Clara Swim Club in 1950. By the time Arnold Spitz realized he had a prodigy on his hands and took young Mark to Santa Clara, Haines already had turned out American Olympic superstars Don Schollander, Steve Clark, Claudia Kolb, Chris von Saltza and Donna de Verona.

Doc Counsilman and Mark Spitz.
Photo courtesy of Indiana University archives.

Spitz's nickname was "Mark the Shark."

Spitz eclipsed them all.

Spitz had a sleek and lithe body that seemed to slide through the water, but there was more.

Counsilman mused one time about how he as a young coach was "teaching the principles I learned the same way everybody else did — out of the Red Cross and YMCA handbooks: 'The most efficient way to swim is to reach out and pull the arm straight through." While at Iowa pursuing the doctorate that gave him his nickname, Doc assisted in the swimming program and had a star who "couldn't swim that way. His arms were all over the place." Wally Ris won a gold as the fastest swimmer at the 1948 London Olympics and the scientist in Counsilman made him study why. Ergo: "You don't go anyplace until you're working with still water. As soon as you start the water going in one direction, you can't get any propulsion from it. You have to contact fresh water. Wally Ris had the right idea all along."

And:

"Mark Spitz was the best at it. He had the tremendous ability to pitch his hands exactly right through the stroke. Mark did more to give us stroke enlightenment than anyone ever has. And he did it naturally."

All that was present and working when Spitz at 18 went to the 1968 Mexico City Olympics favored – and openly expecting – to win six gold medals: four in individual events, two in relays. He didn't win any individually. In one race, the eight-man 200-meter butterfly finals, he finished last. Embarrassed. Ridiculed.

He hadn't chosen a college then. Indiana had just won its first NCAA championship under Counsilman and had the three-gold swimming star of the meet at Mexico City, backstroker-medleyist Charley Hickcox. After the October Olympics and over the Christmas holidays, Spitz sought out Counsilman, enrolled at IU in January, and the two of them started down the road that 43 months later at Munich put Spitz on the winner's spot atop the Olympic medal stand seven times.

This time he went in favored to win seven golds – in the 100- and 200-meter freestyles, swimming's sprints; the 100- and 200-meter butterfly events, and on all three of America's unbeatable relay teams. This time he made no claims in advance. This time his face was on every news journal going in – Time, Life and Sports Illustrated magazines' covers, even the German equivalent Der Spiegel.

> The only person to surpass his achievements was Michael Phelps 36 years later in 2008 when he won eight medals.

First up was the race that typified his crushed psychological state at Mexico City: the 200 'fly, his last-place final. This time his greatest challenger was his three-year teammate on NCAA championship teams at IU, Gary Hall. A "World Swimmer of the Year" is named; from 1969 through 1972, the winner was either IU's Spitz (1969 and '72) or Hall (1970 and '71). For three years, Counsilman kept them in different events, never facing each other. Each had set world records in the 200 butterfly. Each went all-out to win the event that started all swimming finals at Schwimmehalle in Munich.

Spitz won it in a world-record 2:00.70, almost 13 seconds faster than his give-up last-place time at Mexico City. Hall took the silver in 2:02.86, the only 1-2 Olympic finish ever by IU swimmers.

> The world records Spitz set for his seven events in 1972 still stand today.

Spitz won another gold and set another world record with America's 4x100-meter freestyle relay that night, another in the 200 freestyle the next. Two nights later he won golds (and world records) 4 and 5 in the 100 butterfly and 4x200 freestyle relay.

That made him the first five-gold winner in Olympic swimming history, beating four by Schollander at Tokyo in 1964. He still had two events left.

But he had already scaled a personal Everest. The 100 butterfly gold was his biggie. Getting touched out in that event by American teammate Doug Russell at Mexico City was the key to his psychological collapse there, he all but said in a one-on-one 1970 interview in a classroom just outside IU's Royer Pool. He didn't give many of those. Never did he open his true feelings on anything regarding Mexico City, except that day:

"I replayed the Olympics the year after, only for my use and my benefit. I believe in looking ahead, not behind. …

"I remember looking at Russell after the race. I knew how he felt. I had been there.

"You can't describe to a person who hasn't known the feeling what it means to be No. 1. Once you've had it, you can't settle for anything else, and you'll scratch and work and do whatever you have to do to beat the man in the lane beside you to get there.

"And if you were to ask me the same question after the Olympics, and I had won every race between now and then, I would probably answer the question the same way. Or if not, my biggest race would probably be in the same event at Munich."

This was Munich. And a day later, I was with him again and asked how it felt to be the all-time biggest Olympic winner of swimming golds, with more still possible.

"I could quit now and consider my Olympics a success," he said. "Winning the fourth gold medal to tie Don Schollander's record and then winning the fifth to break it – that was the big thrill to me. Everything after that is downhill."

And the question came: in, say, 20 or 25 years, how would you like Mark Spitz the swimmer to be remembered?

"I have no control over that. I'd like for what I've done to be remembered, but who knows?

"I don't think the public remembers Don Schollander … but everybody remembers Jesse Owens and Jim Thorpe."

He won his sixth in the 100 freestyle, his seventh as the last swimming event of the Munich Games swimming the butterfly leg on the medley relay Tuesday night, Sept. 4. And only a few hours later that very night, a matter of blocks away from the place where his Seven Golds and Seven World Records flight into history took place,

> Mark Spitz was named World Swimmer of the Year in 1969, 1971, and 1972 by Swimming World Magazine.

eight Palestinians came over the Olympic Village fence, went straight to Building 31 where the Israeli Olympic team was quartered, shot their way into the building, held the survivors in the Israeli delegation hostage – and all that Mark Spitz had done on his watery stage went into a shadowed and distant second place – for the moment, and forever. About 24 tense hours later, 18 people were dead and

At age nine, Spitz was training at Arden Hills Swim Club in Sacramento with swimming coach Sherm Chavoor, who mentored seven Olympic medal winners including Spitz.

Munich in Olympic reference no longer brought Mark Spitz to mind but terrorism and murder.

How easy, how almost likely, the two headlined figures at Munich – Spitz and the raiders bent on killing Jews – could have come together.

In retrospect, it was apparent that the invasion planners were not sports fans. The man making all the news and sports headlines at Munich was the most prominent Jew in the world. And, in the lax security of the Munich Olympics before the invaders struck, he would have been easy prey.

Spitz was one of five IU swimmers at Munich were billeted together in a four-room second-floor apartment in the quarters assigned to the U.S. team, in Building 12, about a city block from the Israelis' Building 31.

One of those five, sprinter John Murphy, said he knew nothing of it all till told at breakfast – while Spitz was at a press conference. Spitz returned to the apartment before Murphy did, and it was obvious to Murphy when he got back there that Olympic officials had realized Spitz's particular peril.

"There were four guys from the Munich police there standing guard," Murphy said. "One at the door, one inside and two in the room with Spitz … ."

Within minutes after that, they had Spitz out of the Village, ostensibly headed home. By then, Murphy said, they had torn out the Spitz nametag on the door. "They didn't take any chances," he said. "They cleaned out everything referring to Mark."

It was nine Olympics, 36 years later that Phelps won eight golds at Athens and Spitz's numbers were topped.

Seven remains the record for non-professionals. Seven – as in gold medals, as in world records – remains an Olympic synonym for Indiana's Mark Spitz.

Doc Counsilman in 1986.
Photo courtesy of Indiana University archives.

#12 Martinsville's John Wooden

By Tom Kubat

Tom Kubat is president of the Indiana Sportswriters and Sportscasters Association and a member of its Hall of Fame, Class of 2007. He earned a degree in journalism from Indiana University and went on to enjoy a 40-year career covering sports for the Lafayette Journal & Courier, as well as for USA Today and Gannett News Service. He was the J&C's beat writer for Purdue men's basketball and football, in addition to covering the Pacers, Colts, Indianapolis 500, Brickyard 400 and the 1992 Barcelona Olympics for GNS. He has received numerous writing awards, including "Best Sports Columnist" by the Hoosier State Press Association. He is the co-author of the book "Tiller: Not Your Average Joe."

The basic premise of the John Wooden story seems as if it was taken right out of a fictional novel.

A boy from small-town farm country in southern Indiana grows up, travels to glitzy Los Angeles and, in the shadows of glamorous Hollywood, settles in and becomes one of the most successful, and revered, coaches in sports.

Even today, his accomplishments coaching at UCLA are difficult to wrap your head around.

Ten NCAA national championships, during a 12-year period, including a record seven in a row.

A men's basketball record 88 consecutive victories.

Four unbeaten seasons.

All records that probably never will be broken.

Wooden was raised in Morgan County, Indiana, born in 1910 in Hall, Indiana. In 1918, the family moved to a small farm in Centerton, and then to Martinsville when he was 14.

Wooden became a basketball star at Martinsville High School and later at Purdue University.

> As a 5' 10" guard at Purdue University, Wooden was the first to be named basketball All-American three times.

"I think one thing that gets lost, because he was such a great coach, is that he was a great player," said current Purdue coach Matt Painter. "You don't ever think about John Wooden the player. You just don't.

"When he passed away, I said I think it's our place as an institution to make sure we keep that story alive. That he was a three-time All-American, that he was a great player."

As a three-time All-State performer (1926-28), Wooden led Martinsville to three state title games, winning the championship his junior season.

At Purdue, he was a three-time consensus All-American (1930-32), leading the Boilermakers to the Helms Foundation national championship as a senior.

Wooden won wherever he coached.

His 11-year record as a high school coach was 218-42.

He was the athletic director and basketball coach at Indiana State University for two years, leading the Sycamores to a 47-14 record.

And, in 27 years at UCLA, his overall record was 620-147.

Wooden, very quick and extremely strong, was the first player to become a three-time All-American. And he was the first person to be inducted into the Naismith Memorial Basketball Hall of Fame as both a player (1960) and a coach (1973).

John Wooden as a player at Purdue University.
Photo Courtesy of Purdue Athletics.

Along with his unbelievable won-loss record, Wooden was known for his "grandfatherly" image.

Not prone to histrionics on the sideline, during UCLA games Wooden mostly would sit serenely with crossed legs and a program rolled up in one hand.

But Mike Warren, a starting guard for Wooden who played on two national championship teams from 1966-68, saw a different side of the legend.

"What was he like in practice? Let me tell you. He was a taskmaster," said Warren, who was a two-time high school All-State selection at South Bend Central in Indiana.

"There was no clowning around. He had 3x5 index cards, and you went from drill to drill. You didn't talk, you didn't walk, you ran. And when that whistle blew, you stopped and you listened.

"Did he yell? Yeah. He was tough, man. Sometimes, practices were harder than games. His whole thing was you had to be in tip top condition. But he wasn't the kind of guy who would be in your face, screaming at you."

And, being a deeply religious man, cursing wasn't in his DNA.

"He didn't curse and he didn't allow cursing. Absolutely not," Warren said. "His favorite term was 'gracious sakes alive.' That was like cussing somebody out in his own way."

Paul Reed, a former assistant to another legendary coach, Adolph Rupp at Kentucky, spent a couple of years at UCLA (1966-67 and 1967-68 seasons) taking classes and serving as a consultant and scout for Wooden.

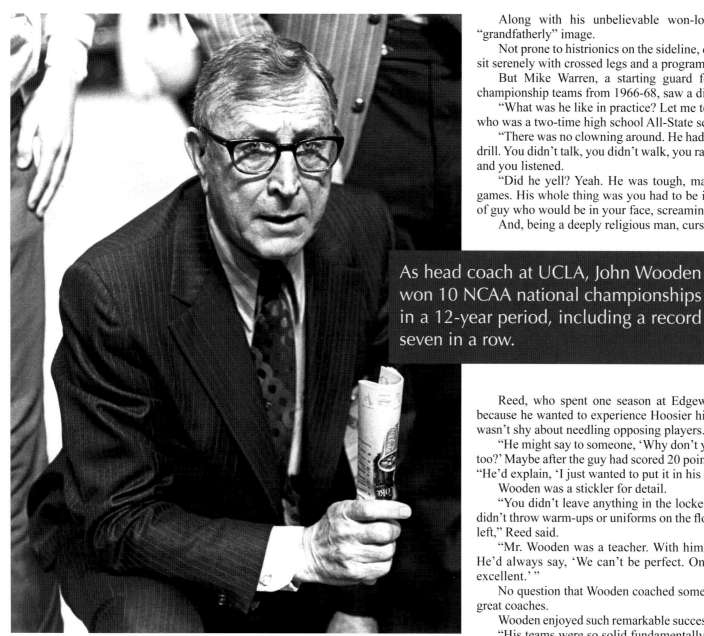

John Wooden. Photo Courtesy of Purdue Athletics.

As head coach at UCLA, John Wooden won 10 NCAA national championships in a 12-year period, including a record seven in a row.

Reed, who spent one season at Edgewood High School in Ellettsville, Indiana, because he wanted to experience Hoosier high school basketball, learned that Wooden wasn't shy about needling opposing players.

"He might say to someone, 'Why don't you let the other four guys play with the ball too?' Maybe after the guy had scored 20 points and hadn't missed any shots," Reed said. "He'd explain, 'I just wanted to put it in his head.'"

Wooden was a stickler for detail.

"You didn't leave anything in the locker rooms. You picked up after yourself; you didn't throw warm-ups or uniforms on the floor. And you turned the lights out when you left," Reed said.

"Mr. Wooden was a teacher. With him, you did what was right, and that was it. He'd always say, 'We can't be perfect. Only the Savior was perfect. But we can be excellent.'"

No question that Wooden coached some excellent talent. But so have a lot of other great coaches.

Wooden enjoyed such remarkable success because he molded that talent into a team.

"His teams were so solid fundamentally, and they played so well as a team," Reed said. "He totally understood team. He didn't just talk team, he was team."

Wooden was named national coach of the year six times.

76

His faith and his devotion to his wife Nell were both Wooden trademarks.

Many of the West Coast coaches never got too close to him.

"He didn't have a good number of friends in basketball – because he didn't run around with the guys," Reed said. "He didn't go out and get drunk with them. He'd rather be at home with Nell."

Wooden, who died on June 4, 2010, just four months shy of his 100th birthday, remained mentally sharp in his later years.

Painter spent a couple of days with Wooden in California, about five years before he passed away.

"It was very educational," Painter said. "More than anything, it was most impressive that anyone could have that kind of memory in his 90s. That is what astonished me, probably more than anything.

"He would talk in some detail about things that happened back in middle school, and that was like 80 years ago.

"He remembered how he courted his wife. He said that she had a couple other boyfriends but he knew that's who he wanted to be with.

"He said that when he was going off to college that she could be with other people but that he wasn't going to do that. He was going to be with her."

Wooden told Painter that he didn't agree with Purdue's setup of having Painter being the coach in waiting, serving as an assistant under Gene Keady, but with the understanding that he would replace Keady the next season.

"It wasn't like he was adamant about it, but he just thought that the players needed to have one head coach, instead of knowing that I was going to be the next guy," Painter said.

Wooden was not happy that Mackey Arena was named after Red Mackey and not Ward "Piggy" Lambert.

Even though Purdue already had Lambert Fieldhouse, Wooden felt strongly that the basketball arena should have been named after his former Boilermaker coach.

"He believed that Piggy Lambert deserved to have the arena named after him," Painter said. "That didn't set right with him. He loved Piggy Lambert. His style of play came from Piggy Lambert.

"A lot of coaches, back when coach Wooden played, didn't push the basketball. Piggy Lambert did. That's where he got his background, in terms of fast break basketball."

Purdue twice tried to hire Wooden as its coach. It wanted Wooden to remain at Indiana State one more year and then take over for then-Boilermaker coach Mel Taube, who eventually resigned in March of 1950.

But Wooden didn't like the idea of Taube being a lame-duck coach for one season, so he turned down the offer.

After Taube resigned, Purdue made another run at Wooden, but he declined again. It was rejected a third time because he was by then settled in at UCLA.

Wooden may have been a taskmaster, but Warren believes that he struck a good balance between hard work and fun.

And he had a sense of humor.

"He would make fun of you in a playful way," Warren said. "He told me a story about one of his players who took a shot and clanked it badly, because he was a terrible shooter.

"In going over that play in practice, the kid said, 'Well, I was open.' And coach replied, 'Well, there was a reason why you were open. If you were a good shooter you would not have been open.'

"He didn't do anything without reason. He was the supreme psychologist. I believe the best coaches are great teachers and great psychologists."

One time Warren felt the wrath of Wooden, and it made a lasting impression on him.

During his first semester on campus, Warren was doing too much partying and not enough studying. He received a note that Wooden wanted to see him.

Warren thought the coach wanted to talk about the upcoming season and what was expected of him.

"I kind of strolled into his office and plopped down, like, hey, what's up coach?" Warren recalled. "And he does not crack a smile. He looks at me and asks, 'Do you know why you're here?'

"I said, 'Yeah, I'm here to play basketball.' And he lit into me about being more responsible and that I was going to get kicked out of school, flunk out of school.

"I couldn't wait to get out of that office. And, man, I turned it all around. I became an academic All-American because of that conversation.

"He was very special. I don't know what my life would have been like had I gone some other place."

#13

A Hoosier Legend – Damon Bailey

By Bob Bridge

Bob Bridge is a columnist for the Bedford Times-Mail and Hoosier Times. A member of the Indiana Sportswriters and Sportscasters Hall of Fame, Bob also served as a columnist for Inside Indiana. A native of Evansville and a graduate of Indiana University, he was named the Bedford Area Chamber of Commerce's Community Service Award winner in 2008. In his spare time Bob strums a guitar and pretends he is James Taylor.

Damon Bailey's Dream Season

amon Bailey's quest to win a state championship had reached critical mass. With his Bedford North Lawrence Stars trailing by six points to the unbeaten Concord Minutemen with only 2:36 remaining in the 1990 state championship game, Bailey saw his lifelong dream ticking away, second by second.

The Stars had advanced to the Final Four but lost there to eventual champions Marion in 1987 and to Muncie Central in 1988. They also fell to Floyd Central in the regional in 1989. Bailey was down to his final chance.

Despite the six-point deficit, he exuded a cool confidence, as did his coach, Hall-of-Famer Dan Bush.

"I remember looking up at the clock," Bush recalls. "I still was confident we were going to do it."

After all, Bush was wielding the ultimate trump card: Indiana's all-time leading scorer.

"Damon had been through the wars and endured everything so gracefully," Bush said. "He deserved the fairy-tale ending, and I just knew he'd find a way."

A record crowd of 41,046 – forty-one thousand, for a high school game – stood and screamed and watched in awe as Bailey, by sheer force of will, scored his team's final 11 points to rally the Stars to a 63-60 victory.

"People may not believe this, but the 41,000 people weren't on my mind," Bailey said. "I was in the moment. Everything else around me didn't matter. I knew what I had to do to achieve the goal.

"So much time and energy had been spent over the course of those four years. This was a community quest. I remembered playing with my dad and some of the older guys who taught us so much about the game. So many people were invested in this. We had to win that game."

In 1986, when Bailey was a 14-year-old eighth-grader, Indiana coach Bob Knight watched two games featuring Bailey's team.

Angelo Pizzo, the screenwriter who penned "Hoosiers," experienced chills as he watched another Jimmy Chitwood deliver in the clutch.

"It's almost like Damon came out of a script," he explained. "This was even better, because it was real."

Seconds after the championship was secured, cameras followed Bailey as he climbed through a sea of humanity to embrace his parents, Wendell and Beverly. His father lifted him onto his shoulders and Damon thrust his fist to the heavens.

"I can remember breathing a sigh of relief when the horn sounded," Bailey recalled. "I wanted to be with the people who had done so much to get me to that point. I was fortunate to have parents who traveled the country watching me play."

He called that precarious-but-perfect, iconically Indiana climb into the crowd "a spur-of-the-moment thing."

Damon Bailey at Bedford North Lawrence.
Photo courtesy of the Indiana Basketball Hall of Fame.

"My father and I had a tough-love relationship," he explained. "He pushed me to be the best and win at the highest level. That was a special moment to thank my parents. We had finally achieved that ultimate goal."

Bailey began playing basketball with his father and friends in Heltonville, just east of Bedford. He took on the challenge of playing against older and tougher athletes.

The stiff competition paid dividends. By the time he enrolled at Shawswick Junior High, every basketball fan in Lawrence County was aware of "Damon." No last name was required.

He was so dominant in junior high that Indiana University basketball coach Bob Knight and author John Feinstein traveled to Shawswick to see him play.

In Feinstein's book "A Season on the Brink," Knight was quoted as saying: "Damon Bailey is better than any guard we have right now. I don't mean potentially better, I mean better right now."

Sports Illustrated declared Bailey the top incoming ninth-grader in the nation. The teen who had played on five AAU national championship squads and earned four MVPs entered BNL as the community's most celebrated 15-year-old. Thus began his life in a fishbowl.

Playing a freshman ahead of more seasoned juniors and seniors is a surefire recipe for a ruckus on most Hoosier hardwoods. But Bush did not mince words.

"Brent Byrer was a sophomore and Damon was a freshman that year," he recalled. "Right after we made cuts, I pointed at Brent and Damon and said they were going to play. I told the other guys if they didn't like it, they probably needed to leave."

Senior guard Ernie Lovell welcomed Bailey with open arms.

"I was fine with it," he recalled. "I always wanted to play for the Stars, and I wanted to win. With his talent, you could imagine the possibilities."

Bush told senior Rusty Garrison to rebound, play defense and leave dribbling and shooting to his teammates.

Like Lovell, Garrison enthusiastically embraced the gifted newcomer.

"I had never played with anyone near that caliber," Garrison said. "Damon played to win, and that was contagious. I don't think we ever stepped on the floor thinking we were going to lose. Damon really fueled our fire."

BNL won its first three games before falling to Indianapolis Cathedral. The Stars bounced back to beat Edgewood but went to Bloomington South as a decisive underdog against the No. 4-ranked Panthers.

"Their point guard was taller than our center," Lovell recalled with a chuckle. "We looked like little kids. Even Damon and Rusty looked small compared to those guys."

Greg Pittman, a junior guard on that squad, said Bailey wasn't prone to trash talking, but the freshman showed his spunk prior to tip-off.

"As we walked to the center circle for the tip, Damon bent over to pull up his socks," Pittman recalled. "One of the South kids leaned in and told him he was going down. Damon looked up at him and said 'Hold on tight, you're going for a ride.'"

Oh, what a resplendent ride it was. Bailey converted 15 of 18 shots, grabbed 11 rebounds and steered the Stars to a stunning 73-62 triumph in Bloomington.

Tales of that stellar performance rapidly rippled throughout the state.

"That was probably the game that woke us up and woke the state up to who we were," Bailey recalled. "I don't know that I was ever as excited to play a game as I was that one. Some of it was the BNL-South rivalry. And, they were one of the top teams in the state. It was such a big game for us. We needed to make a statement.

"They were bigger than us at every position, but we won the tip and we just got in that zone. Winning that game helped us prove to ourselves — and others — that we could compete with anybody."

The Stars lost only two more games during the regular season and rolled through the sectional, regional and semi-state before falling to eventual state champion Marion in the Final Four at Market Square Arena. The Stars played evenly with the mighty Giants for the first three periods, but Bailey fouled out in the fourth quarter and Lyndon Jones and Jay Edwards helped Marion secure its third straight state title.

BNL finished the season 23-4. Bailey averaged 23.6 points and 8.4 rebounds per game while shooting .597 from the field and .721 from the free-throw line.

Every BNL home game was a sell-out that year, and each of the next three seasons as well – approximately 6,300 crammed into the fieldhouse. Athletic directors from opposing schools began leasing larger gymnasiums to capitalize on Bailey's growing popularity.

Cathy Goodin, the secretary in BNL's athletic office, said the phones rang incessantly during Bailey's freshman season and the ensuing three years.

"We would sell out season tickets in a matter of a few days," she explained. "There was always a line at the door and we received phone calls from newspapers and magazines all over the country. Everyone wanted to talk to Damon. It got crazy … and stressful."

Goodin recalled a divorce case in which the right to BNL basketball tickets was at issue. And, an IU season ticket holder offered to exchange his seats at Assembly Hall for a pair at BNL.

During tournament time those intent on experiencing Damon Mania paid princely sums to scalpers to see him play. Though aware of the hoopla revolving around him, Bailey remained distant and remarkably untainted by the circus environment.

"There are three key components to that," he said. "First, there are my parents. No matter how great I thought I was or someone in the community thought I was, my parents weren't afraid to remind me I wasn't so great.

In the 1994 NBA Draft, Damon was a 2nd round pick, 44th overall, and was selected by the Indiana Pacers.

"Secondly, that's just the way I grew up. There were always crowds of people. It was a way of life for me. It's not like it happened suddenly. It just evolved, and I've never known anything different.

"And, the third thing, I'm sure Coach Bush and others protected me from things I didn't need to know about. I just focused on playing basketball."

Bailey averaged 31.1 points and 9.4 rebounds per game during a sophomore season that generated a 26-2 record and a second trip to the Final Four.

His junior season began with a 50-point game against Salem but ended on a frustrating note. Though he averaged 27.2 points and 8.1 rebounds, he fractured a finger during the sectional and the Stars fell to IU-bound Pat Graham and Floyd Central at the Seymour Regional.

Only one season remained.

"I was a senior, and it was my year to lead," Bailey recalled. "I had learned a lot about leadership from guys like Ernie and Greg, and now it was my turn. I tried to make sure we were doing everything as a team. Some of the guys hadn't played varsity yet, so we had to learn to play together. I wanted to bond with these guys and know what they were thinking on and off the floor."

Bailey scored 30 or more points in seven of his first nine games as a senior. The Stars lost just twice during the regular season, dropping one-point decisions to powerhouses Lawrence North and New Albany.

During a 78-58 win over Scottsburg at the Seymour Regional, Bailey converted on a lob from Chad Mills to surpass 1950s star Marion Pierce's 29-year-old state career scoring record of 3,019 points.

Damon made it crystal clear his primary goal remained unattained.

"My goal is to win a state championship," he said that night of nights.

By this time, Bush was familiar with Bailey's business-like approach to basketball.

"A lot of people in the gym were concerned about the record," he said, "but Damon wasn't one of them. What separates Damon from other players is his heart. You can't measure that.

"Of all the remarkable things he's done on the floor, they pale to what he does off the floor, how he handles things, the way he goes about his business."

Damon finished his dream season averaging 31.4 points, 9.4 rebounds per game. After scoring a record 3,134 points in leading the Stars to 99 wins, the 1990 Mr. Basketball and National Player of the Year journeyed up the road to Bloomington and guided Knight's Hoosiers to 108 victories during the next four seasons.

"I've probably been his greatest critic," Knight said at the conclusion of Bailey's senior season at IU, "but I've also been his greatest fan."

Knight noted Bailey never took a day off, despite a string of nagging injuries. And, he marveled at his versatility.

"Was Damon a guard? A forward? A center?" Knight asked the crowd. "What he was … was one hell of a basketball player."

What made Damon so special?

Pittman pointed to his toughness. Lovell appreciated his dogged determination.

"Damon hated to lose … at anything," Lovell insisted.

"For me, it was all about winning," Bailey explained. "It never mattered who did what. I liked having teammates who understood their

Bedford North Lawrence State Champs 1990. Photo courtesy of the Indiana Basketball Hall of Fame.

Briefly, in January 1999, he signed with the Cleveland Cavaliers.

strengths and weaknesses and wanted to win. When it's about winning, individual achievements don't matter as much.

"We genuinely liked each other, and we wanted to win as a team. You have to have that kind of understanding. We were willing to do whatever it takes, and that is very rare. You also need a coach who is honest enough to level with his players."

As for life in the fishbowl …

"Think how hard it might be to be a kid named Damon Bailey," Knight mused.

Damon shrugged and smiled.

"Some of it was great; some of it wasn't," he said. "I've tried to keep it in perspective. My dad told me you're never as good as your biggest supporter says you are, and you're never as bad as your harshest critic thinks you are.

"I always knew basketball was the gateway to be successful in other areas of life. I tried to enjoy the moment while I was in it.

"You know, the fans are the ones who make you popular. So, no matter if I was tired or what kind of a mood I was in, I always wanted the kids to know I cared."

Tough, yet sensitive. Fundamental, yet spectacular.

But his greatest asset?

"If I had a gift, it was probably that ability to stay in the moment and focus on the task at hand," Bailey said.

Even when he was hearing what no high school basketball player in America ever had heard: the roar of 41,406 fans.

After retiring from professional basketball, Damon returned to Indiana to start a series of basketball camps for children.

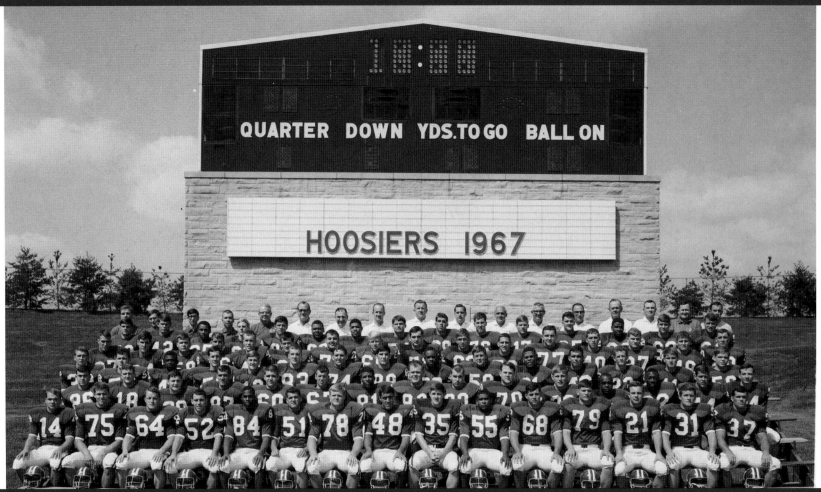

Big 10 Co-Champions 1967. Photo courtesy of Indiana University Archives.

#14 Indiana University's 1967 football team

By Bob Hammel

Maybe it's apocryphal – pure fantasy. But if so, it should feel right at home, as the first "Yeah, it really happened – I swear!" paragraph of the Incredible, Unbelievable, distinctly IU story of The Rose Bowl Season at Indiana.

The Rose Bowl Season ... that very specificity is a good place to start. No other football-playing member of the traditional "Big Ten" Conference can speak of such things so singularly. Only Indiana has made just one trip to Pasadena since the Big Ten started sending its champion there annually in 1946.

The Rose Bowl Season at Indiana was 1967. And the unauthenticated story goes ...

At halftime of the season opener, Kentucky – as disdained in football by its Southeastern Conference partners as Indiana was in the Big Ten – led the Hoosiers, 10-0.

Normally, that would have struck even Hoosiers the way it no doubt did people across the land who heard it mentioned that day on radio or television –ho-hum, what's-new?

But this was different in Bloomington.

> The 1967 IU football team known as the "Cardiac Kids" was coached by John Pont.

This time, hope was in the air. Word had spread that there at last was reason to be excited, that an infusion of sophomores who – as freshmen, ineligible to play on the varsity under rules of the time – had gone to Ohio State of all places the year before and won! Beat the Bucks, in football! At Columbus!

Butcher, Isenbarger, Gonso. Those were the names. And how perfect: even the initials promised a BIG year at Indiana.

Yes, there had been a buzz of new things in the air when John Pont came in as new coach in 1965, and what had followed was a continuation of dreary results: a 2-8 finish in '65, an even worse 1-8-1 in '66.

And, yes, the experts in the Big Ten press had sized this up as another cellar-bound Indiana team. They had come on the annual Big Ten Skywriters' tour; they saw; they voted. And ... didn't Indiana mean basement in Big Ten football?

But John Pont's infectious optimism was hard to ignore or suppress by never daunted loyalists who yearned to be ... something.

They read that this was the start of a New IU in football. They read that top down Indiana now was demanding, not asking, for football improvement, that two days after Rose Bowl-bound Purdue had drubbed the Hoosiers 51-6 to continue domination of the Old Oaken Bucket rivalry, athletic director Bill Orwig had bluntly told returning players at the school's football banquet:

"I'm sick of losing. I was never a loser before I came to Indiana University, and Coach (John) Pont was never a loser before he came here. I'm sick of the attitude some of our players have on the field. I'm sick of seeing some of our players do things off the field that they know the coaches don't expect them to do.

"Boys, if you don't want to play football next year, don't come out. Winning isn't easy. It takes work."

They had read how Pont had picked up on the theme and demanded a reduction of lard – told his team as individuals and a group at the end of spring practice that he'd better see a whole lot less blubber when they reported back in August because the new IU was going to play quick, play fast, and win.

"Rags to Roses..." publication from the 1968/1969 football season. Photo courtesy of Indiana University Archives.

A speed-option I-formation offense was going in, and a new quarterback would be running it. Through the entire spring and well into pre-season work in the fall, the offense was taking shape but the triggerman – the quarterback – wasn't determined. Two of those flashy new sophomores, John Isenbarger of Muncie and Harry Gonso of Findlay, Ohio, were running and passing and executing those last-second pitchouts so impressively that Pont went much later than he wanted in making a choice.

It was crucial because it affected not just one but two key spots in the offense. Whoever lost out at quarterback was going to start at tailback in the same backfield – even though the two best running backs on the 1966 team, Terry Cole and Mike Krivoshia, were still around.

> The 19-14 win over Purdue gave the 1967 Hoosiers a share of the Big Ten Championship and their only Rose Bowl trip in history.

A week before the opener, Pont settled on Gonso as the quarterback, and tall, upright, long-striding Isenbarger learned how to take handoffs rather than make them, to catch passes rather than throw them, to block for the passer occasionally rather than trust somebody else to.

And there was the third part of that BIG new infusion: hometowner Jade Butcher, who had averaged a touchdown catch a game for three years and 29 games at Bloomington High. When recruited, Butcher was listed as a defensive back. When the season opened, Jade Butcher was listed at flanker: technically a back but really a wide receiver, with hands that – three seasons and 30 touchdowns later – had never dropped a pass.

Hoosiers couldn't wait for that season opener.

And here it was halftime, with a zero on the scoreboard, against Kentucky – and, the story goes:

An exasperated, maybe slightly lubricated, red-wearing loud-shouting male fan in the heart of the big-givers' ticket section of Memorial Stadium's west stands stood up, as that dreary first half ended, held his and his wife's student tickets aloft, shouted "That's it – same old stuff. You suckers can stay if you want, but I'm outta here!"

And he dramatically tore both sets of tickets into shreds.

And stomped out.

If it happened … ohhh, did he make a mistake!

Gonso got the option game going in the second half and the Hoosiers pulled out a 12-10 win. They scrambled to an 18-15 win over Kansas the next week, and the game stories already were noting "The last time IU started 2-0 in football was …"

Then it was 3-0 after a 20-7 win at Illinois – in the Big Ten opener! On the road!

Iowa came in, and just before kickoff a delightful banner unfurled in the giddy stands:

WILL THE HOOSIERS EVER LOSE?

A legend was born that day.

Isenbarger, besides developing into a productive runner, was the team's punter. Pont saw Iowa tended to overrush punts, leaving an inviting gap up the middle, so Isenbarger was given an option to run if the opening was there. Leading 14-10 in the fourth quarter, Pont choked on his coffee when the daring sophomore saw that hole, aborted punt plans, and took off. The hole closed a yard short. Iowa, outplayed all day, drove to the touchdown that put the Hawkeyes ahead, 17-14.

Make that two legends. Gonso wasn't ready to lose.

Running and passing and pitching out laterals, he moved the Hoosiers downfield. But time was running out, fourth down came up, and Pont sent in kicker Dave Kornowa for a field goal and a 17-17 escape from defeat. Ostensibly.

The holder, new to the job, was Gonso. Neither Pont nor Gonso was ready to settle for a tie. Gonso took the snap, leaped to his feet and sprinted outside rushers, then shot a pass to Butcher for a first down at the 6. Next play was another pass to Butcher for the touchdown that won the game, 21-17.

Indeed. Will they ever lose?

At 4-0, the "first-time-since" newspaper comparisons required deep digging: only the 1910 Hoosiers, who won their first five in a 6-1 season, had started 4-0 in IU's 80 years of football.

But it was moment-of-truth time. No. 5 was at Michigan, the "Big House" where forever and ever Big Ten dreams have gone to be tested.

Pont pulled out something new. Gonso sprinting toward the corner, keeping the ball and slanting upfield or faking a run and pitching the ball to Isenbarger for an option sweep had become the '67 Hoosiers' new staple. The third option came in at Michigan: the pitch went to Isenbarger but instead of turning the corner and running, he pulled up and lofted a pass to Butcher – all alone, 20 yards behind defenders who had spent a week preparing for Isenbarger on a sweep. Michigan looked lost and didn't adapt quickly. The play worked three times and Indiana bolted out to a 20-0 lead. By then rookie Butcher already had caught six touchdown passes, in his four-game college career.

But in the fourth quarter it was 20-14 and Indiana was punting. Only … not. Iowa memories still fresh, Isenbarger thought he saw a hole, disdained a punt and ran – and got caught, short. Michigan capitalized with a short-field touchdown drive and lined up to kick the extra point that would provide a 21-20 lead and … go back home and be yourselves, Hoosiers.

But the kick was low and blocked. And Isenbarger as a tailback was a man possessed. Time and again he took simple handoffs and slashed to big gains, and ultimately the touchdown that stood up for a 27-20 victory. No. 5, and the Hoosiers' introduction to the national rankings: No. 10. Indiana!

They stepped out of league play to go to Arizona, which had won 14-7 at Ohio State.

Same team lost 42-7 to Indiana, the Hoosiers' only winning rout of their miracle season. No. 7-ranked now, and 6-0 for the first time – ever..

They played much of the Arizona game without Gonso, who tweaked an ankle. He was back the next week but not electric in a 14-9 scrape past

> One of John Pont's biggest challenges was determining who would emerge as the starter between competitive sophomores Harry Gonso and John Isenbarger.

a Wisconsin team that finished winless. Dan Jenkins was there for Sports Illustrated, upstart IU now a national curiosity. His report was titled "Punt, John, Punt" – for a telegram Isenbarger received from his mother before the Tucson game wishing him well with a footnote of Iowa and Michigan memories: " Dear John: Please punt." Yet another legend that never died.

Another prove-it game was next, at Michigan State – "Kill, Bubba, kill" no longer in the air nor Bubba Smith, George Webster and the monsters who had devastated the Big Ten for two years around. But it was still Michigan State, at Spartan Stadium. It was Michigan-soggy and chilly, and the flashy Hoosier offense slogged for 50-some minutes, trailing 13-7.

As much as any game, the final minutes at Michigan State showcased the change of eras, and attitudes. Gonso and Isenbarger cut the Spartan defense more ruthlessly than flashily. Suddenly the ball was near the goal line, and Gonso – the stadium screaming for a Spartan stand – stood at the line and coolly extended his hands in a "quiet" command.

Didn't work at all in East Lansing.

But back in Bloomington, where a few thousand had gathered in the basketball fieldhouse to watch a closed-circuit telecast … the roaring fans, so much into the moment they didn't realize the futility, hushed.

Isenbarger scored, Dave Kornowa kicked, and Indiana won, 14-13.

Now 8-0. And No. 5 in the land. And the Rose Bowl – the Rose Bowl – actually beckoning.

Times were different then. The Big Ten for more than 20 years operated with a policy of never sending a team to Pasadena two years in a row. A "no-repeat" rule, they called it. So although Purdue was blowing everybody away and looked like the runaway Big Ten champion, the Boilermakers – who had made their own first Rose Bowl trip the year

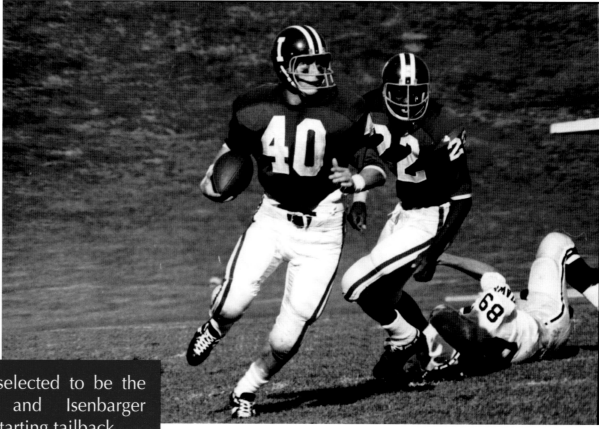

> Gonso was selected to be the quarterback and Isenbarger became the starting tailback.

Jade Butcher in a game in 1967. Photo courtesy of Indiana University Archives.

before as runnerup to national power Michigan State, a "no-repeat" Rose Bowl victim itself – were out of the Pasadena picture for this season and the runnerup would go.

So Indiana on the next-last Saturday of this heaven-ordained season went to Minnesota needing just one more win to go Rose Bowl-ing – the surreal real. The very week before, Purdue had mauled the Minnesotans, 41-12.

It looks like a total pratfall in the record books. Minnesota won, 33-7.

But it wasn't. It was all playing out as the 1967 IU football script had been reading. Two strong defenses dominated play as Minnesota took a 13-7 lead into the fourth quarter. It was a bright and sunny day, but Minnesota-cold, with a strong wind dictating how things would go in that decisive quarter – a wind that was like everything and everyone else that year: directly behind the Hoosiers.

They used it for a drive that carried inside the Gopher 25 but stalled. No big deal. Seven minutes left. Hold here, force a punt that couldn't possibly get past the 50, and drive in the final minutes to victory. Same ol' same ol'.

But on third-and-7, one stop needed to force that punt, Minnesota quarterback Curtis Wilson slipped outside and wasn't caught for 70 yards. The Gophers pushed through the stunned Hoosier defenders for what amounted to a clinching touchdown and capitalized

on two more mistakes by an IU team suddenly in shock. In the papers next morning it looked like an Indiana score of old: 33-7.

With Purdue to come. What a way to go out, Pasadena unpackers in deflated Indiana were thinking.

And what a way to go out it was. What might have been Purdue's best team ever – with halfback Leroy Keyes an All-American and sophomore Mike Phipps an emerged star, each of them eventually a Heisman runnerup, and Chuck Kyle, Tim Foley, Jim Beirne, Perry Williams All-Big Ten caliber in other offensive and defensive spots – had beaten Notre Dame when it was No. 1 and lost only outside the league to Oregon State. It wasn't going bowling, but even a national championship – determined by poll – wasn't out of the question.

Until about 4:30 on the afternoon of Nov. 25, 1967, which usually wins any vote as the greatest day – the greatest game – the greatest victory – in IU football history.

There was no Minnesota hangover. From the start, the Hoosiers carried the fight to the heavily favored Purdues.

This was the day even offense-riveted media folks finally noticed that the Indiana Miracle was at least as much – maybe more so – caused by that slimmed-down, quick, dependable defense that was keeping games so close that last-minute touchdown drives could pull them out.

That, too, had been new. Pont and defensive coordinator Ernie Plank had gone to a 4-4 front keyed on quickness.

And unselfishness.

It had its own leaders. It was more senior than sophomore, short on NFL prospects but long on dogged, defiant determination.

Doug Crusan gave up a lot to be its leader. A lot of weight: Crusan was one of the biggest summer weight-shedders, dropping more than 20 pounds. But he risked giving up a lot more, just to – in the last of what had been a personally successful but miserable 3-16-1 career – win.

Crusan had built a reputation among NFL scouts as an offensive lineman to watch. Pont asked him to give up that scouting status, get quicker with weight loss, and move to defense, at tackle, as a 4-4 anchor. He did it, his teammates elected him captain, and the defense he led was at its best against Keyes, Phipps, Williams and Purdue. A few months later, NFL evaluators put him back on offense, Miami took him in the first round, and he was a starter on the only unbeaten Super Bowl champion, the 1973 Dolphins.

There was another senior who had sacrificed. Terry Cole had come to IU as a small-town back with big-time power and speed. He was moved aside when the offensive focus went to the extra dimensions Isenbarger could provide. The I-formation had only one primary running back. The other back was the fullback, basically the blocker. That became Cole's role.

Until Pont's last surprise. With the Purdue defense primed to streak outside and counter the Gonso-Isenbarger option threat, Pont waited until that game – and until just the right moments of that game – to slip the ball to fullback Cole, "blocking back" Cole,

John Pont's decision to switch two-year starting offensive tackle (and captain) Doug Crusan to defense, is said to have been a move that laid a winning foundation and solidified the team.

running straight up the wide-open middle. By halftime, his bolts for 63 and 42 yards had IU ahead 19-7. By day's end, he had a career-high 155 yards, and IU was Pasadena-bound with a 19-14 victory.

Oh, it had its perilous points.

Purdue finally got its weapons firing as the clock moved inside 10 minutes. From the IU 4, fullback Williams was met at the line by linebacker Ken Kaczmarek, whose tackle shook loose a fumble that safety Mike Boughman recovered at the IU 1.

Those irrepressible sophomores on offense took it from there. No be-careful in them. There was Gonso, disdaining a time-killing run up the middle, sprinting across the end zone to launch a first-down pass that just missed.

And then on fourth down, there was Isenbarger, in the end zone, punting – and delivering under the most extreme pressure the punt of his life: 63 yards, over safetyman Foley's head, pushing the Boilermakers back to their 40 for a game-ending drive that never reached the 20.

Suddenly, the Big Ten had a three-way tie for the championship: bowl-ineliglble Purdue, Minnesota and Indiana. The 10 athletic directors voted in a telephone poll to pick the Pasadena team: Minnesota, which had beaten IU by that 33-7 margin, or Indiana, which had beaten Purdue. Cinderella won. Indiana went west, lost gallantly 14-3 to All-American O.J. Simpson and national-champion Southern Cal, and the Dream Season was over.

But not at all forgotten.

And as its numerical sum-up, there is that Bucket Game score: 19-14.

When everything was added up from a 9-2 year and a No. 4 season-ending national ranking, the whiz-bang, exciting, sophomore-led offense averaged 19 points a game;the senior-studded new-look defense averaged giving up 14. The Purdue game score, exactly.

#15 The ABA Indiana Pacers

By Ashley Steeb

Ashley Steeb is a student at Franklin College of Indiana with a major in Multimedia journalism and a minor in History. During the summer she works for TheStatehouseFile.com, a news website powered by Franklin College journalism students. During her work at the website, Ashley was able to cover major events like the Republican National Convention. After she graduates, Ashley has plans to travel the world and see a baseball game in every major league baseball stadium.

Editor's Note:
Although not a Hall of Fame writer yet, Ashley was invited to participate in this project as a representative of the outstanding journalism school at Franklin College.

I was born and raised in Indiana. Therefore, like many other Hoosiers, that meant I grew up in a household that watched every NBA Indiana Pacers game.

Unfortunately, in the beginning, I only cared about Reggie Miller, not the Pacers. For me, watching a game was purely for entertainment purposes, or a way to stay up a little bit later on a school night.

For the longest time, the history and the origins of the team was a mystery to me. As a child, I do not recall ever hearing about the ABA Pacers. Thankfully, after I grew up a little bit, and my love for history grew, I began to slowly uncover the interesting story and importance of the early Pacers to Indiana.

The National Basketball Association Pacers is the team everyone knows the most, but the American Basketball Association Pacers are the ones who started everything.

The American Basketball Association was created in 1967 and merged with the National Basketball Association in 1976. The league offered a chance for high school and college basketball players to make a living of doing what they loved to do – play basketball.

Despite Hoosiers' love for the sport, the state of Indiana never had a professional basketball team before the ABA Pacers, even though the NBA was around since 1946. The Pacers team was created in 1967 and funded by a group of Hoosier business men.

Billy Keller, a three-time champion with the ABA Pacers, never felt like the ABA was a stepsister to the NBA.

"Once I started playing for the Pacers, I didn't really even think about the NBA," said Keller. "We had our own schedule. We had our business to take care of. So, I didn't really think much about it.

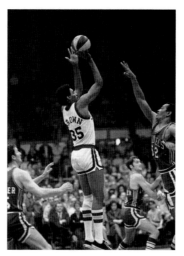

Reggie Brown elevates for the shot. Photo courtesy of the Indiana Pacers.

Mel Daniels adds two! Photo courtesy of the Indiana Pacers.

> **The Pacers were first established in 1967 as a member of the American Basketball Association (ABA) and became a member of the NBA in 1976 as a result of the ABA–NBA merger.**

"My concern was to play well individually, fit in with the team, do my job and play pro ball."

The Pacers may be an odd name, but there a couple of interesting theories on how the team received the name.

Indiana is known for the Indianapolis 500, a very famous motorsports race. Some people say the team is named after the race cars used in the race.

Indiana also was famous for harness horse racing. The horses used in that sport are called pacers because they can only run at a certain pace. Therefore, some people claim this was the origin for the basketball team's name.

Then, there are those who say it is a mixture of both theories.

The ABA Pacers played their first seven seasons at the Indiana State Fairgrounds Coliseum, now known as the Indiana Farmers Coliseum.

The first year's roster included Freddie Lewis, Bob Netolicky and the coach was Larry Staverman.

During their first season, the ABA Pacers did relatively well, making it to the semifinal round of the playoffs.

After a lackluster start to the second season, Staverman was replaced by Bobby Leonard as the head coach.

Leonard is probably known more by his nickname of "Slick". He received the nickname during his days as a basketball player for the Minneapolis Lakers. On a trip to an exhibition game, Leonard was playing Hollywood Gin with George "Hot Rod" Mikan on the team's bus. During the card game, Mikan and Leonard decided the team should stop at a truck stop for food.

"When the bus stopped and the driver turned on all the lights on the bus, at that time I blitzed George Mikan all away across in the gin game," said Leonard. "Here's what he said when the other players started getting up, 'How about buying me a cup of coffee? You're too slick for me'. The other guys heard him say slick and they started calling me that."

Leonard never expected to be the Pacers coach for 13 years.

"When they asked me to come in, it was pretty simple," said Leonard. "I looked at the ABA at that particular time and I thought 'A red, white and blue ball and three-point line?' I just didn't think it would last."

However, Leonard now says the ABA had the most talent he has ever seen in his basketball career.

Keller said Leonard brought a special dynamic to the team.

"He brought enthusiasm. He brought experience. He brought the knowledge to play the game," said Keller. "He just brought so much to it."

Keller contributed Leonard's experience and knowledge to his time as a professional basketball player.

During his time as the head coach, "Slick" Leonard became known for his famous catchphrase "Boom Baby!" He still uses this phrase as a sports broadcaster for the NBA Pacers.

Keller said Leonard first uttered his famous phrase during a game in which Keller made a last- second, game-winning, three-point shot

> **During the merger, the league charged a $3.2 million entry fee for each former ABA team.**

The team is named after Indiana's history with the Indianapolis 500's pace cars and with the harness racing industry.

- one of Keller's favorite memories from his playing days.

Under Leonard's guidance, the Pacers were able to make it to the championship round.

The 1969-70 season could be considered as the breakout performance season for the ABA Pacers. They drafted Keller out of Purdue University and won their first ABA Championship.

Keller said the excitement and joy the team felt after winning their first championship could not compare to other wins and major moments during his career. Leonard said every championship was memorable and exciting.

The Pacers went on to win the next two ABA titles.

"To be able to win three championships out of four years, we just felt that was a great accomplishment for our team," said Keller. "It was great for our city. I don't think you ever get tired of winning championships because that's what you're playing the game for. To be competitive, to win and be the best you can be."

Leonard said winning championships cannot be accomplished unless everyone on the team plays together.

"A championship team, of course, is made up with talent and we always used the idea that the players need to govern themselves where they wouldn't let each other down," said Leonard. "If they did they would be called out by their own teammates. We made it a family affair."

Keller said that the ABA Pacers had all of these traits.

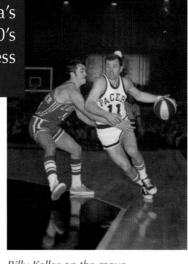

Billy Keller on the move.
Photo courtesy of the Indiana Pacers.

"We had great teams. We had great coaching. We had great players. But, more importantly, we had players who really got along," said Keller. "They loved the game. They enjoyed being around one another."

Leonard also said it was important for the head office members, floor crew and those who sold memorabilia to be considered on the team.

Shortly after their third championship, the team was nearing the end of its run. Even after a televised fundraiser where Hoosiers donated money to keep the Pacers in Indiana, the team had financial issues.

Due to financial reasons, ABA teams had to merge with the NBA or close their doors. More and more basketball players preferred the NBA over the ABA.

By 1976, the ABA League went completely bankrupt. The few remaining teams were forced to make the decision of continuing on as an NBA team or ending the franchise.

The Pacers decision was to join the NBA and continue to compete.

Leonard said he was saddened the ABA had to merge with the NBA, but knew it was inevitable. However, he said the ABA is still making its mark on the sport today.

Both Keller and Leonard want the ABA Pacers to be remembered by today's sports fans.

"The ABA is fun, is family and its community," said Keller. "I think it was all of that. For us players it was tremendous fun."

Leonard said the ABA Pacers helped pave the way for professional sports in Indiana.

"I would like the Pacers to be remembered as a kind of pioneer for the rest of the city," said Leonard. "For the growth of Indianapolis. There's no question that we're [Indianapolis] a major league city. We [the ABA Pacers] kind of started it."

The Pacers proved that Hoosiers were willing to attend games, buy memorabilia and even donate their own money to keep the team in Indiana.

Unfortunately, a majority of the younger generation has just a basic understanding of the ABA Pacers. Most of them never heard of Billy Keller, Roger Brown, Mel Daniels or Bob Netolicky.

However, Keller and Leonard believe the ABA Pacers will never truly be forgotten because there will always be fans who want to keep their story alive.

Bobby "Slick" Leonard.
Photo courtesy of the Indiana Pacers.

Fairgrounds Coliseum.
Photo courtesy of the Indiana Pacers.

For their first seven years, the Pacers played in the Indiana State Fairgrounds Coliseum. In 1974, they moved to the plush new Market Square Arena in downtown Indianapolis, where they played for 25 years. Today, they play at Bankers Life Fieldhouse.

Indiana Sportswriters and Sportscasters Association

After World War II, someone had the idea of creating the Indiana Sportswriters and Sportscasters Association. In 1946, the ISSA was born. And 70 years later, it's still a vibrant and much appreciated organization.

The original idea was for the state's sports media to gather in Indianapolis the night before the high school basketball finals, which then was a boys only, single-class tourney. The mood was festive, with food, drink and poker, while honoring ISSA members. The turnouts were large and the meetings successful. But things started changing. Members began covering Indiana and Purdue teams in the NCAA tourney on the night before the state finals instead of coming to the ISSA meeting. Plus, the introduction of class basketball diluted the media's interest in the high school finals. Attendance started sagging at the ISSA meetings.

To save the ISSA it was clear change was necessary. So 21 years ago the ISSA decided that the key purpose of the organization would be to create a Hall of Fame, and to induct members annually. The yearly Hall of Fame induction banquet has become a tremendous success. There is a lot of personal satisfaction in being honored by your peers. It is from these people that you get your greatest respect.

Prospective ISSA members ask what they get from joining the ISSA. What they get is the satisfaction of associating with and earning the respect of their peers. That is what happens at the yearly Hall of Fame induction ceremony, where the state's sportswriters and sportscasters (both active and retired) gather to reconnect with each other and to honor their peers. With the induction of six newcomers in 2016, the ISSA's Hall of Fame grew to more than 100 members.

The ISSA honors the best in the business. Besides the Hall of Fame inductions, the association also annually honors the Corky Lamm Sportswriter of Year and the Marv Bates Sportscaster of the Year, in addition to also giving out the Bob Williams Helping Hand Award. Periodically, the ISSA presents the Lifetime Achievement Award, which in 2016 was renamed the Ron Lemasters Lifetime Achievement Award. Ron is a past president of the ISSA and, along with Rex Kirts, another past president and current member, are credited with playing key roles in creating the Hall of Fame. Lemasters passed away in 2015.

ISSA
Indiana Sportswriters and
Sportscasters Association
Since 1946

ISSA Hall of Fame

2017
Bill Benner
Jim Brunner
Dan Egierski
Reggie Hayes
Arv Koontz
Bob Simmers

2016
Kent Hormann
Pete DiPrimio
Matt Kopsea
Dan Korb
Chris Denari
Bob Nagle

2015
Bill Beck
Bob Jenkins
Mark Morrow
Blake Sebring
Jason Whitlock

2014
Andy Amey
Mike Chappell
Tracy Dodds
Tom Rust

2013
Mark Boyle
Mike Emrick
Andy Graham
Bill Robertson
Ben Smith

2012
Bill Bilinski
Mike Knezevich
Dave Niehaus
Steve Warden

2011
Dick Denny
Bob Lovell
Joe McConnell
Dean Pantazi
Phil Richards

2010
Jerry Birge
Paul Condry
Walt Ferber
Lynn Houser
Jack Lorri

2009
Howard Kellman
Mike Lopresti
Pat McKee

2008
Al Hamnik
Dave Kitchell
Bob Lamey

2007
Jan Clark
Fred Inniger
Tom Kubat

2006
Bob Forbes
John Harrell
Dick Mittman

2005
Bob Bridge
Bob Ford
Don Hein
Tony Roberts
Max Skirvin

2004
Don Fischer
Bill Fowler
Don Jellison
Rex Kirts
Forest Miller
Stan Sutton
Vic Tanguy
Ben Tenny
Luke Walton
Carl Wiegman

2003
Dennis Kraft
Dave Krider
John Mutka
Joe Smith

2002
George Bolinger
Bob Chase
Jim Costin
Paul (Bud)
   Gallmeier
Dick Ham
Morry Mannies
Tom Reck

2001
Jerry Baker
Bill Fluty
Ron Lemasters

2000
Don Bernhardt
Joe Boland
Joe Edwards
Kurt Freudenthal

1999
Jimmie
   Angelopolous
Charlie Jenkins
Chris Schenkel

1998
Marv Bates
Bob Hammel
Sam
   Simmermaker
Bob Towner

1997
Joe Doyle
Hilliard Gates
Corky Lamm
Bob Williams

1996
Bob Barnet
Dale Burgess
Don Burton
Tom Carnegie
Bob Collins
Sid Collins
Johnny DeCamp
Bill Fox
Gordon Graham
Dan Scism

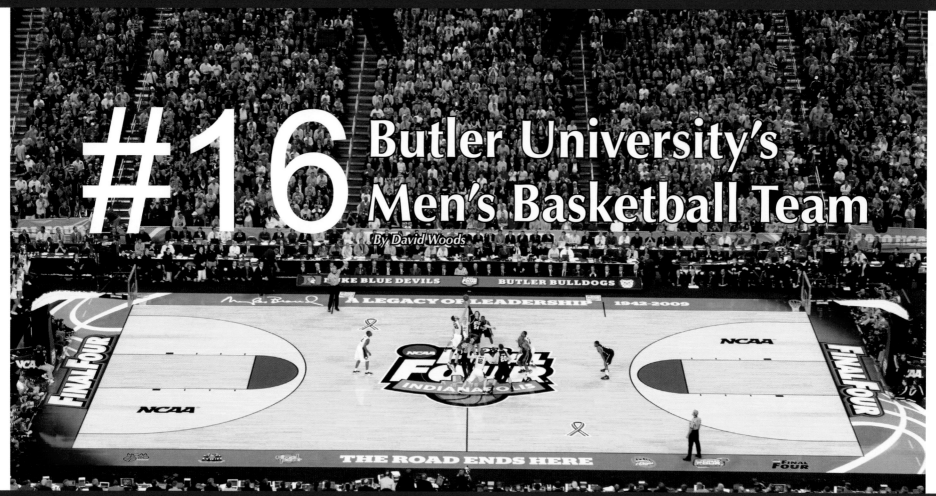

#16 Butler University's Men's Basketball Team

By David Woods

Photo by Brent Smith, courtesy of Butler University.

David Woods, an Urbana, Ill., native and University of Illinois graduate, has been an Indianapolis journalist since 1994. He has covered Butler basketball for The Indianapolis Star since 2001 and has written three books on the subject, including "Underdawgs: How Brad Stevens and Butler University built the Bulldogs for March Madness." He has covered eight Olympic Games and is the first four-time winner of the Jesse Abramson Award from Track and Field Writers of America for journalism excellence.

The difficulty in placing Butler's back-to-back tournament runs in perspective is that there is no comparable occurrence. There was no one shining moment. Rather, there was a series of moments. The Bulldogs' legacy is that of prolonged underdog achievement.

Even in 2016, it might be too soon to appreciate what Butler achieved in reaching NCAA basketball championship games in 2010 and 2011. Mathematics can supply context.

Ken Pomeroy is the statistician whose numbers are a tool used in game plans assembled by Brad Stevens and other coaches. Based on season resume, Butler had a 1.5 percent chance of reaching the NCAA Tournament's championship game in 2010 and 0.02 percent in 2011. In oddsmaking, that's 500-to-1 in the second year.

Using Pomeroy's figures, Butler had 0.003 percent chance of reaching back-to-back championship games. In oddsmaking, that's 33,333-to-1. The statistician acknowledged that is probably overstated. Still, if odds were badly miscalculated by a factor of 33, that is 1,000-to-1. There is nothing analogous to it in college basketball or any other sport.

That doesn't address Butler's back story. When the NCAA separated into divisions in 1973, Division I featured the biggest programs and athletic scholarships. Alexander E. Jones, then the university president, considered bringing Butler into Division III – the lowest level and without scholarships.

When Duke and Butler played each other in the 2010 tournament final, it was the first title game between private universities in 25 years.

Butler's recruiting budget was $3,000. The team traveled not on a conventional bus, but on a black limousine painted blue, the "Blue Goose." Butler didn't have a secretary for the athletic department until 1970, a sports information director until 1981 or a marketing director until 1989. There were once 15 paid season tickets. *Fifteen*. From 1980 to 1991, Butler lost in the first round of the Midwestern Collegiate Conference tournament every year: 0-12.

A new president, Geoffrey Bannister, brought a new vision. He was no Hoosier basketball sophisticate. He was born in England and raised in New Zealand. But he hired 34-year-old Barry Collier as coach and oversaw a $1.5 million renovation of Hinkle Fieldhouse, built in 1928.

Photo courtesy of Butler Athletics.

In Collier's first season, 1989-90, the Bulldogs went 6-22 and set a school record for defeats. In response, Bannister awarded the coach a four-year contract extension.

Collier's teams improved, but not enough to satisfy him. At a 1995 summer retreat, he had what amounted to an epiphany. He had long admired the way coach Dick Bennett's teams played at Green Bay, an MCC rival, but Bennett had moved on to Wisconsin. Collier sought advice. Butler's coach adopted five principles from Bennett – humility, passion, unity, servanthood, thankfulness – that came to be known as the Butler Way. It was a foundation for everything that followed.

The Bulldogs reached the NCAA Tournament in 1997 and 1998 and lost decisively in the first round. When they made it again in 2000, they lost to Florida 69-68 in overtime in a gut-wrenching outcome. Collier left for Nebraska thereafter, but that defeat galvanized the Bulldogs in a way that victory could not have. The next year, in 2001, they made it back under coach Thad Matta and crushed Wake Forest 79-63. It was Butler's first NCAA Tournament victory since 1962.

Stevens was director of basketball operations for that Butler team – travel secretary, essentially -- but was an eyewitness to March Madness. It was Matta who encouraged Stevens to think like a head coach.

"It may have been as enjoyable a year as I've ever had," Stevens said. "I didn't know what was going on. I was just so happy to be there."

Lucas Oil Stadium in Indianapolis hosted the Final Four games for the first time in 2010.

Hoosiers has been produced. Perhaps Butler's story resembles that too much for Hollywood to film another Indiana basketball movie. There would be no shortage of potential opening scenes:

>> Stevens and his then-girlfriend, Tracy Wilhelmy, meeting with Stevens' parents over dinner to tell them he was leaving his marketing job at pharmaceutical giant Eli Lilly to take an unpaid position at Butler.

>> A 15-year-old Gordon Hayward standing in front of a mirror, rehearsing what he would tell his Brownsburg High School basketball coach: I quit. Then 5-foot-11, Hayward was thinking of dropping the sport to concentrate on tennis.

>> A young Ronald Nored learning about servanthood before he ever heard of the Butler Way. His father, Ronald Sr., was an African Methodist Episcopal pastor who helped transform a Birmingham, Ala., community. Each Christmas morning, the father and his two sons distributed gifts to needy children before opening any packages under their own tree. Nored's father died of pancreatic cancer when he was in eighth grade.

>> Matt Howard, son of a mail carrier and the eighth of 10 children, growing up in a three-bedroom house in Connersville and sharing one bathroom for the entire family.

There is enough to Butler's story to give it a fictional quality. If an author or screenwriter had submitted the script, it would have been rejected as implausible. Fiction must be believable.

There were many factors influencing Butler's run to the first Final Four, but the two most important were these: Collier's decision to promote a 30-year-old Stevens to head coach after Todd Lickliter left for Iowa in 2007, and Stevens' first full recruiting class featuring Shelvin Mack, Hayward and Nored. Mack was a Lexington, Ky., guard snubbed by his hometown Kentucky Wildcats.

Two foreign trips in the summer of 2009 propelled the Bulldogs into the next winter. Hayward and Mack were chosen to the USA Basketball team for the under-19 World Basketball Championship at Auckland, New Zealand. They helped the Americans win the gold medal for the first time since 1991.

Later, those two accompanied Butler's team to Switzerland and Italy. In Rome, the players toured two 2,000-year-old structures, the Colosseum and Pantheon temple. The architecture prompted Stevens to remind them that the ancient engineers intended their work to last. Last for eternity. The coach introduced a slogan, "Build for Eternity." Those words were imprinted on gray practice T-shirts as a reminder of what the Bulldogs were trying to do.

Duke's and its 2010 tournament win was its first national championship since 2001 and fourth overall.

★★★★

After being underrated for so long, the Bulldogs went into the 2009-10 season overrated. Never had they been in the preseason rankings, and here they were in the Top 10. Some in the media were picking them to go to the Final Four. Could they handle the hype?

No.

They lost twice – to Minnesota and Clemson – in the 76 Classic at Anaheim, Calif. Then they fell behind Georgetown by 17 points in a 72-65 loss at New York's Madison Square Garden.

In the locker room afterward, Nored went on a tirade lasting several minutes.

"I've never been more fired up in my life," Nored said months later. "The more I yelled, the more fired up I got."

If the Bulldogs didn't get that message, they got the next one, delivered by Stevens. Practices after Christmas break were so poor, he had the locker room stripped bare. Chairs were gone. Trophies were gone. Quotes were gone. One symbol remained in the middle of the room: The second-place Horizon League Tournament trophy from 2009. Keep this up, Stevens told them, and that's what we'll be: runners-up.

Not in 2010. After an 18-0 league season, Butler underscored its dominance by crushing Wright State 70-45 to win the league tournament. The Final Four was in Indianapolis, home of Butler's campus. Still, it was unimaginable that the Bulldogs could get there, as good as they were.

Butler (28-4) was awarded a No. 5 seed and dispatched to San Jose, Calif., to play UTEP in the NCAA West Regional. At 26-6, and 15-1 in Conference USA, the Miners were almost certainly under-seeded. Given the fact there is an upset almost annually in the 5/12 game, UTEP was a trendy pick.

UTEP led 33-27, marking the seventh time in 21 games that the Bulldogs trailed at halftime. They did not lose the 20 other times, and they didn't lose this time. Butler outscored UTEP 22-4 to begin the second half and rolled to a 77-59 victory. Mack sank seven 3-pointers, scoring 18 of his career-high 25 points in the second half. Butler again trailed in the second half but beat Murray State 54-52, and it was on to Salt Lake City.

Coincidentally, Butler was pitted against No. 1 seed Syracuse and coach Jim Boeheim, chairman of the committee that put Hayward and Mack on the U.S. junior team less than a year before. The Bulldogs pounced on Syracuse early and led 12-1.

Eventually, the Orange recovered, built a 54-50 lead and appeared set to pull away. With the Bulldogs wobbling and the shot clock expiring, Nored was left open at the 3-point line – where he was shooting 17 percent. He swished it. That started the Bulldogs on an 11-0 run, and they won 63-59. They were one victory from Indianapolis.

Next was Kansas State, coming off a 101-96, double-overtime victory over Xavier. The Wildcats were exhausted from that and never matched Butler's intensity. Stevens made a curious substitution, inserting 6-foot-11 freshman Andrew Smith, who had played all of three minutes over the past month. Smith, who six years later would inspire so many with a heroic fight against cancer, did his job. DYJ – Do Your Job – had long been a Butler catchphrase. After Kansas State tied the score at 54, the Bulldogs went on a late spurt, as they did against Syracuse. A 9-0 run led to a 63-56 victory and a berth in their first Final Four. Hayward scored 15 of his 22 points in the second half and was the West Regional's most outstanding player.

Back on campus, students spilled out of residence halls and Greek houses. They crowded around the university president, Bobby Fong, who climbed on the shoulders of a football player and raised four fingers on each hand. Indianapolis media covered the Bulldogs as they did the Colts in the Super Bowl two months before. Joining Butler (32-4) in the Final Four were Michigan State (28-8), West Virginia (31-6) and Duke (33-5). So many fans attended the Bulldogs' open practice at Lucas Oil Stadium that the lower bowl seating 29,000 was nearly full.

The magic that the Bulldogs produced in Salt Lake City didn't desert them during the flight home. They defeated Michigan State 52-50 in the first semifinal, playing the kind of smash-mouth basketball for which coach Tom Izzo's Spartans were known.

"You're used to people saying that Michigan State pushed them all over the floor," said Indiana's governor, Mitch Daniels "And for them to say that these Butler kids were too physical for them was terrific."

Butler became the smallest school in 40 years to play for a national championship. The climactic game against Duke was an instant classic, made more so by how close Hayward came to winning it on a half-court 3-pointer at the buzzer. The Blue Devils' 61-59 victory came by two points, and by three inches – the estimated distance by which Hayward's shot missed off the glass. Butler's 25-game winning streak was over.

"We almost had an aura of we thought we were going to win every game," Stevens said.

Entering the tournament, the top four seeds were Kansas, Duke, Kentucky, and Syracuse.

Photo courtesy of Butler Athletics.

Hayward, after two college seasons, left Butler and was chosen No. 9 by the Utah Jazz in the NBA draft. What were the Bulldogs going to do? Go to the Final Four again?

Well, yes.

Butler's 2011 advance to the championship game would have been more astounding, but minds were conditioned because of what happened in 2010. Butler, once 6-5 in the Horizon League, came close to missing the NCAA Tournament altogether.

The Bulldogs (23-9) qualified by winning the Horizon's automatic berth, beating No. 1 seed Milwaukee 59-44. They reached the Sweet Sixteen with victories over Old Dominion, 60-58, on Howard's buzzer-beating layup, and No. 1 seed Pittsburgh, 71-70, on Howard's free throw.

The Pittsburgh game should have ended on Smith's basket sending the Dawgs ahead 70-69 with seven seconds left. But in what Mack said was "the dumbest mistake in my life," he ran into Pittsburgh's Gilbert Brown with 1.4 seconds on the clock, fouling him 45 feet from the basket. Mack had scored 30 points, and he was going to lose the game for Butler. Except Brown missed the second of two free throws, and in a gaffe worse than Mack's, Pittsburgh's Nasir Robinson fouled Howard on the rebound. With 0.8 on the clock, Howard made one free throw, purposely missed the second, and the Bulldogs returned to the Sweet Sixteen.

"I've never seen anything like that. I doubt I'll ever see anything like that again," Nored said, speaking for everyone.

In New Orleans, the Bulldogs beat Wisconsin 61-54 (it wasn't really that close) and erased an 11-point deficit in overtaking Florida 74-71 in overtime. Mack dropped 27 points on Florida.

In a semifinal at Houston, Mack scored 24 in a 70-62 victory over VCU, setting a Final Four record by shooting 5-of-6 on 3-pointers. The two-year run came to an ignominious conclusion two nights later. The Bulldogs shot 18.8 percent – worst ever in a championship game and worst in any tournament game since 1946 – in a 53-41 loss to Connecticut. They led 23-17 early in the second half but were rendered impotent thereafter by UConn's defense.

What Butler could not accomplish should not diminish what it did:

– Win as an underdog, by seeding or betting line, in seven of its final 10 tournament games.

– Became the first team outside the six major conferences to reach successive Final Fours since UNLV in 1990 and 1991, and the first small school to do so since San Francisco won national championships in 1955 and 1956.

– Tie for the lowest seed, No. 8, to reach the championship game.

– The first to reach successive Final Fours without being a No. 1 or 2 seed in either year. Butler was the first to knock off both a No. 1 and No. 2 seed before the Final Four in consecutive years.

"Looking back on it, who has ever experienced that?" Nored asked. "Who has ever experienced what we have experienced?"

A study commissioned by Butler's athletic department estimated that the two tournament runs generated $1 billion worth of publicity in television, print, and on-line news coverage. Factoring in social media, the audience reach exceeded 69 billion. Student applications increased, as did enrollment and merchandise sales. Butler left the Horizon League in 2012 for the Atlantic 10, then a year later joined the Big East.

There has never been anything like it. Not in Indiana or in any of the 49 other states.

Kansas entered the tournament as the overall number one seed but was defeated on the opening weekend by Northern Iowa.

#17 Indiana Pacers & Reggie Miller

By Conrad Brunner

Conrad Brunner's first big assignment was writing a 2,000 front-page feature about an old lard bucket a farmer had dug up while plowing his field. His editor at The Statesboro (Ga.) Herald figured if this neophyte could find something interesting to write about that, he could cover just about anything. Nearly four decades later, Brunner is still producing buckets of copy for IndysSportsCenter. com, the homepage of 1070 the Fan radio. Brunner covered the Pacers for The Indianapolis News, and later the Star, from 1988-95, winning four Pro Basketball Writers Association of America contests in the process. He moved into the digital world in 2000, pioneering Pacers.com as the first news-driven team site in the NBA. He joined 1070 the Fan in 2011 to serve as the station's analyst for the Pacers and Colts. The winner of 26 national, regional and state sportswriting awards, Brunner and his wife Jane live in Indianapolis.

As they prepared for the most significant game of their lives, Reggie Miller gathered his Indiana Pacers teammates in the locker room and posed a question that, in truth, was a challenge.

"If the league called you up and asked you if you only had to play one game and you could pick the spot where you want to play and if you win the game you go to the Finals, would you take it and where would you want to play?'"

In unison came the response:

"The Knicks in the Garden."

In just the right place, against just the right opponent, and in just the right way – with Miller scoring 17 of his 34 to break it open in the fourth quarter – the Pacers beat the Knicks in the Garden, 93-80, in Game 6 of the 2000 Eastern Conference Finals to advance to the NBA Finals for the first time in franchise history.

With that one game, that one moment, finally burying the one team that had proved their greatest rival, these Pacers took the final step in a long, arduous, improbable journey that began before many of them were born.

This had been the franchise that couldn't win, even when it won.

The reward for dominating the ABA, winning three championships in four years, was an enormous toll exacted by the NBA for the privilege of membership. Joining the NBA cost the Pacers $4.5 million up front: $3.2 million to the league, plus $1.3 million to the owners of the two surviving teams not included in the merger, the Kentucky Colonels (John Y. Brown) and St. Louis Spirits (Ozzie and Dan Silna). But the biggest hurt came when the Silnas shrewdly negotiated a deal for one-seventh of each merging team's TV revenues, including the phrase "in perpetuity."

At the time, few NBA games were carried live, and it wasn't unusual for the Finals to be tape-delayed, so it didn't seem like that big a deal. But it wound up netting the Silnas nearly $1 billion, including $500 million from a settlement in 2014. Each of the four surviving ABA teams – the Pacers, Spurs, Nuggets and Nets – forked over more than $100 million to the Silnas prior to the settlement.

In 1968, Bobby "Slick" Leonard became the coach of the ABA Pacers, a position he held for nearly 12 years – the last four after the franchise moved to the NBA. Leonard led the Pacers to three ABA championships before the ABA-NBA merger in June 1976.

The Pacers also couldn't participate in their first NBA Draft, and it just so happened 1976 was a national championship year for Indiana University, thus they were unable to select Scott May, Quinn Buckner or Bobby Wilkerson, who all went in the first 11 picks.

The misfortune of the years that followed, however, was more a combination of bad luck and bad judgment. The Pacers had draft picks that, with a little foresight and luck, could've been used on Larry Bird and Michael Jordan, but instead netted Rick Robey and Tom Owens. They lost the 1983 coin flip for Ralph Sampson, settling for Steve Stipanovich at No. 2. They wound up second in the famed 1985 lottery, with Patrick Ewing going No. 1 to the Knicks and Wayman Tisdale the consolation prize.

Small wonder the team averaged 32 wins from 1976-86, reaching the playoffs just once, needing a fan-driven telethon in 1977 to prevent the franchise from either folding or moving.

But things began to turn in 1986, when fledgling owners Melvin and Herb Simon pulled young Donnie Walsh off the bench, where he had been George Irvine's assistant coach, and made him general manager. Walsh drafted Reggie Miller in 1987, Rik Smits in '88, landed Antonio Davis in the second round in '90 and Dale Davis in 91, thus forming a nice nucleus.

With the hiring of Larry Brown as head coach in '93, the team leapt to prominence, reaching the conference finals for the first time in '94 and returning in '95. Brown wanted a defensive identity for his team and urged Walsh to trade crowd favorite Detlef Schrempf for the enigmatic Derrick McKey, whose lockdown ability at forward turned out to be a critical element. Walsh traded for Mark Jackson in '94, traded him away in '96, and got him back six months later.

But when Brown left following a tumultuous 1996-97 season, Walsh made his most important move. He brought one of the state's greatest basketball legends, Larry Bird, back home again, finally, to serve as head coach. Bird had a firm hand without being domineering, leaving most of the in-game adjustments to offensive coordinator Rick Carlisle and defensive coordinator Dick Harter. But Bird let the players know his rules would be enforced, once leaving Dale Davis

Reggie Miller Court (above) and Reggie Miller dunk highlight (left). Photos courtesy of the Indiana Pacers.

Five Hall of Fame players – Reggie Miller, Chris Mullin, Alex English, Mel Daniels, and Roger Brown – all played with the Pacers for multiple seasons.

and Travis Best on the tarmac as they arrived only minutes late for a team flight.

With Bird's emphasis on professionalism on and off the court, a stout defense anchored inside by the unrelated "Davis Brothers" (Dale and Antonio), and Miller emerging as one of the great clutch scorers in league history – a trait that would ultimately make him the first player from the team's NBA era to reach the Hall of Fame – the Pacers established themselves as one of the most successful teams of the '90s. They reached the playoffs all but one season (1996-97), advancing to the conference finals five times and posting four seasons of at least 52 victories.

But they just couldn't take that Finals step.

The Knicks weren't the only team to stand in the way, but they were the one that always seemed to be there, taunting their Midwestern rivals with Big Apple arrogance, swagger, and toughness.

After Miller scored 25 of his 39 points in the fourth quarter to rally the Pacers to a 93-86 victory in Game 5 of the conference finals in '94 – in the Garden, of course – the underdogs led the series 3-2 and seemed poised to advance. But the Knicks won the next two games to reach the Finals.

The following year, Miller scored eight points in 8.9 seconds near the end of Game 1 as the Pacers stole a 107-105 victory – again in the Garden – and this time it propelled them to a 4-3 series victory, albeit in the second round. Indiana wound up losing to Shaquille O'Neal, Penny Hardaway and the Orlando Magic in the conference finals.

In Bird's first season, 1997-98, the Pacers dominated the Knicks in the second round, winning in five games, but this time Michael Jordan had returned from his brief hiatus and the Bulls won in seven, then went on to win another title.

But nothing was more frustrating, or more baffling, than '99. The season was shortened to 50 games by a lockout and the Pacers looked unstoppable, going 33-17 (a 54-win pace), and then sweeping Milwaukee and Philadelphia in the first two rounds.

The Knicks, meanwhile, were concocting a little magic of their own. Early injuries to Patrick Ewing and Latrell Sprewell, combined with the short season, conspired to leave them in the No. 8 seed. But they shocked No. 1 Miami in the first round, swept No. 4 Atlanta in the second, and once again faced the Pacers in the conference finals.

Though Indiana had homecourt advantage, it lost it quickly as the Knicks took the opener in Market Square Arena. After the Pacers squared

Reggie Miller against New York Knicks. Photo courtesy of the Indiana Pacers.

A five-time All-Star selection, Miller led the league in free throw accuracy five times and won a gold medal in the 1996 Summer Olympics. He holds many of the Pacers scoring records.

really got off the ground due to chronic knee problems. The gifted but inconsistent Jalen Rose moved into the starting lineup, replacing respected veteran Chris Mullin.

Even their home court changed, with Conseco Fieldhouse – The House Reggie Built – taking the place of the demolished Market Square Arena.

These Pacers would be different, and the suspicion was they would not be better.

But with Rose emerging as the first person other than Miller to lead the team in scoring since 1989, and Austin Croshere providing more offensive punch off the bench than Davis, the Pacers thrived during the regular season, winning 56 games, the Central Division, and the top seed in the conference for the first time.

When the playoffs rolled around, however, the fine line between triumph and failure was never made clearer than in the first round. Tied 2-2 heading into the determining Game 5, the Pacers just couldn't shake the upstart Bucks and appeared on the verge of disaster. But Miller scored 18 in the fourth quarter and Dale Davis's offensive rebound led to Travis Best's game-winning 3-pointer, and the Pacers escaped with a 96-95 victory.

It seemed to breathe life into a team that found the will to push through the accumulated doubts of all those years of postseason frustration.

Miller and Rose each scored 40 in Game 1 of the second-round series against the Sixers and suddenly the Pacers found themselves, winning in six games.

And then, one more time, came the Knicks.

This time, there was little more than token resistance from the New Yorkers. The Pacers won all three home games and closed it out in the Garden in Game 6, thanks to Miller's 17-point fourth quarter.

After the final buzzer, Miller leapt into Rose's arms in a tight embrace as the players celebrated their long-awaited, hard-earned breakthrough.

In his walk-off interview with Jim Gray of NBC, Miller revealed the story of his pregame talk with his teammates, paid heartfelt tribute to the Knicks for all of the battles through the years, and took a peek at what was to come.

"We had to exorcise some demons. My God, this is beautiful."

They won the East, but not the 2000 NBA championship. Shaquille O'Neal, Kobe Bryant and the Lakers won the title in six games, and the Pacers would never again be quite the same. After that season Bird followed through on his pledge to coach only three seasons and resigned, Smits retired, Jackson and Mullin departed as free agents and Dale Davis was traded to Portland for a young talent named Jermaine O'Neal.

What they accomplished, however, was nothing short of transformational for the franchise and the city. Once a laughingstock team of castoffs and misfits that needed donations from fans and local businesses to stay afloat, the Pacers had evolved into one of the most respected organizations in professional sport.

By beating the Knicks, in the Garden, to reach the NBA Finals for the first – and thus far only – time in franchise history, the Pacers didn't get rings, but they didn't need jewelry to feel like champions.

Photos courtesy of the Indiana Pacers.

Over the Pacers 49 seasons of play they have made the playoffs 32 times (23 in the NBA and 9 in the ABA).

things in Game 2, another moment tipped the balance of the series, only this time Miller wasn't involved. Larry Johnson converted a controversial four-point play in the closing seconds of Game 3, with a questionable foul called against Antonio Davis, and the Knicks pulled a 92-91 stunner. The underdogs went on to win the series in six games over the demoralized favorites, becoming the first No. 8 seed ever to reach the Finals.

It looked more and more as if these Pacers were forever doomed to life on the doorstep.

The sensation of a receding tide was strengthened when Antonio Davis, whose rebounding, defense and toughness off the bench had contributed mightily to the team's personality, was traded away on draft night. He went to Toronto for the No. 5 pick, used on a lithe, talented but long-term prospect, Jonathan Bender, whose career never

The Pacers have appeared in the NBA Eastern Conference Finals seven times and advanced to the NBA Finals in 2000.

#18 The Shooter–Rick Mount

By Tom Kubat

During his professional career, Mount played for the Indiana Pacers, Kentucky Colonels, Utah Stars, and the Memphis Sounds.

"I think I was the greatest shooter to ever live. I've got to believe that. Nobody ever stopped me. I stopped myself."

Those are pretty strong words – uttered by an arrogant, cocky, stuck-on-himself athlete?

Nope. The words belong to Rick Mount. He didn't just talk the talk. He definitely walked the walk. Or shot the shot, as it were.

During his three-year career at Purdue, "The Rocket" averaged 32.3 points a game, most of them the result of a deadly jump shot from long range.

He closed out his Boilermaker career with 2,323 points, still the most in Purdue history.

Remarkable considering that Mount played during an era when freshmen weren't eligible for varsity competition AND the three-point shot was not yet part of the college game.

During Mount's senior season, he exploded for 61 points – still a Purdue record – in a 108-107 loss to Iowa.

He made 27 of 47 shots against the Hawkeyes – and later research showed that 13 of his baskets would have come from beyond the original 3-point line.

In today's game, that would have added up to 74 points.

Still, Mount (who played from 1967-68 to 1969-70) left Purdue as the Big Ten Conference's career scoring leader and remained so until 1981.

Today, he's No. 6 on the Big Ten's all-time scoring list – and the five ahead of him, record-holder Calbert Cheaney (Indiana), Shawn Respert (Michigan State), Glen Rice (Michigan), Mike McGee (Michigan) and Steve Alford (Indiana) – all played four years of varsity basketball.

Alford played one season

Rick Mount's father, Pete, was an avid basketball player who urged Rick to learn how to play.

with the 3-point shot, and the others had it as a weapon all four seasons.

Mount could score in a variety of ways but he was, first and foremost, a shooter. The bulk of his points came from his laser sharp jumpers.

"To be honest with you, I think Rick shot the ball better when there was a guy hanging all over him," said Billy Keller, a teammate and point guard on Purdue's 1969 Final Four team. "He was so used to guys being physical with him, getting in his face when he'd shoot it.

"Rick had a shooter's mentality. He always believed his next shot was going in. Rick was a great shooter."

With Mount's deadly sniping leading the way, the Boilermakers won the Big Ten title and advanced to the NCAA championship game in his junior season.

It was Mount's buzzer-beating baseline jumper versus unranked Marquette that propelled Purdue to a 75-73 victory and its first (of only two) Final Four appearances.

And it was his 36 points that led the Boilermakers to an easy 92-65 victory over third-ranked North Carolina in the semifinals.

That set up a championship game between No. 1 UCLA (28-1), coached by former three-time Boilermaker All-American John Wooden, against No. 9 Purdue (23-4).

But Mount suffered through a rare off night (making only 12 of 36 field goal attempts) in a 28-point effort, and the Bruins prevailed 92-72.

UCLA center Lew Alcindor (who became Kareem Abdul-Jabbar two years later) dominated with 37 points and 20 rebounds.

Mount played prep basketball at Lebanon High School, just a long jump shot south of Purdue's West Lafayette campus. He started and scored in double figures every game in four seasons for the Tigers.

His career high was 57 points against Crawfordsville, and he averaged 27.3 points over 94 games, finishing with 2,595 points – second on the state's all-time scoring list at the time.

Voted Indiana's Mr. Basketball in 1966, Mount became the first high school athlete to be featured on the cover of *Sports Illustrated* (Feb. 14, 1966 issue).

Photo courtesy of the Indiana Basketball Hall of Fame.

Mount's college decision came down to Miami (Fla.) and Purdue. He originally picked the Hurricanes but then changed his mind.

It didn't take him long to offer up a preview of what was to come during his three seasons as a Boilermaker.

As a sophomore, he made his debut in the inaugural game in Mackey Arena. Although Purdue lost 73-71 to – you guessed it – top-ranked UCLA, Mount poured in 28 points.

He went on to earn first-team All-Big Ten and second-team All-American honors. In each of his final two seasons, Mount was voted the Big Ten's Most Valuable Player and a first-team All-American.

"What helped Rick, he shot the ball high over his head, and he was about 6-4," Keller said. "The smaller guards would be all over him, but they really couldn't get up high enough to block his shot.

"The other thing that made him so good, he was one of the best at coming off screens. There are three guys who I think were great at using a screen. Rick obviously was one. Steve Alford was another. And Reggie Miller was another."

Asked about a story that claimed Purdue coach George King, before the Final Four season, told Keller and Herm Gilliam they had to get the ball more to Mount – because the Boilermakers needed him to shoot more if they were going to reach their potential.

Although Keller didn't recall that conversation with King, he did say, "I do know that it was important for Herman to understand his importance and his role, and to know that Rick was going to be the marquee shooter," Keller said.

"I knew what my job was and that was to facilitate the ball. To get the ball to Rick, to Herman, to the people who could score. I knew what my job was and accepted it."

Mount played at the same time as two other prolific scorers – Pete Maravich and Calvin Murphy. While they ended up with more career points, Mount had the much better shooting percentage, 51.5 percent compared to 45.2 for Maravich and 43.7 for Murphy.

Mount was the first overall draft pick by the Indiana Pacers of the fledgling American Basketball Association in 1970.

But he never blossomed as a pro, playing five seasons with four different teams – the Pacers, Kentucky Colonels, Utah Stars and Memphis Sounds.

Keller said that Mount and Pacer coach Bobby "Slick" Leonard did not mesh.

"It was a different setting for Rick with the Pacers, because they had a lot of guys who were already established and had won a championship," Keller said. "Slick was not going to change his offense and his philosophy. So Rick wasn't going to have the same luxury he had at Purdue.

"I believe that Rick wasn't Slick's kind of player. As a player, Slick was a hard-nosed, in your face, scrap and fight kind of guy. That's what he liked. I just don't feel like Rick was that kind of player for Slick."

After Mount's career ended he became estranged from his high school and Purdue. He stopped going to Lebanon games and stayed away from West Lafayette.

An avid hunter and fisherman, he opened an outdoor shop in his hometown but that went under in four years. He applied for the coaching job at Central Catholic High School in Lafayette but was turned down because he hadn't earned his Purdue degree.

Over the years, several stories have been written about what caused the fallout with Purdue.

Some speculated that he was upset with former Boilermaker coach Gene Keady for not playing his son, Richie, enough. Richie eventually transferred after only one year at Purdue.

> When it was time to try out for the school basketball team, Rick wasn't able to make a standard left-hand lay up (a requirement for the team), so Rick practiced for hours the night before the tryouts, mastered the shot, and made the team.

Rick Mount at Purdue University. Photo courtesy of Purdue Athletics.

Others wrote that, although Mount's number 10 was never formally retired, he was upset when Woody Austin showed up wearing his former number in 1988.

Although it had nothing to do with Purdue, another story centered on when Mount was selected in 1999 as one of the Top 50 players in Indiana history, he turned down an invitation to the banquet because Leonard would be there.

Mount finally did return to Purdue this past season (2015-16) for a "Rick Mount Bobblehead Night." At that time he was quoted in a story saying part of his problem with Purdue was that he and George King didn't always get along.

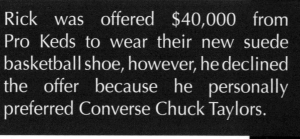

Rick was offered $40,000 from Pro Keds to wear their new suede basketball shoe, however, he declined the offer because he personally preferred Converse Chuck Taylors.

Keller remembers one incident between the two that resulted in Mount quitting the team for a couple days.

"Rick came out in the paper one time after a game, kind of saying that his teammates froze him out – didn't get him the ball," Keller said.

"So the next day at practice, it was my understanding that George went up to him and said, 'You have a right to be upset if that's the way you feel, but you can't say that in the newspaper.'

"And then he and Rick had some words and Rick quit the team. He left and went home."

Keller asked King if there was anything he could do, and he went to the locker room to talk to his teammate, but to no avail.

"George told me that he was not going to talk to Rick about coming back," Keller said. "George was not going to initiate a phone call. Rick had to initiate the phone call."

Keller added, "But only Rick knows what his conflict was with Purdue."

One thing's for sure, to this day Rick Mount remains a Boilermaker legend and one of the all-time great shooters in college basketball history.

Rick Mount Indiana All-Star. Photo courtesy of the Indiana Basketball Hall of Fame.

#19

The Legend of Tony Hinkle

By Pete DiPrimio

Pete DiPrimio is an award-winning sports writer for the Fort Wayne (Indiana) News-Sentinel, a freelance writer and a member of the Indiana Sportswriters and Sportscasters Hall of Fame. He's been an adjunct lecturer for the National Sports Journalism Center at IUPU-Indianapolis and for Indiana University's School of Journalism. He is the author of three nonfiction books pertaining to IU athletics (two on basketball, one on baseball) and more than 20 children's books. He's a Heisman Trophy voter and a long-time member of the USBWA and FWAA. He has finished one novel (unpublished) and is working on a second. Pete is also a fitness instructor and wellness coach.

They don't name basketball arenas after nobodies.-

That's the first thing you should know about Tony Hinkle.

It's not the only thing, of course, when talking about a man who built a legacy at Butler University few can match, but let's start there.

Butler Fieldhouse was built in 1928, renamed for Hinkle in 1965, and it wasn't because he donated a ton of money.

Hinkle was a legend in his time, and if his impact sometimes gets overlooked against me-first 21st Century drama, it never gets forgotten.

Butler is a success in so many ways today because of Hinkle.

That's the second thing you should know about him.

He played; he coached; he conquered.

Simple concepts for a not so simple man.

Hinkle started coaching during the Roaring Twenties. He ended just after men landed on the moon. He lived 92 years and made the most of every single one, most of them with a name not his own.

Yes, we'll get to that.

Overall, Hinkle's teams won 17 conference championships in football and 10 in basketball, with most of those coming between 1952 and 1964.

In 1929, a decade before the NCAA tourney started, Butler was considered the national basketball champion. It came via declaration from a third-party organization called the Veterans Athletic Association of Philadelphia rather than postseason tournament triumph, but it came from solid logic -- the Bulldogs went 17-2 with wins over defending national champ Pittsburgh (ending the Panthers' 27-game winning streak), Purdue, North Carolina, Missouri, Illinois and Notre Dame.

Not bad for a small, private school wedged into Indianapolis's northwest side on what was once an amusement park.

Along the way, Hinkle served as president of the National Collegiate Basketball Coaches Association, and was Rules Committee Chairman for the National Basketball Committee of the United States and Canada (he was a major influence in getting rid of the center jump after every made basket, and changing the color of the ball from dark brown to orange). He was a force on a national scale despite his small-school status and was inducted into the Naismith Memorial Basketball Hall of Fame (as a contributor rather than a coach), the Indiana Basketball Hall of Fame and the Indiana Football Hall of Fame.

How's that for a triple crown.

Hinkle didn't win with gimmicks or overwhelming talent, although standout players came to Butler because of him – All-Americans such as Jerry Steiner, Ralph "Buckshot" O'Brien, Bob Dietz, Jimmy Doyle, Ted Guzek and, at the end, Billy Shepherd.

Tony attended the University of Chicago, where he won varsity letters in three sports

Tony Hinkle. Photo courtesy of Butler University.

Hinkle captained the Chicago Maroons basketball team for two seasons and was twice selected as an All-American, in 1919 and 1920

Milan hero Bobby Plump was a Butler Bulldog good enough to score 1,439 career points.

Still, Hinkle wasn't excited about recruiting, didn't devote all waking hours to it as modern coaches do, and lacked the money and resources other programs had, which meant he often won without superstars. He did it because of fundamentals, because of a belief in doing things the right way. It was a substance-over-flash approach famously known as "The Butler Way" that continues to this day despite the emergence of three-point shots, shot clocks and one-and-done players.

That is memorialized underneath a bust of Hinkle outside of Hinkle Fieldhouse (between Gates 2 and 3), and it consists of these five principles:

1 Humility – know who we are, strengths and weaknesses
2 Passion – don't be lukewarm, commit to excellence
3 Unity – team first
4 Servanthood – make teammates better, lead by giving
5 Thankfulness – learn from every circumstance.

Hinkle thrived with a coaching versatility that has long since disappeared. He went 560-392 in basketball, 165-99-13 in football and 335-309-5 in baseball. One black-and-white photo shows him standing atop the football stadium in a white Butler t-shirt holding a basketball, a football and a baseball.

It was the ultimate coaching juggling act, and no one appreciated it more than John Wooden, the UCLA coaching legend (and former Purdue All-American), who once called Hinkle the greatest coach of all time because he won in multiple sports.

For Hinkle, even all that wasn't enough.

He was also the Bulldogs' long-time athletic director, joining with the administration to balance academics and athletics in an era when many schools had no interest in that. Butler would never be just a sports factory, although in recent years it has become a basketball power, with consecutive national championship game appearances in 2010 and 2011, an amazing accomplishment for a mid-major school.

Beyond that, Hinkle taught classes at Butler, including Theory and Practice of Basketball, and Theory and Practice of Football.

With the demands of recruiting and year-long player development, that could never happen now – at least not at the major college level.

Specifically, Hinkle coached for nearly 50 years, from 1921 to 1970, and the only reason he stopped was because then-university president Alexander E. Jones forced him out using a mandatory retirement age of 70 as an excuse, although three losing records in Hinkle's final four seasons set the stage.

The result – Butler went into a two-decade basketball funk.

Actually, Hinkle did leave Butler for four years in the 1940s while serving in the Navy in World War II, and, of course, he coached. He directed the Great Lakes Navy teams.

While Hinkle won in every sport he coached, he achieved his greatest success in basketball. Under him, Butler appeared in one NCAA tourney, in 1962, when the Bulldogs went 2-1 in the NCAA Regional with the loss to Kentucky and a win over No. 8 Bowling Green. They also played in the NIT in 1958 and '59.

The Bulldogs excelled with the Hinkle System, which was a disciplined, pass-and-cut attack that led to the motion offense Bob Knight later used to championship-winning effect at Indiana. In fact, Knight once said Hinkle, "May well be the most remarkable coach in American collegiate athletic history."

As a player at Chicago, Hinkle lettered three times in basketball, was team captain twice, and was a member of the Big Ten Conference championship team in 1919–20, losing the national championship to Penn.

Tony Hinkle. Photo courtesy of Butler University.

Hinkle was a passionate coach who didn't publicly rip players, although intense one-on-one discussions behind closed doors sometimes happened.

He coached men, not saints.

Hinkle inspired many of his players to become coaches. In fact, Hinkle was sometimes called the "Dean of Indiana College Basketball Coaches" because at one point 55 of his former players coached basketball in Indiana. That included Marvin Wood, who coached tiny Milan to the 1954 state championship and a place in Hoosier lore (and become the inspiration for the movie, "Hoosiers").

Before he was a successful coach, Hinkle was an outstanding player. He was born Paul Hinkle just outside of Logansport, and graduated from Calumet High School on Chicago's south side while excelling in basketball, baseball, golf and soccer (Calumet had dropped football). He attended the University of Chicago and played for Hall of Famers Amos Alonzo Stagg and Harlan "Pat" Page, earning nine letters in football, basketball and track from 1917-20.

That was when Chicago was a member of the Big Ten Conference. Hinkle played on Chicago's 1920 Big Ten title team while earning All-American honors. He also was team captain, twice made the all-conference team and earned a new name – "Tony."

According to legend, after a road game, Hinkle left a restaurant carrying extra spaghetti. Coach Page found that funny enough to call him "Tony" because it sounded Italian.

The new name stuck. Paul became Tony.

Hinkle graduated from Chicago in 1920, and spent a year as an assistant coach under Stagg. The next season he headed to Butler to become an assistant under Page, who had taken the Bulldogs' head coaching jobs in basketball and football.

Tony Hinkle. Photo courtesy of Butler University.

It was a multi-sport example Hinkle quickly followed once Page left in 1926

His first three basketball seasons set the tone for the future. Butler went 17-4, 19-3 and 17-2 against a schedule full of far bigger teams. That peaked during the 1959-60 season, when its first 10 games consisted of eight Big Ten squads and UCLA.

Butler went 5-5 in that stretch and finished 15-11.

Butler won often enough against Big Ten teams to become known as Big Ten killers. Three times the Bulldogs won the Hoosier Classic, that era's equivalent of today's Crossroads Classic, going 6-0 against Indiana, Purdue and Illinois in that event in the 1947, '48 and '60 seasons.

After the 1960 season, tired of losing to Butler, IU and Purdue pushed to discontinue the Hoosier Classic.

And so it was.

Hinkle was once asked to name some of his best players. His answer reflected the Butler Way as nothing else could.

"We never had any great players, only great teams," he said. "The kids did what I told them, and we played as a team. That is why we could win so often."

Perhaps that's the best thing to know about Tony Hinkle.

Hinkle Fieldhouse. Photo courtesy of Thomas Mueller.

#20 Coach Knute Rockne

By Matthew VanTryon

Matthew VanTryon is a student at Butler University in Indianapolis. He has done freelance work and internships with the Hendricks County Flyer, Journal Review, the Indianapolis Star and Sporting News. He has also served in various capacities on the staff of the Butler Collegian, Butler's student newspaper.

Editor's Note:
Although not a Hall of Fame writer yet, Matthew was invited to participate in this project as a representative of the outstanding journalism school at Butler University.

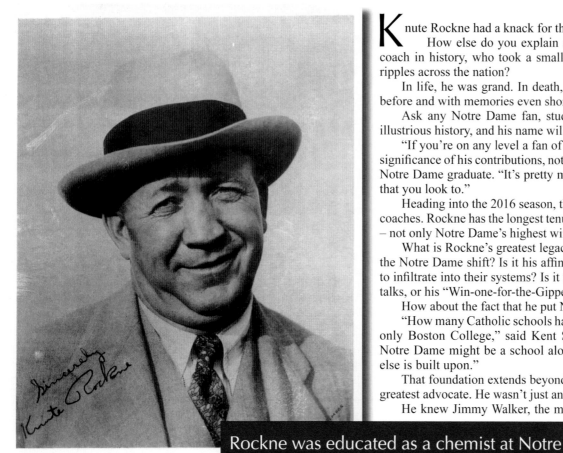

Halftone portrait signed by Knute Rockne. c. 1920s. Photo courtesy of Notre Dame Archives.

Rockne was educated as a chemist at Notre Dame, and graduated in 1914 with a degree in pharmacy.

Knute Rockne had a knack for the grandiose.

How else do you explain a man who won a higher percentage of football games than any other coach in history, who took a small Catholic school in Indiana to national heights, and whose death sent ripples across the nation?

In life, he was grand. In death, he was grand. Even today, in a world speeding faster ahead than ever before and with memories even shorter, the name Rockne reverberates.

Ask any Notre Dame fan, student, player or alumni about the most important names in the Irish's illustrious history, and his name will immediately surface.

"If you're on any level a fan of the football program or university, you begin to appreciate not only the significance of his contributions, not only to the football program, but to the university," said Pat Reis, a 1985 Notre Dame graduate. "It's pretty much Father Sorin, Father Hesburgh and Knute Rockne are your figures that you look to."

Heading into the 2016 season, the Irish have won 892 games in their illustrious history. They've had 23 coaches. Rockne has the longest tenure (13 years), the most wins (105) and the highest win percentage (.881) – not only Notre Dame's highest winning percentage, but all of college football's.

What is Rockne's greatest legacy? Is it his on-field strategy that led to never-before-utilized things like the Notre Dame shift? Is it his affinity for the passing game, something that few teams had ever attempted to infiltrate into their systems? Is it the five undefeated seasons? The three national titles? Is it his fiery pep talks, or his "Win-one-for-the-Gipper" speech?

How about the fact that he put Notre Dame on the map?

"How many Catholic schools have big-time college football programs? Other than Notre Dame, there's only Boston College," said Kent Stephens, College Football Hall of Fame curator. "Without Rockne, Notre Dame might be a school along the lines of Xavier or DePaul. He built the foundation everything else is built upon."

That foundation extends beyond the borders of South Bend, Indiana. Rockne became college football's greatest advocate. He wasn't just an icon in football circles, either. He was a national celebrity.

He knew Jimmy Walker, the mayor of New York. He knew Babe Ruth. He knew Lou Gehrig. As the image of Rockne grew, so did the name of Notre Dame and the sport of college football.

"He was a great promoter, not only of the team and the school, but of himself," Stephens said. "He was very humorous, he was one of the first guys to use mass media such as radio and the mass print publications of the time. Since Notre Dame was not restricted by a conference schedule, he was able to transform Notre Dame into a national team by playing a national schedule."

While Rockne's exploits on the field are well known, what cannot be understated is his role in continuing Notre Dame's success even after his death in 1931.

Hunk Anderson, who coached the Irish for three years following Rockne's death, played for Rockne.

Elmer Layden, who coached the Irish for seven years after Anderson's departure, was one of the "Four Horsemen" under Rockne. Frank Leahy, who won five national titles as coach of the Irish, was a tackle on Rockne's final three teams.

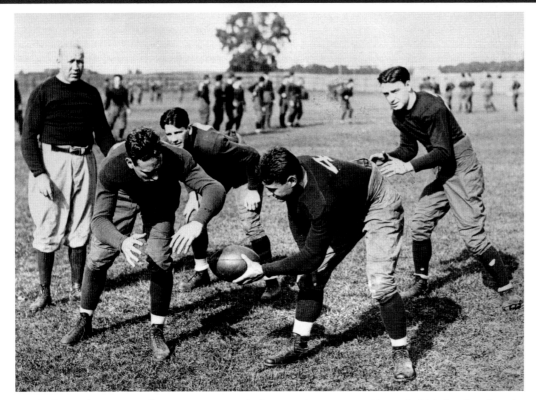

Football Coach Knute Rockne at practice with the Four Horsemen – Harry Stuhldreher handing the ball to Don Miller; Jim Crowley is behind Stuhldreher; Elmer Layden is behind Miller, c. 1924. Photo courtesy of Notre Dame Archives.

"That's one of his greatest legacies," Stephens said. "They always talk about coaching trees. You look at the number of Hall of Fame coaches that came from Rockne, it's unbelievable."

Yet as great as Rockne's numbers and legacy are, there are so many "what-ifs" that hang in the balance. Just as his career was reaching its climax, tragedy struck.

During Rockne's 13 years as head coach for Notre Dame, Rockne led the Fighting Irish to 105 victories, 12 losses, five ties, and three national championships, including five undefeated seasons without a tie.

Rockne helped to popularize the forward pass and made the Notre Dame Fighting Irish a major factor in college football.

In the two seasons prior to Rockne's death in March, 1931, the Irish went 19-0 and won two national titles. Based on several Sports Reference metrics, the 1930 team was Rockne's best team by a wide margin, and that was also a season in which they faced the toughest schedule of his 13-year career.

Rockne was on TWA Flight 599 bound for Los Angeles to participate in the filming of "The Spirit of Notre Dame." The plane crashed near Bazaar, Kansas, killing him and seven others. It was a loss like few others the nation had experienced.

President Herbert Hoover declared Rockne's death "a national loss." Countless coaches and celebrities from across the nation sent their condolences. King Haakon VII, then king of Rockne's native Norway, sent a personal envoy to attend Rockne's funeral.

Will Rogers, the famous columnist of that generation, wrote:

"We thought it would take a President or a great public man's death to make a whole nation, regardless of age, race or creed, shake their heads in real, sincere sorrow. Well, that's what this country did today, Knute, for you. You died one of our national heroes. Notre Dame was your address but every gridiron in America was your home."

One of the first responders to the crash was 13-year-old James Easter Heathman, who lived on his family's farm near the crash site. Heathman arrived at the site with his father and several brothers. What he saw – bodies strewn about the ground – would change his life.

"Being so young with eight dead bodies, it was a horrible, gruesome sight to see," said his daughter, Sue Ann Brown. "Things like that stay with you forever."

Heathman wouldn't return to the site until he retired. Yet the traumatic event was always on his mind.

"When I was a little girl, I used to ride my horse up there not knowing, just because it was a beautiful place," Brown said. "My folks told me that a famous football coach died in a plane crash there. I never dreamed in a million years that it would affect my life as it has."

For many years, the crash site was accessible to the public. But when a family built a house on the adjacent property, they put locks on the gate.

However, they gave Heathman keys so he could take visitors to the site.

"They don't want to deprive the Notre Dame or Rockne fans or the people that really want to visit the crash site," Brown said.

Notre Dame, took it upon themselves to embrace their responsibility to protect that site and to make it accessible to the families and the many people who admire and adore Knute Rockne."

Attendance has waned during each of the last two memorials, which Brown attributes to the passing of her father. Heathman died in 2008.

"There's a lot less people who are called to go up to the monument since dad passed away," Brown said. "He was very busy his last couple of summers. People wanted to do that while an eyewitness was there to tell them. It meant so much more to hear it from somebody that was there that day."

The Chase County Historical Society and Museum near the site has multiple pieces of Rockne memorabilia, including a Rockne Studebaker, a propeller from the plane and audio of a Rockne halftime speech.

Rockne's legacy continues in a plethora of other ways. The film "Knute Rockne, All American" was released in 1940 and tells the story of his life. Dozens of books have been written about him. Yet perhaps the most visible tributes to him come in the form of sculptures. Jerry McKenna has sculpted 11 life-size Rockne figures that reside around the world.

His original Rockne sculpture resides in South Bend, where the College Football Hall of Fame was located until it moved to Atlanta in 2011. An identical sculpture is also in Voss, Norway, Rockne's birthplace.

Other McKenna sculptures of Rockne reside in downtown South Bend, in Rockne, Texas, and at various places on Notre Dame's campus, including one at Notre Dame Stadium.

Knute Rockne at practice coaching, c.1925.
Photo courtesy of Notre Dame Archives.

Rockne died in a plane crash (TWA Flight 599) in Kansas on March 31, 1931. He was en route to participate in the production of the film The Spirit of Notre Dame (released October 13, 1931).

For many Notre Dame fans and alumni, making a trek to Chase County, Kansas, has become a way to honor Rockne and the others who lost their lives in the crash. One of those was Reis, who is an active Notre Dame alumnus in the Minnesota area.

While in college, Reis and several of his friends decided to make the trek to see the site. Several times after he and his friends graduated, they made return trips.

Soon, they became known to the locals in the area. When it came time for the 75th memorial in 2006, the locals asked Reis if he would be willing to organize a more official memorial. That year, 250 people showed up on March 31 to honor the Notre Dame legend, including family members of the other seven people who died.

"It's a small-part Graceland," Reis said. "It's a little bit of an odd way to honor a man at the very location (he died), but it is hallowed ground. It is a special place. The people in the area, who at the time had little or no connection to Knute Rockne and

McKenna has also sculpted smaller Rockne busts for the last several Notre Dame football coaches to have in their office.

"Brian Kelly said, 'I get these recruits in my office and they can say no to me, but it's awfully hard to say no to Rockne who's right there next to me,' " McKenna said.

Rockne has been gone for eight decades, yet he has transcended time in the hearts of the Notre Dame faithful. Maybe, if possible, his status has increased. For all the success Notre Dame has had since his passing, and for all the success yet to come, it can all be traced back to one man.

"Even if you know him in this caricature-type manner, this bigger-than-reality charismatic figure, I don't think anybody who ever graduated from Notre Dame doesn't have appreciation and knowledge of who Knute Rockne is," Reis said.

'HOOSIERS' INTRODUCED MILAN TO THE WORLD

By Lynn Houser

It's almost impossible to talk about The Milan Miracle without also talking about the movie, "Hoosiers." Since the release of the film in 1986, those two story lines have been largely inseparable.

Milan's story was begging to be told, and it is hard to believe anybody could have told it better than Hoosier native Angelo Pizzo.

"The reason I wrote 'Hoosiers' is that I couldn't have somebody from outside the state, somebody who didn't know the people, write it," Pizzo said in a 2016 interview. "I wanted somebody who knew how the people walked, how they talked, how they chewed their gum."

Although Pizzo took a lot of creative license in telling Milan's tale, it was obvious his Hickory Huskers were essentially the Milan Indians, and that Jimmy Chitwood was the equivalent of Milan hero Bobby Plump.

Using former Indiana high school basketball players and shooting the film at various locations in Indiana, the movie authentically captured the heart and soul of Indiana high school basketball, back in the day when the big dogs had to fear the underdogs.

"Underdog stories work in all cultures, but they are particularly salient in America because even the over-dogs think they are underdogs," Pizzo said.

Another thing that has made the movie so timeless is that it depicts a period in which the little towns and their little high schools still mattered.

"There is certainly a nostalgic component to it," Pizzo said. "A producer who grew up in Manhattan said it was something he felt like he missed, the natural goodness of people emerging in that environment, a natural assumption of worth."

Pizzo and director David Anspaugh, a fellow Hoosier native, didn't set out to make a period piece as such, but they did take measures to give it some longevity. The musical score of Jerry Goldsmith had a timeless quality to it, as proven by the fact that you can still hear it playing in high school gyms today.

"We deliberately chose not to use contemporary songs," Pizzo said. "That always dates a film in a negative way, taking you back to a certain time and place. We wanted a soundtrack that could come from any era."

Choosing rural Indiana locations to shoot the film was just as important to Pizzo and Anspaugh, who also purposely filmed "Rudy" (1993) right on the campus of Notre Dame.

As Pizzo explained it, "My approach to making 'Rudy' and 'Hoosiers' was that 'place' is as important as 'character.' I thought of Indiana and Notre Dame as my characters."

Along the same lines of authenticity, Pizzo and Anspaugh were just as determined to take Indiana high school players and make them into actors, rather than trying to take professional actors and make them into high school basketball players. It wasn't just about having realistic action scenes, but also about having individuals who looked and spoke like Hoosiers.

"It's knowing who the people are," Pizzo said. "Casting is huge. People in England don't know what Hoosiers are like, but certainly David and I did."

No wonder the movie has enjoyed a long shelf life.

On its 100th anniversary in 2007, the American Film Institute ranked "Hoosiers" the No. 4 sports movie of all time, and the No. 13 most inspirational movie of all time. More recently, the film was selected for preservation in the U.S. National Film Registry by the Library of Congress, hailing it as "historically and aesthetically significant."

"I am continually surprised," Pizzo said. "Nobody can plan for anything like that."

GENE HACKMAN

CASTLE THEATRE NEW CASTLE, IND.

HOOSIERS

It'll go straight to your heart.

BARBARA HERSHEY

DENNIS HOPPER

SPECIAL PREMIERE ENGAGEMENTS
BEGIN FRIDAY, NOVEMBER 14.

Ten Indiana Sports Movies That Belong In Your Library

Just one writer's opinion, and some of these are a stretch, but let the countdown begin:

10. Winning (1969)
The world is still waiting for that one great movie about auto racing, but at least you get to see a lot of the Indianapolis Motor Speedway in this one. Paul Newman is believable as driver Frank Capua.

9. Season On The Brink (2002)
John Feinstein's book was way better, and Brian Dennehy doesn't do Bob Knight justice, but any movie about Knight is enough to hold your interest.

8. Eight Men Out (1988)
Although the story is about the 1919 Chicago Black Sox, it was filmed at old Bush Stadium in Indianapolis. Very well done.

7. Knute Rockne: All –American (1940)
Pat O'Brien as "Rock" and Ronald Reagan as "The Gipper" make a darn good pair in this story of the iconic Notre Dame coach.

6. Madison (2005)
A year after playing Jesus in Mel Gibson's "Passion of the Christ," Jim Caviezel is hell bent on winning the Madison Regatta. Based on a true story, it is surprisingly good, sort of a "Hoosiers" on the banks of the Ohio River.

5. Blue Chips (1994)
Nick Nolte spent an entire season hanging around the IU basketball program, hoping to recreate a character in the mold of Bob Knight. Good luck with that, but Knight saves the movie in a cameo role where he coaches several former Hoosiers (Calbert Cheaney, Eric Anderson, Greg Graham, Chris Reynolds, Jamal Meeks, Keith Smart). Larger roles went to Shaquille O'Neal, Penny Hardaway and Matt Nover. The movie got panned, but it grows on you.

4. A League Of Their Own (1992)
Although the film is based on the Rockford Peaches of women's professional baseball fame, it was shot at Evansville's storied Bosse Field. Tom Hanks is a hoot as the drunken sot of a coach, spouting the immortal line, "There's no crying in baseball." Geena Davis, Rosie O'Donnell and even the Material Girl herself, Madonna, have you rooting for the Peaches.

3. Rudy (1993)
Seven years after "Hoosiers," screenwriter Angelo Pizzo and director David Anspaugh created another sports gem. It tells the story of Dan "Rudy" Ruettiger, a Notre Dame walk-on (played by Sean Astin) who goes to great lengths to have his 15 seconds of fame. Shot right on campus, the film captures the Notre Dame mystique. If the climactic ending doesn't give you a lump in your throat, check your pulse.

2. Breaking Away (1979)
Based on the Little 500 bike race and filmed in Bloomington, you can still recognize the town landmarks so many years later. The movie won a Golden Globe Award, and Steve Tesich won an Oscar for his screenplay. The four lead actors, no-names then, are well known now: Dennis Quaid, Dennis Christopher, Jackie Earle Haley and Daniel Stern. You have to laugh when the used car dealer, played by Paul Dooley, has his meltdown, screaming "Refund! Refund! Refund!"

And the winner is … (as if there was any doubt)

1. Hoosiers (1986)
From the screenplay of Angelo Pizzo, to the directing of David Anspaugh, to the musical score of Jerry Goldsmith, to the acting of Gene Hackman, Dennis Hopper, Barbara Hershey and a cast of real Hoosier basketball players, this film never gets old. As one critic put it, "it succeeds by staying small." USA Today once called it "The best sports movie hands down," and it continues to show up on the lists of best sports movies. At one time, Sports Illustrated, USA Today and ESPN had it at the very top. Admit it: You know all the lines by heart.

– Lynn Houser

Coach Richard "Digger" Phelps, players and fans celebrating on the court. Photo courtesy of Notre Dame Archives

#21 1974 Notre Dame's Men's Basketball Team

By Mike Lopresti

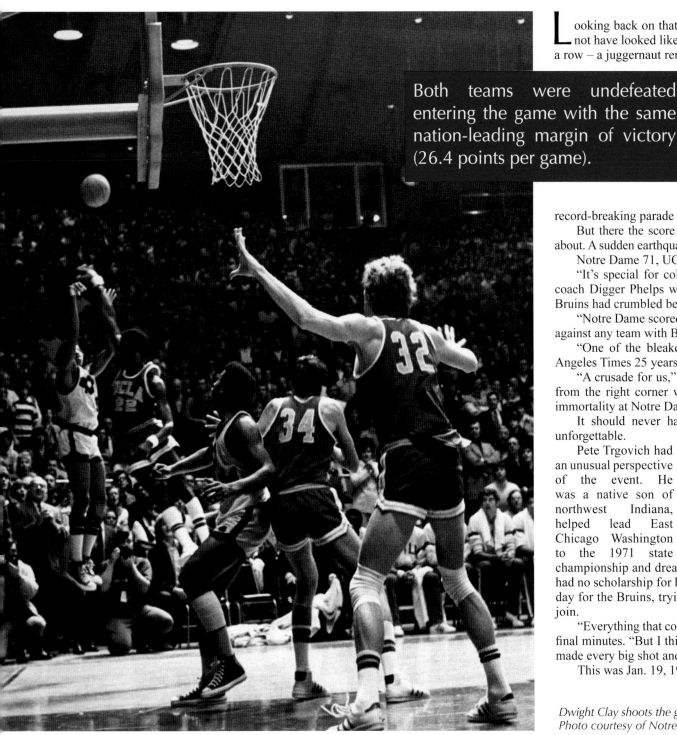

L ooking back on that remarkable Saturday at Notre Dame in 1974, it could not have looked like a surer thing. A UCLA team that had won 88 games in a row – a juggernaut renowned for its relentless purpose and unshakable poise – held an 11-point lead with only 190 seconds left.

Both teams were undefeated entering the game with the same nation-leading margin of victory (26.4 points per game).

Think about it. The Bruins had the best player in the nation on the floor, and one of the most hallowed coaches in the history of college athletics on the bench. There was no 3-point line, to be used as firewood for an Irish comeback. Absolutely no reason to expect anything but for Bill Walton to put the last touches on yet another UCLA victory, and for John Wooden to drop his rolled-up program and shake hands with yet another victim. The Bruins' record-breaking parade would march on; invulnerable and unstoppable.

But there the score stands, decades later, to be marveled at and wondered about. A sudden earthquake that in some ways, altered the flow of an entire sport.

Notre Dame 71, UCLA 70.

"It's special for college basketball. Special for everybody," Notre Dame coach Digger Phelps would say that day when it was over, after the mighty Bruins had crumbled before a 12-0 Irish run in the last three minutes.

"Notre Dame scored 12 straight points, and I didn't think that was possible against any team with Bill Walton on it," Wooden would say 10 years later.

"One of the bleakest days in my life," Bill Walton would tell the Los Angeles Times 25 years after the fact, having never quite let that moment go.

"A crusade for us," Dwight Clay would one day call it, long after his shot from the right corner with 29 seconds left beat the Bruins, and assured his immortality at Notre Dame.

It should never have happened. But it did, and that's what makes it unforgettable.

Pete Trgovich had an unusual perspective of the event. He was a native son of northwest Indiana, helped lead East Chicago Washington to the 1971 state

UCLA had won each of the last seven NCAA championships and 218 of its last 223 games, dating to the 1966-67 season.

championship and dreamed of going to nearby Notre Dame. Except the Irish had no scholarship for him, so he headed for UCLA, and was on the floor that day for the Bruins, trying to hold back the team he had grown up wanting to join.

"Everything that could have went wrong went wrong," Trgovich said of the final minutes. "But I think you need to give the Notre Dame guys credit. They made every big shot and made every big play. And we obviously didn't."

This was Jan. 19, 1974 in South Bend.

Dwight Clay shoots the game-winning shot to end UCLA's 88 game winning streak. Photo courtesy of Notre Dame Archives

The Notre Dame campus was still aglow from the football season. Only nineteen days before, the Irish had beaten Alabama 24-23 in the Sugar Bowl to win the national championship. Hence, this banner held up in the stands by students, in clear view of the UCLA bench: "Dear John Wooden, God DID make Note Dame No. 1. Sincerely, Paul (Bear) Bryant."

Strange vibes were in the air. This was the very place UCLA had last lost before the monumental winning streak began, 89-82 three years before, with 46 points from Austin Carr. Plus, Walton was playing in a brace, having broken a bone in his back against Washington State nearly two weeks earlier.

Clearly, Notre Dame was a dangerous opponent. The Irish were ranked No. 2 and 9-0, having already beaten the likes of Ohio State, Indiana and Kentucky, all on the road. Most of all, the Irish had the confidence they could pull it off. At the end of the practice the day before, Phelps told his players to hoist captains Gary Novak and John Shumate on their shoulders, and handed each a pair of scissors. It was a dress rehearsal for cutting down the nets, which Phelps was certain his team would be doing the next day, post-upset.

"Coach Phelps, he made us believe," Novak said later.

At 6:30 a.m. game day morning, according to Frank Dolson's story in the Philadelphia Inquirer, Irish center Shumate – the minister's son who would be facing Walton – was on the phone with his parents, in prayer.

At the Saturday morning team mass, Notre Dame executive vice president Rev. Edmund P. Joyce proclaimed, "This is not just an ordinary day. The chances are good that years from now, you will look back on this day as one of the memorable ones in your life."

Everything and everyone seemed ready for Notre Dame to shake down some true thunder from the skies. Phelps. His players. Their parents. The student body. The scissors for the nets.

But only 14 minutes into the game, UCLA led by 17 points. So much for Irish karma.

At halftime, it was 43-34. With 3:22 left in the game, a Tommy Curtis jumper from the corner pushed the Bruins lead to 70-59. Walton had 24 points. Bad back? What bad back? Rev. Joyce had apparently gotten it all wrong. This looked like a most ordinary day for UCLA after all.

But suddenly, the game and college basketball did a back flip. Phelps made a change in his pressing defense, putting the taller Shumate in front of Walton to protect against inbounds passes. Shumate scored over Walton, scored again after a steal, and Adrian Dantley scored again after another steal. The lead was cut to 70-65 in 45 seconds.

"Suddenly," Phelps said years later, "we felt we could win."

As Dick Vitale would shout, time for a T.O., baby. But Wooden did not like to call timeouts, preferring to rely on his players to sort out any problem. Phelps had learned that reading a book about UCLA basketball, so he kept the Irish attacking, guessing there would be no Bruins' timeout to stem the charge.

Famed player Bill Walton of UCLA stood tall, but came up short in 1974 against the Irish.
Photo courtesy of Notre Dame Archives

When Notre Dame ended UCLA's winning streak, it had been 1,092 days since it had lost a game.

The last game UCLA had lost was coincidentally in South Bend to Notre Dame in an 89-82 Irish victory.

There wasn't. UCLA committed yet another turnover, and Gary Brokaw hit from the corner. After a Bruins miss, Brokaw scored again. When Keith Wilkes was called for charging, UCLA had its fourth turnover in just over two minutes. And Notre Dame, down 70-69, had the ball and a chance for the lead, with 45 seconds left.

The ball went to Brokaw, who had scored 25 points. But instead of forcing a move, he spotted an open Clay in the corner – Curtis had left Clay some space, to help inside. Clay had not scored a point in the second half.

"I was waving my hand feverishly when Brokaw read it and passed me the ball," Clay said. "Curtis tried to recover but he couldn't. I knew the shot was good as soon as it left my hands."

It was only his second field goal of the game. The score that would live for the ages was there on the board, 71-70. UCLA finally – finally – called a timeout.

There was nearly a half-minute left for Bruins salvation – an eternity – but fate had tipped its hand and was not changing its mind. Curtis missed, then Walton missed a follow-up, then UCLA missed three more tip-in attempts. The Bruins, for once, had run out of time, and magic.

UCLA shot nearly 52 percent that day. Walton was 12-for-14, playing all 40 minutes in his brace. It had not been enough. If one statistic explained the shocker, try 18 Bruins turnovers.

First, Alabama in football, and now this. For the second time in three weeks, the Irish faithful were waving their We're-No. 1 fingers in the air. The stands emptied upon the court in a tidal wave. And yes, the players did cut down the nets.

"When you think about it, this is the No. 2 team in the country playing on their homecourt," Trgovich said. "And it was that big of an upset. That just shows you the dynamics of UCLA at that time, and how the whole basketball world felt about UCLA."

The Notre Dame football team from that year is still No. 1 in the record books, and always shall be. Not so much, the basketball team. One week after their fantasy came true, the Irish played a return match at UCLA. The Bruins were waiting for them, and won 94-75. In March, Notre Dame fell to Michigan in the Sweet 16, never matching the adulation from that Saturday afternoon.

But Phelps and his players will always have that day, and the inspiration it taught. "If you work hard and prepare and believe, you can do anything you want," Phelps said later. At a place that cherishes its history of upsetting top-ranked opponents – it's happened 11 times – that one is the brightest.

Notre Dame advanced to the 1978 Final Four, but has never played in a national championship game. Jan. 19, 1974 could be called its One Shining Moment.

As for UCLA, it was that most rare occasion in the Wooden dynasty when the Bruins were not asked to share the glory, but the blame. These were Wooden's words the day after, per the Los Angeles Times.

"We lacked something in those last minutes, which we'd always been credited for having – our poise. I know I was guilty. I permitted myself to become complacent, perhaps more than I should have. I thought we had it safely in hand."

He had returned to his home state and endured a day that showed that even wizards can be wrong.

The game also was the first sign that something was amiss with his supposedly invincible UCLA team. Trgovich said Wooden began tinkering with the lineup after that game, and things were never the same.

Later in the season, the Bruins would lose back-to-back games at Oregon and Oregon State. In March there would be another blown lead, this one far costlier, when North Carolina State came from seven points back in the second overtime in the Final Four to beat UCLA 80-77, and end its run of seven consecutive national titles.

"It really changed the course of UCLA that year," Trgovich said of the Notre Dame loss. "It was a bigger event than I think people really realized. It wasn't just one game. It led us into losing a championship that year. It didn't have to be that way."

Decades later, Walton – who won two national championships and lost only four games in his Bruins career – still is pained by the winter of '74.

"The losses are what you remember. The failures, the mistakes, and how it could have been so different," he said. "We could have, we should have won them all, and we didn't get it done.

"That's the timelessness of pain and suffering; the agonizing, the reflection and the endless questioning for yourself. When it's right there for you and the whole world is watching, and it's recorded as history that can never be changed."

No, 71-70 is still there. Always will be.

UCLA had won 72 of the 88 games by double digits during the streak, and the average margin of victory came in at 23.5 points per game.

#22

Purdue Cradle of QBs

By Tom Kubat

Drew Brees left college as one of the most decorated players in Purdue and Big Ten Conference history, establishing two NCAA records.

Joe Tiller and Drew Brees.
Photo courtesy of Tom Campbell.

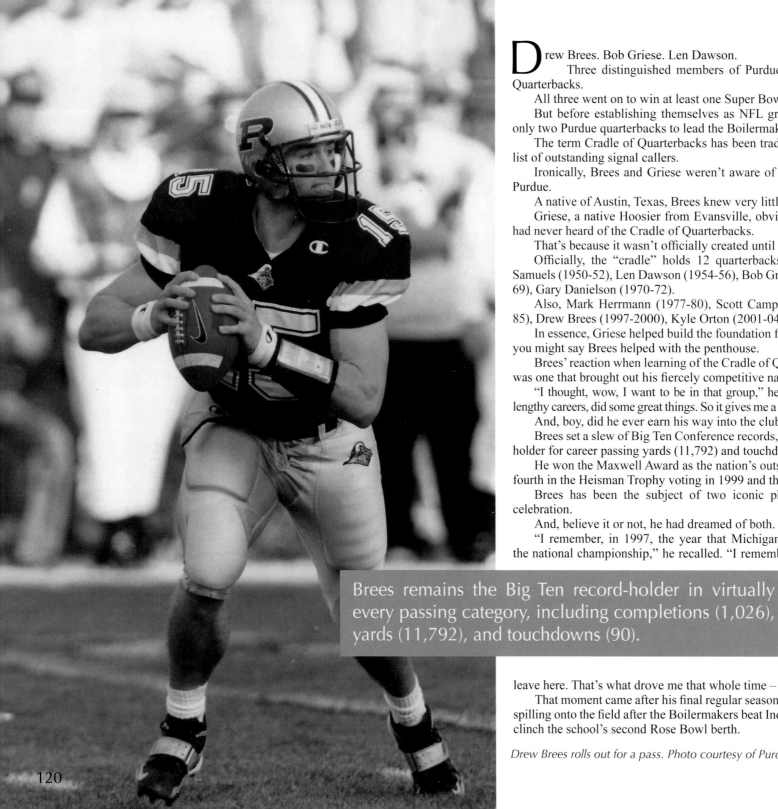

Drew Brees. Bob Griese. Len Dawson.

Three distinguished members of Purdue University's illustrious Cradle of Quarterbacks.

All three went on to win at least one Super Bowl.

But before establishing themselves as NFL greats, Brees and Griese became the only two Purdue quarterbacks to lead the Boilermakers to the Rose Bowl.

The term Cradle of Quarterbacks has been trademarked by the school to honor its list of outstanding signal callers.

Ironically, Brees and Griese weren't aware of the elite club when they arrived at Purdue.

A native of Austin, Texas, Brees knew very little about Purdue.

Griese, a native Hoosier from Evansville, obviously was aware of Purdue. But he had never heard of the Cradle of Quarterbacks.

That's because it wasn't officially created until after Griese left Purdue.

Officially, the "cradle" holds 12 quarterbacks – Bob DeMoss (1945-48), Dale Samuels (1950-52), Len Dawson (1954-56), Bob Griese (1964-66), Mike Phipps (1967-69), Gary Danielson (1970-72).

Also, Mark Herrmann (1977-80), Scott Campbell (1980-83), Jim Everett (1981-85), Drew Brees (1997-2000), Kyle Orton (2001-04) and Curtis Painter (2005-08).

In essence, Griese helped build the foundation for the Cradle of Quarterbacks while you might say Brees helped with the penthouse.

Brees' reaction when learning of the Cradle of Quarterbacks after arriving at Purdue was one that brought out his fiercely competitive nature.

"I thought, wow, I want to be in that group," he said. "Every one of those guys had lengthy careers, did some great things. So it gives me a ton of pride. It's really a special club."

And, boy, did he ever earn his way into the club.

Brees set a slew of Big Ten Conference records, and he remains the league's record-holder for career passing yards (11,792) and touchdown passes (90), among others.

He won the Maxwell Award as the nation's outstanding player in 2000, and he was fourth in the Heisman Trophy voting in 1999 and third in 2000.

Brees has been the subject of two iconic photos – both snapshots of joyous celebration.

And, believe it or not, he had dreamed of both.

"I remember, in 1997, the year that Michigan went to the Rose Bowl and won the national championship," he recalled. "I remember seeing Charles Woodson on the field after they beat Ohio State, to clinch the Rose Bowl berth, with a rose in his mouth.

Brees remains the Big Ten record-holder in virtually every passing category, including completions (1,026), yards (11,792), and touchdowns (90).

"I sat there watching that moment, over and over again. Just saying, 'I. Want. That. Feeling.' I want to have a rose in my mouth by the time we leave here. That's what drove me that whole time – to be able to have that moment."

That moment came after his final regular season game in 2000, with the Purdue fans spilling onto the field after the Boilermakers beat Indiana 41-13 in Ross-Ade Stadium to clinch the school's second Rose Bowl berth.

Drew Brees rolls out for a pass. Photo courtesy of Purdue Athletics.

Between 1967 and 1974, Purdue quarterbacks Len Dawson and Bob Griese started five Super Bowls, winning three.

There was Brees, celebrating with coach Joe Tiller, both beaming smiles of overwhelming elation.

"We knew the dream had come true," Brees said. "I got to put the rose in my teeth.

"That senior year was so crazy. Think about this – our fans rushed the field three times. We only played six home games, so half the time – the Michigan game, the Ohio State game, the Indiana game. That's incredible."

The other snapshot of pure happiness occurred after Brees led New Orleans to its Super Bowl victory, leading the Saints to a 31-17 victory over the Indianapolis Colts in 2010.

"Obviously, the Super Bowl, that's what you're striving for in your pro career, to hold up the Lombardi Trophy," Brees said. "But more important for me, I've always envisioned that happening with my child.

"The fact that our (first-born) son, Baylen, was born a year earlier and he was there on the field and I held him up – that was a dream come true. I wanted that so much to happen. And all of a sudden, it was happening."

Brees, of course, is still active, and hoping for a second trip to the Super Bowl.

While Brees' 14th-ranked Boilermakers lost their Rose Bowl, 34-24 to fourth-ranked Washington on Jan. 1, 2001, Griese led No. 7 Purdue to victory in its first Rose Bowl, 34 years earlier, edging Southern California 14-13 on Jan. 2, 1967.

It's been written that Tiller and New Orleans coach Sean Payton were a perfect match for Brees.

He agrees.

"Coach Tiller was one of those guys who could really motivate you in different ways," Brees said. "He could do it through a humorous comment; he could do it by just being a hard-nosed football coach.

"He always had a plan, always trying to get the best out of his team. He was going to challenge you, he was going to force you to compete – put you in a position where you would have to grow up a little bit. I felt like he helped us all grow up.

"I feel the same way about coach Payton. He was the one who wanted me here in New Orleans, at a time when no one else really wanted me. Coming out of high school, I had two options. And then, coming out of San Diego, through free agency, I had two options, New Orleans and Miami."

Ironically, neither Brees nor Griese were highly recruited. Brees, mainly because of a knee injury his junior year of high school, only received two scholarship offers – from Purdue and Kentucky.

Griese, who was inducted into the College Football Hall of Fame in 1984 and the Pro Football Hall of Fame in 1990, never played organized football until his freshman year of high school.

Bob Griese at Purdue University. Photo courtesy of Purdue Athletics.

Bob Griese as a sports commentator. Photo courtesy of Purdue Athletics.

An outstanding Little League, Pony League and American Legion pitcher, Griese was offered a contract by the Baltimore Orioles but chose to play football at Purdue.

His father, a plumber, died when Griese was 10 years old, forcing his mother to work. The family didn't have much, and Griese placed a high value on getting a college degree.

During his first Purdue training camp, Griese was buried on the depth chart – seventh among the quarterbacks.

But by the time spring practice ended, he had moved up to No. 1.

After his professional football career, Griese worked as a television commentator for college football for ESPN and ABC.

Purdue's head coach was Jack Mollenkopf, but Griese gives DeMoss, his quarterback coach, credit for helping him reach his potential.

Griese was throwing the football like a baseball pitcher, with a three-quarter motion, instead of coming over the top. DeMoss brought in former Boilermaker great Cecil Isbell to teach Griese the correct delivery for a quarterback.

The rest, as they say, is history.

As a senior, Griese led Purdue to a 9-2 overall record, losing only to eventual No. 1 Notre Dame and No. 2 Michigan State.

At 6-1 in the Big Ten, the Boilermakers finished second to the 7-0 Spartans, but they earned the Rose Bowl bid by virtue of the so-called no repeat rule.

Michigan State had won the Big Ten title and played in the Rose Bowl the year before, and thus was ineligible to make a return trip to Pasadena.

Back then only one Big Ten team went bowling, and Boilermaker fans were ecstatic about their first bowl trip ever.

"I almost felt like Moses leading all our people to the Promised Land," Griese said at the time.

The game in Pasadena went down to the wire, Purdue not clinching the victory until defensive back George Catavolos intercepted a 2-point conversion pass in the final minutes.

"What we did at Purdue, first of all, was the highlight of my college career, obviously," Griese said. "It was my senior year and it was the last game I was going to play for Purdue.

"So, the highlight of my college career was not being All-American my junior and senior years, or second in the Heisman Trophy voting and all that, it was going to the Rose Bowl, and winning."

Bob Griese was inducted into the College Football Hall of Fame and the Indiana Football Hall of Fame in 1984, and the Pro Football Hall of Fame in 1990.

After leaving Purdue and being drafted by Miami, Griese figured he'd play two or three seasons with the Dolphins and then use his degree to land a job with a major company.

But his NFL career blossomed into a stellar 14-year career.

Griese won two Super Bowls, guiding Miami to a 14-7 victory over the Washington Redskins in1973 – still the only NFL team to win the Super Bowl to cap an undefeated season.

Then he led the Dolphins to another championship the following year, defeating the Minnesota Vikings 24-7 in the Super Bowl.

Griese actually suffered a dislocated ankle and broken leg in the fifth game of that undefeated season. But Earl Morrall took over at quarterback, the Dolphins kept winning and Griese returned for the playoffs.

"We would have never gone undefeated if it weren't for Earl Morrall," Griese said.

Following his football career, Griese became a noted college football broadcaster for 30 years, working beside legendary play-by-play man Keith Jackson.

"The highlight of my pro career was going to the Super Bowl – and winning those," Griese said.

"The highlight of my broadcasting career was working with Keith Jackson, doing the Rose Bowl many times. But the real highlight was doing the Rose Bowl when my son Brian was in it, playing quarterback for Michigan.

"They won the game and the national championship. And Keith Jackson says, at the end of the game, 'You want to know who the MVP is? I'm standing right next to his proud daddy.' "

PURDUE™
ATHLETICS

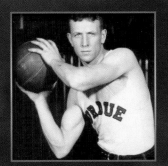

Purdue University Athletics has been a significant part of the sports fabric of the state of Indiana since 1880. As a founding member of what is now the Big Ten Conference, we celebrate the spirit of competition. Our student-athletes, both men and women, have provided millions of Indiana fans with the excitement of sports, been champions in competition, scholars in the classroom and leaders throughout the world. Join us in honoring our state's Bicentennial, our rich athletic history as well as the Greatest Sports Stories in the History of Indiana™.

BOILER UP! HAMMER DOWN! HAIL PURDUE!

#23 Fort Wayne's Rod Woodson

By Rex Kirts

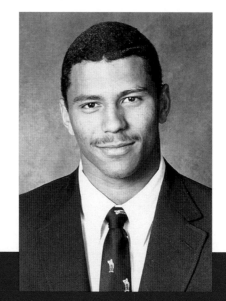

Roderick Kevin Woodson played in the NFL for 17 seasons.

Photo courtesy of Purdue Athletics.

A native of Lafayette, Indiana, Rex Kirts graduated from Lafayette Jefferson High School in 1960 and Indiana University in 1964. He was sports editor at the Crawfordsville Journal-Review for a year and a half and worked at the Bloomington Herald-Times and Bloomington Courier-Tribune since January of 1966. He primarily covered high schools, IU and auto racing. He is a former president of the Indiana Sports Writers and Sportscasters Association and is in the association's Hall of Fame. Four times he was named Sports Writer of the Year in Indiana, and the Indiana Football Coaches Association named its media award after him.

Rod Woodson is, at least, a contender for Number 1.

Somebody has to be the greatest athlete the state of Indiana has ever produced. And that just might be Fort Wayne Snider High School's Woodson.

He excelled for 17 years as a defensive back and kick returner in the National Football League, 11 times making the Pro Bowl.

In addition, Woodson was a five-time state champion and an Olympic-caliber hurdler. In basketball, he didn't come out for the team in high school until his junior year but made all-conference as a senior.

Playing football for Purdue, as a senior he went both ways, at running back and defensive back, in the Old Oaken Bucket victory over Indiana. He was in on an astounding 137 plays.

An assistant coach with the Oakland Raiders and living in Pleasanton, California, heading into the 2016 season, Woodson likes to spend free time with his family. That's wife Nickie and their five children – Marikah, Demitrius, Tia, Jairus and Nemiah. He fishes and plays golf but isn't into an exotic lifestyle. "I'm kind of boring, just a country boy from Indiana," he said.

There are lots of receivers and running backs who, having suffered bruises from his hits, wouldn't describe Rod Woodson as boring.

He grew up in Fort Wayne and liked football from the start.

"I grew to love the game no matter where I played," he said. "In the park, in the street, in a stadium with a couple of hundred people or in the Super Bowl. I just love the game, love what it teaches you. I love the competitive aspect of going against other good athletes."

Few people loved football longer. Seventeen years in the NFL is about three careers for many players. From 1987-2003 he played 10 years with the Pittsburgh Steelers, one year with the San Francisco 49ers, four years with the Baltimore Ravens and two years with the Oakland Raiders. He was on the Ravens 2000 Super Bowl championship team.

The NFL Defensive Player of the Year in 1993, Woodson had 71 career interceptions, which was the third best in history when he retired. His 12 interceptions returned for touchdowns is the best in NFL history. At age 37 in 2002 his eight interceptions led the NFL.

He was inducted into the NFL Hall of Fame in 2009 and was inducted into the College Football Hall of Fame in December of 2016.

He was named to the NFL's 75th Anniversary Team, in 1999 was ranked 87th on the top 100 list of all-time players by the Sporting News and was named one of the top 100 college players of the 20th century by College Football News.

Woodson had a 10-year run with the Pittsburgh Steelers and was a key member of the Baltimore Ravens' Super Bowl XXXV championship team.

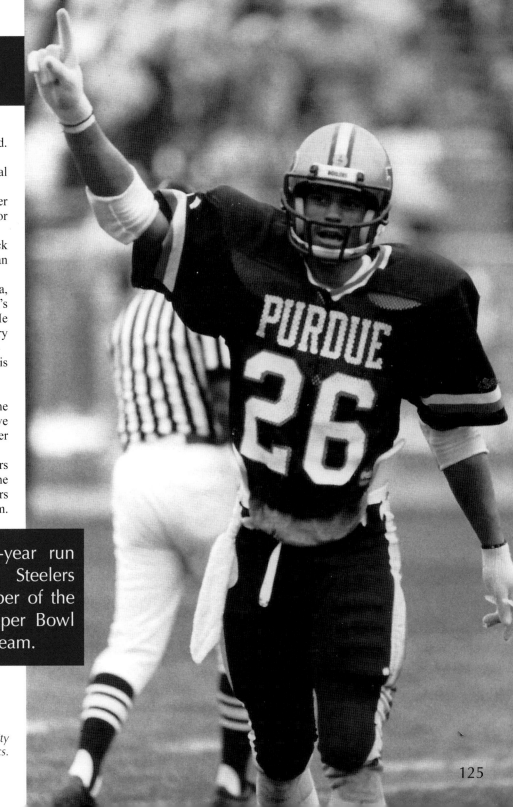

Rod Woodson at Purdue University
Photo courtesy of Purdue Athletics.

Rod Woodson at Purdue University Photo courtesy of Purdue Athletics.

Woodson also played for the San Francisco 49ers and Oakland Raiders, wearing the jersey number "26" throughout his career.

"I'm really proud of the NFL Hall of Fame," he said "It's known for the many great players who played at a great level. Knowing that a kid from Fort Wayne making it is kind of remarkable. And it's an honor going into the College Hall of Fame with the many great players who have been inducted."

Woodson was fast, tough and smart and credited his football development to many coaches.

"I had a really good coach in Dave Brody in youth football," he said. "And the coaches at Snider did a wonderful job of teaching football.

"And I had some really good coaches at Purdue. I was really blessed when I got to Pittsburgh with Chuck Noll and Tony Dungy."

At Snider High School, the head football coach was Mike Hawley.

"We knew Rod coming out of Blackhawk Middle School was an outstanding talent, from his track," Hawley said. "We played him on our JV team as a sophomore." Woodson, though, felt he should have been on the varsity, and it took some persuasion to keep him in football.

"His track coach, Jim Gurnel, convinced him football was a way to make a living, convinced him to stay with football, and Rod played both ways (at slotback and defensive back) for us his junior and senior years," Hawley said. "Rod invited me and Russ (Isaacs, assistant coach) to his Hall of Fame induction, which was really neat."

While still living in Pittsburgh, Woodson kept in close touch with his Fort Wayne roots and sponsored a multi-sport camp for kids.

"Rod is a phenomenal athlete," said Hawley.

"He had great speed, and his vertical leap is unbelievable," Hawley said." We played him at safety because he could get anywhere on the field, and we played him at slot for reversals. We threw him the ball – if you got the ball near him he was going to catch it. He has huge hands." Woodson also returned kicks, just as he did at Purdue and the NFL.

Isaacs later became Snider's head coach. He joked that the coaches' main jobs were "to give Woodson the equipment and tell him when the bus was leaving. He was as talented as anyone ever in Fort Wayne. He won five state track titles, was all-state, was a high school All-American. Woodson came out for basketball for the first time as a junior. "I did basketball to stay in shape for track, did it to keep myself busy," he explained.

Gary Crawford was the Snider basketball coach.

"Rod was just a good athlete," Crawford said. "For his size (6-0, 200) he was a heck of a rebounder, and his leadership abilities were first rate – he was a tri-captain. When the bell rang Rod was ready to go. We won a sectional with him."

Major colleges from across the country wanted Woodson to play football. He picked Purdue.

"Purdue just fit me," he said. "Fit who I was. I knew I wanted to play in the Big Ten. The other schools had all those blue chippers, and I didn't want to be just another guy. Purdue was a good academic school and was the one school that said I would start as a freshman – I wanted to play right away."

Leon Burtnett was the Purdue coach.

"Rod is real polite, he worked hard and is a super kid with super parents," Burtnett said.

He could have added super talent.

"The thing I remember most was a buddy of mine on the Dallas Cowboys said Rod was the fastest guy he'd ever seen.

He ran a 4.3 (in the 40). We played him on defense because that was his temperament."

Well, Woodson wasn't bad on offense, either. He had badgered Burtnett during his career to play offense, too, and the coach agreed in Woodson's final game in college. It was against Indiana in the Old Oaken Bucket game at Purdue's stadium.

"It was a great experience," Woodson said. "One of the defining moments of my career was that I never lost to IU in the bucket game."

He helped beat IU, 17-15, on both sides of the ball. With only a couple of practices and learning only a couple of offensive plays, Woodson carried 15 times for a team season high of 93 yards and caught three passes for 67 yards. On defense he had 10 tackles, one pass breakup and one forced fumble, and he returned three punts for 30 yards and two kickoffs for 46 yards. He also recovered a blocked field goal attempt with about two minutes left in the game.

Joe Tiller, who later became Purdue's head coach, was an assistant that year.

"The reason we played Rod on offense that game was almost like a gift from Leon. He and Rod were very close," Tiller said. "Leon Burtnett loved him. We wanted to give the Hoosiers something they hadn't seen, and Rod was a glutton for punishment."

Woodson was probably as good in track as football. He qualified for the U.S. Olympic trials but never went because he had been drafted by the Steelers and went to football camp instead.

"Rod was an incredible competitor," said Mike Poehlein, Woodson's track coach at Purdue. "He was the first guy to practice and the last to leave. He never lost a race in the Big Ten."

Woodson ran only indoors until his senior year. Outdoors he had one of the two fastest times in the world. He and Roger Kingdom tied in a 110-yard high hurdles race, and three months later Kingdom won the Olympics.

"Rod was a great guy to coach. He never gave me any grief," Poehlein said.

Comments like Poehlein's about Woodson's ability and character come from many people.

"Without a doubt he'll go down as one of the greatest players to ever play the game," said Bill Cowher, his coach with the Steelers.

"You could see the specialness," then-Steeler assistant Tony Dungy said after first watching Woodson on the first day of camp. "We felt he'd be a multi-year Pro Bowler.

Rod Woodson as a track star. Photo courtesy of Purdue Athletics.

He was very determined. You couldn't measure that pride, the determination, the desire to be the best."

Said assistant coach Dick LeBeau: "Woodson had size, he had strength, he had speed, he had reaction, he had great instinct, and he was very, very smart."

Woodson said: "Without coaches like that at Pittsburgh I don't think I'd be in the NFL Hall of Fame. I was naturally gifted, but how many times do you see naturally gifted guys who don't do anything?"

From his retirement in 2003 to February 2011, Woodson worked as an analyst for the NFL Network (on NFL Total Access and Thursday Night Football) and for the Big Ten Network.

#24

The Zellers –
The First Family of Indiana
High School Basketball

By Tom Kubat

Luke, Tyler and Cody Zeller were all named Indiana's Mr. Basketball.

The Zeller brothers are the nephews of former NBA player, Al Eberhard.

W hat are the odds?

What are the odds of parents raising a son who becomes an academic all-star, is voted Indiana's Mr. Basketball and leads his high school team to a state championship?

Pretty high, you say?

What about raising three sons who each accomplish those impressive feats?

Those odds would be nothing short of astronomical.

Yet that's exactly what the sons of Steve and Lorri Zeller did.

Luke, Tyler and Cody, playing for the Washington Hatchets, were McDonald's All-Americans and then went on to play major college basketball – Luke at Notre Dame, Tyler at North Carolina and Cody at Indiana.

Luke had a brief pro career, while Tyler and Cody are still playing in the NBA.

But what they accomplished in high school is unprecedented.

If Angelo Pizzo, the screenwriter and producer of *Hoosiers*, arguably the greatest sports movie ever, would tell the Zeller story on film, many would assume it was a figment of his imagination.

"At the time, when I was going through it, I just had a passion for basketball," Tyler said. "Our family just had fun with it. As it turned out, we were 7-footers, we were very blessed.

"All the accomplishments just kind of came along with our passion for basketball."

Washington High School, situated in a burg with about 12,000 people in southwestern Indiana, won state championships in 1929-30, 1940-41 and '41-42.

The town may be small but the gymnasium – affectionately called the Hatchet House – seats more than 7,000.

Washington had gone 22 years without even winning a sectional, the first round of the state tourney. But fans had good reason to fill the place during the Zeller era.

It all began with Luke, who averaged 19.6 points and 8.9 rebounds as a senior and led his team to the Indiana 2005 Class 3A state championship.

Tyler was a little-known freshman on that team. The talk of the town centered on Cody, the youngest Zeller.

But after Tyler had a good first game as a sophomore, fans began to take notice.

"Some lady came into the athletic office and said to Lorri, 'I didn't even know you had a middle son,'" recalled Gene Miiller, then in his first season as Washington's athletic director and coach.

Lorri worked in the athletic office and she picked up on a renewed spirit among the fans.

"Luke's team winning the state championship kind of opened the door, creating the mentality that we could do this," she said. "The fans kind of had the mentality that when a Zeller is a senior, we're going to win state."

Tyler followed that script, averaging 33.1 points and 11.0 rebounds as a senior, and Washington won the 2008 Class 3A title.

But Cody, a freshman on that team, was about to one-up his brothers. He didn't wait until his senior year to lead the Hatchets to another state crown.

Cody Zeller at Washington High School.
Photo courtesy Mike Myers.

Cody Zeller became the 26th Mr. Basketball from the state of Indiana to play for the Hoosiers.

Regarding Cody Zeller, Tom Crean noted, "He's the most mentally focused kid I've ever recruited...I see a young man that has mental toughness that is not normal."

As a junior, Cody averaged 20.5 points and 11.4 rebounds a game as Washington won the 2010 state championship.

Then he capped off his career, and the Zeller family's incredible Indiana high school basketball story, by averaging 24.6 points and 13.1 rebounds en route to the 2011 championship.

If you're keeping score, that's one state championship for Luke, two for Tyler and three for Cody.

Six in all.

The Zeller resume ended up being so much bigger than their respective heights – Luke 6-10 ½, Tyler a little over 7-foot and Cody a tad over 6-11.

For the record, Steve is 6-4 and Lorri is 6-0.

"If the '05 team had not won, I think it would have been much more difficult for the others to win," Miiller said.

"Being around it, I never felt the pressure and I didn't sense that the players did. It just made them more determined."

There's no debate when it comes to each of the brothers' signature moment on the court. They all occurred in a championship game.

For Luke, it was "The Shot." His half-court game-winner as time expired in overtime to beat Plymouth 74-72 in the title game.

"I've probably watched *Hoosiers* too much," said Luke. "Because in the huddle before the last play of our state championship game, I told coach to give me the ball and I'll score."

He, of course, was referring to Jimmy Chitwood's comment to his coach in the movie before hitting the winning basket for Hickory.

The Hatchets had to inbound the ball under their own basket with 1.8 seconds remaining, trailing 72-71.

"The coach (Dave Omer) told me, 'Do not heave that ball. Take one dribble, get your feet set and shoot it, I don't care where you're at.'

"So I wasn't going to heave it, I was going to shoot a jump shot. That was pretty cool."

Luke just missed a triple double, with 27 points, nine rebounds and a then-record 11 assists for a title game.

In Washington's 84-60 victory over Fort Wayne Harding in the 2008 championship game, Tyler dominated with 43 points and 16 rebounds.

The 43 points broke the overall state finals scoring record that had stood since 1970.

As a senior, Cody scored 20 points and had 18 rebounds to lead Washington to a 61-46 victory over Culver Academies in the 2011 title game.

But the year before, he also scored 20 points – and tied the state finals record with 26 rebounds – in the Hatchets' 65-62 overtime victory over Gary Wallace.

In the four seasons that the Zellers led Washington to a state title, the Hatchets were 97-11.

Each of the brothers wore number 40 in high school, in honor of their maternal grandfather, Marvin, who wore number 40 while winning a state high school championship in Iowa.

"After we won state and I was Mr. Basketball, they wanted to retire my jersey," Luke said. "They had a ceremony ready to go, but I called and said I didn't want that.

"I wanted Tyler to wear my jersey. I wanted the jersey to be retired as a family jersey."

Today there are three No. 40 jerseys retired in the Hatchet House.

As if their basketball exploits in high school weren't enough, the Zellers excelled in the classroom too.

Luke graduated with a perfect 4.0 grade point average and was valedictorian of his class. Tyler and Cody finished with 3.99 GPAs and were salutatorians.

"Tyler and I both got an A-minus in the same English class our freshman year," Cody said. "Luke didn't have that teacher, so that's something we always kid him about.

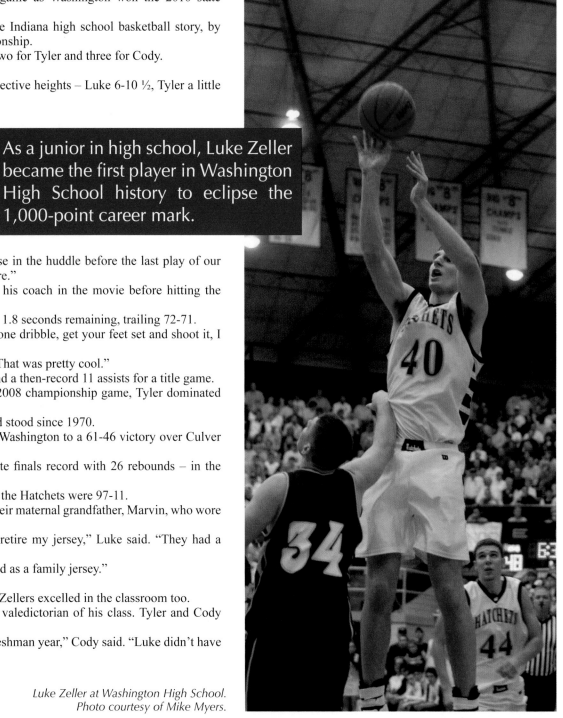

As a junior in high school, Luke Zeller became the first player in Washington High School history to eclipse the 1,000-point career mark.

Luke Zeller at Washington High School.
Photo courtesy of Mike Myers.

"The teacher who gave us both an A-minus, she's the sweetest lady. She's a big Zeller fan; a big basketball fan. She hates when we tell this story. She doesn't want to be labeled as the one teacher who gave us an A-minus."

The boys were competitive in everything, but surprisingly never seemed to feel the pressure of trying to live up to their older brother's accomplishments – except for that Welcome to Washington sign on the edge of town.

Besides the mayor's name, the sign also advertised Washington as the home of three Mr. Basketball winners – Steve Bouchie, Luke Zeller and Tyler Zeller.

"We lived just outside of town, so for three years I drove to school past that sign, wondering if my name was going to be up there one day," Cody said.

"I didn't put too much pressure on myself but it was definitely one of my goals to join them on that sign."

Steve added, "I don't think they would have performed as well as they did if they had felt the pressure."

Maybe that's because Steve and Lorri made sure their sons kept basketball in perspective.

The day after it was announced that Cody also had been named Mr. Basketball, a neighbor spotted him mowing the lawn.

Surprised, he asked Steve why the boy wasn't out celebrating.

"Oh, we'll celebrate," Steve said. "But he's got to get his chores done first."

And then there was the time that Tyler scored 18 points in his first game at North Carolina, but then suffered a broken wrist in the next game.

"A reporter said he heard that it could be a career-ending injury and asked Tyler what he would do if that turned out to be the case," Steve said.

"And Tyler's answer was, 'Well, I guess I'll be successful in something other than basketball.'"

Excellent parenting, the family's faith, good coaching – and the benefits of living and playing in a small town – combined to keep the Zeller brothers grounded.

"Playing in Washington was pretty special," Luke said. "I knew the person in the second row was struggling with cancer. I knew the person sitting in the fourth row just had a kid. I knew the person sitting in the 10th row, their kid looked up to me and I had a responsibility to do the best I could."

Miiller capsulized the love affair between the Zeller boys and the people of Washington.

"Sometimes people are jealous of others who have a lot of success, but I don't see any of that here, I think because of the way the boys represented the school and the community," he said. "They're held in such high regard here."

It's difficult to find the proper words to describe the magnitude of the Zeller story.

But Hall of Fame writer Bob Hammel managed to do just that in his foreword in Steve and Lorri's book *Raising Boys the Zeller Way.*

"I can say what Steve and Lorri can't: There has never been anything like their sons in Hoosier basketball accomplishments," Hammel wrote.

"I grew up disciplined in journalism to never say never. I repeat, about the Zellers: *never, anything* like them."

That's why it's a slam dunk to refer to the Zellers as The First Family of Indiana High School Basketball.

Tyler Zeller at Washington High School.
Photo courtesy of Mike Myers.

Considered a four-star recruit by Rivals.com, Tyler Zeller was listed as the No. 7 center and the No. 33 player in the nation in 2008.

#25 Franklin High School's "Wonder Five"

By Bob Hammel

The boys had started playing together
as children, developing synergy.

Turn back time a hundred years. To when cars weren't common. And TV? There was barely even radio.

In Franklin, Indiana, a town of not quite 5,000, there was a Holy Grail Athletic League for Sunday School boys, and the competition was brisk. That's where young Robert Vandivier (Presbyterian), the Friddle brothers, Burl and Carlyle (Methodist), Paul White and Ralph Hicks (Baptist), Johnny Gant and Ike Ballard (Christian) got to know each other and a thing or two about this game called basketball. A Sunday School teacher at Grace Methodist, Ernest Wagner – called "Griz" since little boyhood when an older brother said he looked like a grizzly bear – was a new man in town as a high school business teacher but he had been exposed to basketball in his own early years so he coached the boys in the league from Grace Methodist.

When all those kids he had watched moved up in school he asked to be junior high coach, and when they moved up to high school, he already was there, Franklin's third-year head coach.

Yes, the listed Sunday School names total seven. Numbers are incidental in the classically Indiana story of "the Franklin Wonder Five" – five in this sense not a number at all but a synonym for team, as in that era "the Crimson eleven" would have been a reference to the entire Indiana University football team.

Credit Phillip Ellett for putting together a 1986 book called just that, *The Franklin Wonder Five*, for amassing through scrapbooks and newspapers and interviews a year-by-year, game-by-game account that demythologizes maybe Indiana's most misinterpreted sports legend, while giving it its just due – which makes it greater.

For years, for generations, "Wonder Five" to Hoosiers raised foggy mental images of a great player named Fuzzy and the long-unequaled Franklin feat of winning three straight state high school basketball championships, in 1920, '21 and '22.

In so doing it comprised its own mystery. A simple look at the three championship-game box scores showed that no "Five" was there on all three teams.

The "Wonder Five" included Burl Friddle, Ralph Hicks, Paul White, Robert "Fuzzy" Vandivier, Sima Comer, Johnny "Snake Eyes" Gant, Harold Borden, Pete Keeling, and coach Ernest "Griz" Wagner.

Photo courtesy of the Indiana Basketball Hall of Fame.

133

One name was. Vandivier.

"Fuzzy" to everyone but his mother from his own early childhood nicknaming, Vandivier was at the heart of all three championship teams and, as a freshman, the one before – which got to the State but lost its first game. He never felt the punctuation of tournament elimination again.

He won with four older players in 1920, and as the sole starting returnee won again in '21 and with a re-altered combination in '22.

Ellett contrived his own "Wonder Five" delineation: "any Franklin team that had both Fuzzy Vandivier as a player and Griz Wagner as a coach" and "a player on at least one of the three high school state championship teams." The first two parts span eight years – Vandivier's four playing years at Franklin High, then four more under Wagner at Franklin College. Altogether Ellett's "Five" add up to 14: Vandivier plus Franklin High/College teammates Ike Ballard, Harold Borden, Sima Comer, Hubert Davis, Burl Friddle, Carlyle Friddle, Johnny Gant, Ralph Hicks, Pete Keeling, Harry King, Jimmy Ross, Paul White and Butter Williams.

Gant and Burl Friddle are with charter inductees Vandivier and Wagner in the Indiana Basketball Hall of Fame. Vandivier also is in the Naismith International Basketball Hall of Fame – and not, as has generally been assumed by today's generations, solely because of his long-unprecedented high school championship feat. He, Friddle, Gant and many of the 13 other "Wonder Five" qualifiers were also outstanding achievers in the next four years at Franklin College.

All were part of what indeed really was "The Roaring Twenties" in Franklin, Indiana.

It was such a different time.

High school basketball was played with 20-minutes halves, but the clock stopped only for timeouts. The game started with a center-court jump ball, and restarted with one after every point scored. Players fouled out with No. 4. One player could shoot all his team's free throws. Traveling and double-dribble were technical fouls that brought a free throw. A substituted player could re-enter, once – only. And there was of course no three-point shot, no shot clock. Team scores in the 20s, even the teens were common, which makes Vandivier's 1,540-point career point total and near 15-point average astonishing, a time warp.

The 14-year-old Fuzzy was in the starting lineup with juniors Paul White, Clifford Crowell and captain Burl Friddle and senior Roy Bridges when the "Wonder Five" era began Nov. 15, 1918, with a 42-6 victory over Spiceland. Vandivier scored the first basket, then came back with 28 points the next time out when Franklin clouted Indianapolis Broad Ripple, 60-9. Franklin as a town, high school or basketball team wasn't used to state prominence; its tournament history showed just one sectional championship up to then. But when Griz Wagner's new group followed its fast start by winning at Indianapolis Tech, 33-17, beating Indianapolis Shortridge, 43-19, and then – in the first of what became common: a game scheduled for the 500-capacity Franklin High gym was moved to the 1,200-seat Franklin College gym to handle the new crowd – defending state champion Lebanon was handled, 23-20, the Franklin *Evening Star* crowed: "Franklin high school has a team that will be satisfied with nothing less than the state belt."

And a few months hence, in a 12-hour stretch on Saturday, March 13, at Indiana University's Men's Gymnasium in Bloomington, Franklin beat Bedford 28-12, strong Anderson (for a third time) 14-12 in a tense overtime, and Lafayette Jeff (31-13), and the championship was won.

Oh, the town went crazy. An estimated 300 cars met the team's arrival by train at Bargersville – to a fireworks display – and formed a procession that stretched the 15 miles from there into downtown Franklin, where a bonfire and 1,500 more people awaited. The next Monday there was a victory parade; the next day presentation of $1,000 to Wagner, raised by fans, and gold watches to each player on a team whose 29-1 record was the best by any of the state's 10 champions up to then.

And Franklin was just beginning to frolic.

Paul White, who had shared team scoring leadership with Vandivier all season and made the All-State tournament team with him, was gone to his own outstanding career at DePauw when the next season began. But it ended with another state championship, which didn't come easily. This team lost some games, one when Vandivier was at home with a heavy cold, and was on the brink of defeat in the State quarterfinal game against Rochester when sub Hubert Davis turned an in-bounds pass into a short-range shot that just beat the buzzer and Rochester, 19-18. Wagner took his team home to Franklin to sleep in their own beds after that escape, and they came back to handle Lafayette Jeff and Anderson a little more comfortably in repeating their championship.

By then, Franklin's citizenry was hooked. The Opera House had installed a giant electric apparatus that, with colored lights portraying game action, could convey almost instant relay of road-game action to fans back home. The first game so carried was a 19-11 rivalry victory at Martinsville, the Artesians' first home loss in four years, and for a full house at the Opera it was like being there. Opera crowds have rarely been so raucous.

And, after a scheduled game against Martinsville had to be canceled because the college gym wasn't available and Martinsville declined to play in the tiny high school gym, public subscription forwarded enough money to convince the school board to build a 2,500-seat new gym. It was up and opened – with 3,000 crammed in and 300 turned away – Jan. 3, 1922, with a 39-20 victory over Shelbyville. Senior Fuzzy Vandivier scored the gym's first basket.

That third state championship came with Vandivier scoring 12 points and Gant 10 in a 26-19 victory over Terre Haute Garfield at the chilly Indianapolis Coliseum March 18, 1922 – the end of one era. But not *the* era – the "Franklin Wonder Five" Era.

Really, it was about to begin. Nobody ever used the team "Wonder Five" in the high school run.

Wagner resigned at Franklin High to take the college job in town, and Vandivier led the parade of his players there. Wagner inherited some players without a "Wonder Five" link, but it didn't take long for his clearly best lineup to be carryovers from his high school program.

> The leading scorer on the Wonder Five was "Fuzzy" Vandivier.

What also carried over was winning. By Ellett's math, the "Wonder Five" won 50 straight games, bridging their last 14 high school games and first 36 in college.

There is an asterisk game. Indiana University's records show a 36-18 victory over Franklin Dec. 15, 1922.

Not a "Wonder Five" game, Ellett says.

The Big Ten – from formation in the late 1890s until the 1970s – operated with a freshman-ineligibility rule, and a requirement for both teams to follow that was, probably with awareness of what was coming in at Franklin, written into its 1922-23

Photo courtesy of the Indiana Basketball Hall of Fame.

game contract with Franklin. Franklin had no such rule, but for that game the freshmen had to sit out. Ellett covers the situation in one paragraph headlined "The Non-Wonder Five Game." The holdovers Wagner inherited were beaten, not the "Wonders."

There certainly was a difference. At full strength, Vandivier and friends rolled and reigned in college as they had in high school. Butler, DePauw, Wabash – all considered near-equals of IU, Purdue and Notre Dame – couldn't handle the new scourge at Franklin.

The Wabash game introduced the "Wonder" name. The Cavemen had beaten Washington and Vanderbilt in a 12-2 start to their season, but when Franklin went to Crawfordsville and handled Wabash, 20-16, the state's most distinguished sportswriter, Bill Fox of the Indianapolis *News*, was there and used the W word in a story that began:

"CRAWFORDSVILLE, Ind. – Well, it's time to drag out the word 'wonder.' If the Interstate Special of two cars that pulled out of this historic little old village Tuesday night didn't haul a 'wonder five,' there never was one.

"Just figure it out for yourself. The Franklin College five that defeated Wabash College last night is composed of four high school lads and one sophomore, all light but fast, backed up by five substitutes at least two of whom are freshmen and the rest sophomores or juniors. The entire first string … played under Wagner at Franklin High School."

The name stuck and the word spread.

Colleges didn't play only other colleges then. Wagner booked a game against a team of professional players sponsored by the Omar Bakery of Indianapolis. The "Omars" included former Chicago All-American Tony Hinkle, not yet started on his own legendary coaching career at Butler, and they had beaten strong opponents. After Franklin edged them 32-31 in overtime at Indianapolis and 36-29 two weeks later at Franklin, a Cleveland *News* columnist wrote: "The (professional New York) Celtics are considered the best in the world with a record of 125-4. One of the defeats was to Omar, 25-19. Franklin has beaten Omar twice." And in the Detroit *Free Press*: "Not only has this team been the best Franklin College ever had, but it is considered the best collegiate team ever seen in Hoosierdom, the basketball center of the world."

Take that, "Big Three" – Indiana, Purdue and Notre Dame.

Even the Indianapolis Athletic Club's magazine included the line:

"Franklin, beyond any doubt, was the best basketball team in the United States last year."

There was no national-championship tournament to prove it, of course, but in 1980, a banner was unfurled at Franklin College claiming the national championship of 1923.

The streak continued the next year, and this time included a 19-12 win at Notre Dame – and a South Bend newspaper review: "Franklin is to the hardwood court what Notre Dame is to the gridiron."

And when the string finally ran out at Butler Feb. 28, 1924, by a solid 36-22 score, it was reported poetically by Thomas A. Hendricks in the Indianapolis *News*:

Don't be surprised!
If the sun rises in the west
If White River runs uphill
If a duck crows and a chicken swims …
If anything happens,
For the impossible has happened, the irresistible force has been
    stopped, the immovable body has been kicked about.
Franklin has fallen
Butler 36 Franklin 22

(The poem-writer was a *News* sportswriter, not the 19th-century Vice President Thomas A. Hendricks from Indiana. But, the Eugene Pulliam who wrote a 45-line poem celebrating the second of the three straight state high school championships in 1921 – "We won! We won! By golly, we won!" – was the Eugene C. Pulliam who was at the start of his journalism career then as the young owner and editor of the Franklin *Star* and went on to national celebrity as the owner and publisher of the Indianapolis *Star* and *News*, both newspapers in Phoenix, Ariz., and a string of other newspapers in Indiana.)

The "Wonder Five" era ended two years later, Vandivier injury-slowed much of an almost anti-climactic senior season. More than half his collegiate defeats came that senior year (13-6), after his team went 18-0 (the loss to IU without the Franklin freshmen not counted), 19-1 and 17-4 the first three seasons – 67-11 altogether after a composite 107-11 in high school.

Vandivier never attempted a professional career, never left Franklin. Straight out of college he began teaching and coaching at Franklin High. He took his 1939 team to the state championship game but lost there to Frankfort. He declined several head coaching offers from colleges, reportedly including Michigan State. After coaching he stayed on as athletic director at Franklin and retired in 1978. By then, he had been inducted – and seemed genuinely surprised – in basketball's grandest Hall of Fame at Springfield, Mass. He died at 79 July 31, 1983.

No player of his era had more accolades. After his freshman season a Chicago *Tribune* headline proclaimed him "U.S.' LEADING BASKET PLAYER." A kid who came along right after him in high school, John Wooden of Martinsville, UCLA and the Hall of Fame, called him "the greatest basketball player I have ever seen." Tony Hinkle, who saw them all in Indiana from the tournament's earliest days into the 1980s, named as his own all-time Indiana All-Star team Oscar Robertson, George McGinnis, Johnny Wooden, Homer Stonebraker and Fuzzy Vandivier. "Wonder Five" Fuzzy. From a time long ago, and unforgotten.

Most of the data for this story came from the book, The Franklin Wonder Five, *by Phillip Ellett, and some from* Hoosier Hysteria, *by Herb Schwomeyer. Both can be purchased at the Indiana Basketball Hall of Fame.*

The Day ~~Indiana~~ the Nation Stood Still for a Sports Radio Show

On July 14, 2016, the *Greatest Sports Stories in the History of Indiana*™ was revealed to the state of Indiana, and many across the nation tuned in to the streaming show via Internet. Memorable moments are the best part of sports and Executive Producer of the program Greg Rakestraw, along with some of the most celebrated voices in sports journalism, told great stories of our time.

The three-hour program, (almost unheard of in today's programming) captivated listeners with stories, replays, and sub plots that make Hoosiers proud. Few radio programs have captured an audience's attention like this one with stories that will resonate for years to come—and inspire future generations to attempt the same astonishing feats.

Program includes narratives by:

Bob Lovell	Michael Grady
Chris May	Joe Staysniak
Eddie White	Conrad Brunner
Jack Nolan	Mike Chappell
Kyle Neddenriep	Curt Cavin
Bob Hammel	Jim Brunner
Angelo Pizzo	Tom Kubat
Justin Sokeland	Lynn Houser
Rex Kirts	Ted Green
Todd Lickliter	David Woods

You can find a link to each hour of this program on ESPN's 107.5 The Fan's website at http://www.1070thefan.com/blogs/25-greatest.

Greg Rakestraw has now been a part of the Indy sports-media scene for over two decades. Currently, Greg is the program director for 107.5 & 1070 The Fan in Indianapolis and manages affiliate relations for Network Indiana, which boasts more than 60 affiliates statewide. In addition to that, Greg serves as the television voice of the Indy Eleven, IUPUI men's basketball, and is the post-game host on the Colts' Radio Network. In addition, Greg also is one of the lead anchors of the IHSAA Champions Network, calling state championship games in soccer, volleyball, football, basketball, wrestling, softball, and baseball. Greg hails from Lanesville in Harrison County, but has called Indianapolis home since attending the University of Indianapolis. Greg and his wife Amy along with children Mia and Jack live in the Broad Ripple area.

Contributions

There is a common thread between these great sport stories and this documentary: teamwork. When people have a shared vision, coupled with commitment, success is the natural order of things. This project is the sum total of countless people simply coming together to pay respect to our Indiana sports history. Each selfless in the pursuit of ensuring these stories be told.

I am fortunate to have worked with exceptional people coming from diverse backgrounds and experience, which also includes several outstanding Hall of Fame Journalists. Without four gentlemen in particular, this project would not be a reality. Thanks to Bob Hammel and Angelo Pizzo (our prized sports storytellers of all time) for your counsel, commitment and shared vision. Without hundreds of hours of work by Tom Kubat and Doug DeFord, this project would still just be an idea. Without an advisory board of individuals that I leaned on for counsel and advise for nearly two years, this project would not be. To Greg Rakestraw for putting together a wildly entertaining 3-hour radio broadcast: *The 25 Greatest Sports Stories in the History of Indiana*, as part of this project, your voice and work carried this project to another level of entertainment for thousands of people.

A person could not ask for a better group of advisors and friends.

Project Advisory Board

Doug DeFord - Project Advisor and V.P. Indiana Sports History, LLC

Bob Hammel - Indiana Hall of Fame Sports Writer and author

Lynn Houser - Indiana Hall of Fame Sports Writer and author

Honorable Joe Kernan - American politician and 48th Governor of Indiana

Tom Kubat - Indiana Hall of Fame Sports Writer and author

Judge Edward W. Najam, **Jr.** - Indiana Court of Appeals

Angelo Pizzo - Screenwriter and film producer: "Hoosiers" and "Rudy"

Greg Rakestraw - ISSA Board Member and Production Advisor

Sandy Searcy – Former Assistant Commissioner Indiana High School Athletic Association

Joe Smith – Hall of Fame sportscaster

Mark Thompson – President of MT Publishing Company, Inc.™

This project is dedicated to those athletes, coaches and spectators we lost along the way, doing what they loved.

- **Brent Slinkard** – Project Visionary and President of Indiana Sports History.

If you would like to write a fan letter to a sports legend, writer or contributor in this book, we've made it easy...

It's easy to show your appreciation!

Visit www.indiana25.com

1. Find the link to your favorite sports legend, writer or contributor.

2. Write your note or letter and hit send.

3. We will forward your personal e-mail.

Pre-1900

- Civil War veteran Arthur Twineham was one of nine lettermen on the first Indiana University sports team: baseball, in 1866. Allison Maxwell, first dean of the IU School of Medicine, also lettered on that team.

- Bobby Mathews pitched the hometown Kekiongas to a 2-0 victory over Cleveland at Fort Wayne May 4, 1871– the first professional baseball game. The Kekiongas, a charter member with franchises from New York, Philadelphia, Boston, Chicago, Washington, Cleveland, Troy, N.Y., and Rockford, Ill., in the National Association of Professional Base Ball Players, won the right to play the first game on a coin flip. Mathews, 20, went on to win more than 100 games in three different leagues and is credited with inventing the spitball. The Kekiongas' future wasn't as bright; they won only seven games before the franchise folded in mid-season.

- Indiana, Purdue and Notre Dame each played its first football game within a 29-day stretch in 1887, and all lost – IU to Franklin Oct. 25, 89-10; Purdue to Butler, 48-6, Oct. 29, and Notre Dame to Michigan, 8-0, Nov. 23. Purdue's first victory was 34-10 over DePauw Nov. 16, 1889; Notre Dame's, 20-0 over Harvard Prep Dec. 6, 1888; IU's, 20-0, over the Louisville Athletic Club in 1891.

- 20-year-old Amos Rusie of Mooresville pitched a no-hit game for the New York Giants against Brooklyn July 31, 1891. Nicknamed "The Hoosier Thunderbolt," Rusie's blazing fastball was considered the reason baseball moved the pitching slab from 50 feet to the present 60 feet, 6 inches, effective in the 1893 season. He had season highs of 36 wins, 548 innings and 289 strikeouts. In 1901, after he sat out two seasons with head injuries from being hit by a line drive, the Giants traded him to Cincinnati for young pitcher Christy Mathewson. Rusie was 0-1 for the Reds before retiring at 31. In 1977, Rusie joined charter member Mathewson in baseball's Hall of Fame.

- After Purdue won at Wabash, 44-0, Oct. 24, 1891, a Crawfordsville newspaper headline called the conquerors "burly boiler makers." Hitherto known as "the Gold and Black," the name was received popularly at Purdue and stuck.

- Purdue president James H. Smart met with presidents from Illinois, Michigan, Minnesota, Northwestern, Wisconsin and Chicago at the Palmer House in Chicago Jan. 11, 1895, to begin formation of the present Big Ten – the first intercollegiate conference in America. The league was officially chartered Feb. 8, 1896. Indiana and Iowa were admitted in 1899, and Ohio State in 1912.

- The first great Indiana pacer, Dan Patch, was foaled April 29, 1896, in Oxford, Indiana, which still has an annual "Dan Patch Festival" in his honor. "Dan" began his racing career in 1900, and never lost a race – lost just two heats and was so dominant other owners stopped competing against him. He went against the stopwatch before crowds of 100,000. Dwight Eisenhower as a boy saw him at the 1904 Kansas State Fair. Little Harry Truman in Missouri wrote a fan letter to the horse. He retired undefeated in 1909, holder of 9 world records. At the height of his career, he earned his owner more than $1 million a year. And more than half a century later, in Meredith Willson's hit Broadway and movie musical "Music Man," professor Harold Hill warned townsfolk their boys were hearing about horse race gamblin' – *"Not a wholesome trottin' race, no, but a race where they sit down right on the horse! Like to see some stuck-up jockey boy sitting on Dan Patch? Make your blood boil? Well, I should say!"*

1900-10

- Ray Ewry, a polio victim as a child in Lafayette, conquered the paralysis and in the decade won eight Olympic track and field gold medals: in the standing long jump and standing high jump in the 1900, 1904 and 1908 Games and the standing triple jump in 1900 and 1904.. In one day, July 16, 1900, at Paris, he won golds in the long jump (10-6¼), triple jump (34-8½) and high jump ((a world-record 5-5). The standing events were discontinued after the 1912 Games, but no one matched Ewry's eight individual Olympic golds in any sport until swimmer Michael Phelps a full century later.

- Headed for their annual rivalry game with Indiana at Indianapolis, the Purdue football team was aboard a 14-car train that crashed into a section of coal cars just inside Indianapolis Oct. 31, 1903. Killed were 13 players, an assistant coach and a team trainer. A 14th player was pronounced dead at the scene, but morticians detected a pulse, Harry Leslie recovered from grave injuries, and in 1928 he was elected the 33rd governor of Indiana.

- After two preliminary meetings, the Indiana High School Athletic Association was formed Dec. 29, 1903, with the stated purpose of bringing interscholastic competition under the control of high school principals. Principal George W. Benton of Indianapolis Shortridge was named chairman of the first Board of Control. Charter schools in the organization (according to the IHSAA Handbook of 1928) were Anderson, Alexandria, Bloomington, Eaton (in Delaware County, now part of the Delta system), Fairmount, Goshen, Huntington, Indianapolis Manual, Indianapolis Shortridge, Kokomo, Marion, Noblesville, North Manchester, Salem and Wabash.

- Captain Fred Seward won both hurdles races to lead Bloomington to the state high school track and field championship, the first competition run by the IHSAA, on May 13, 1904, at Indiana University's Jordan Field.

- James Lightbody of Muncie and the University of Chicago set a world record in winning the 1,500 meters race at the 1904 Olympics at St. Louis. It still is the only time an American has ever won the "metric mile" at the Olympics.

- In the 1907 and 1908 World Series, Mordecai "Three-Finger" Brown of Nyesville, Ind., pitched shutout wins to lead the Cubs to championships – the team's last of that century.

- The first Newport Hill Climb – from downtown in the small Western Indiana county seat up an 1,800-foot hill – in 1909 brought automobile owners from all around to town. That began a tradition that, after a 50-year break, resumed in the late 1960s and still draws an estimated 200,000-plus participants and spectators on the first weekend in October.

- In the only World Series involving charter Hall of Famers Honus Wagner and Ty Cobb, the Series hero was Wagner's Tipton-born Pittsburgh Pirates teammate, pitcher Babe Adams. He won 3 games, including a seventh-game shutout. Cobb went 1-for-11 against him, a single.

- On Nov. 9, 1909, Notre Dame football broke into the big time with an 11-3 victory at haughty Michigan.

1910-1919

- Captain Elmer Oliphant won the mile to lead Linton's four-man team to the state track championship May 21, 1910. Oliphant, also a football, basketball and baseball star, went to Purdue where he was a two-time basketball all-American, set a still-standing record with 43 points in a football game, won seven varsity letters in football, basketball, track and baseball, and also swam and wrestled. On graduation, he received an appointment to West Point. For Army, he was a two-year

football all-American, set a still-standing record by scoring 125 points in a season, set a world record in the 220-yard low hurdles on grass, was the first Cadet to letter in four sports, didn't letter but won monograms in hockey, boxing and swimming, was football captain and recipient of the outstanding senior athlete award. In 1969, the 100th anniversary of college football, the Football Writers Assn. of America named him and Jim Thorpe backs on their All-Time All-America team for the college game's first 50 years.

- Dave Charters of Peru, playing for Purdue, in 1910 was the first Indiana native named to the Consensus All-America college basketball team.

- Some enterprising Indiana University students, organized as a Boosters Club, in 1911 got IHSAA permission to bring high school teams selected as the best from areas all around the state to Bloomington. A 12-team field arrived, played two days to work down to two finalists, and on March 11, 1911, Carroll Stevenson scored 14 points and Crawfordsville defeated Lebanon, 24-17, to win the first State High School tournament at IU's first Assembly Hall.

- Just a matter of weeks after the basketball tournament began, Carl Fisher invited the world to the Indianapolis Motor Speedway on Memorial Day 1911 for the first 500-Mile Race, won by Ray Herroun.

- Indiana punter Mickey Erehart, a sophomore halfback from Huntington, from deep in the end zone dodged an onrushing Iowa defender, slipped outside and ran all the way to a touchdown: officially 98 yards on a play that started at the IU 2. Erehart's run, tied once (75 years later) but never topped, is the Big Ten's oldest major offensive record. It was IU's only score in a 13-6 loss Nov. 9, 1912, in a game played at Indianapolis.

- Herman "Suz" Sayger of Culver scored 113 points in a 154-10 win over Winamac March 8, 1913 – still considered the state record. Sayger, who had other games of 79, 55 and 52, averaged 29.5 as a senior in 1914. He was inducted posthumously into the Indiana Basketball Hall of Fame in 2015.

- Notre Dame used the new-fangled forward pass and introduced college football to Knute Rockne as the Irish captain and end caught the throws of Gus Dorais to shock mighty Army, 35-13, in 1913.

- New Albany won two games and made it to the final day of the 77-team fourth state high school basketball tournament before losing to Clinton March 14, 1914. New

Albany's coach was science and math teacher Edwin Hubble, better known later for the Hubble Space Telescope when he was world renowned in cosmology.

- Little Wingate, which had only an outdoor court of its own, got 18 points from star center Homer Stonebraker to rout Anderson, 36-8, in that 1914 championship game to become the first team to win two straight titles. Wingate, with 9 points from Stonebraker, had beaten South Bend 15-14 in five overtimes to win in 1913 – still the longest championship game in state history.

- Oscar Charleston in 1915 began a baseball career that carried him, despite being kept out of the major leagues by race, to the Baseball Hall of Fame. Charleston, from Indianapolis, played most of his career with the hometown ABCs with a lifetime average of .354. Baseball historian Bill James rated him the sport's all-time No. 4 player.

- Purdue overwhelmed Rose Poly, 44-9, Dec. 9, 1916 – the first of 371 Purdue victories for coach Ward "Piggy" Lambert. A player at Crawfordsville High before there was a state tournament, Lambert was 28 when he started a 26½-year Boilermaker career that included 11 Big Ten championships and put him in the Naismith Basketball Hall of Fame.

- Outfielder Edd Roush of Oakland City had three hits and drove in four runs as the Cincinnati Reds beat the Chicago White Sox, 10-5, to clinch the World Series title Oct. 5, 1919. Evidence came out later that the favored White Sox had thrown the Series, but Roush – National League batting champion in 1919 and a lifetime .323 hitter – went to his grave insisting the Reds were the better team and earned their victory over the team known ever after as "the Black Sox." Elected to the Baseball Hall of Fame in 1962, he died at 94 in 1988.

1920s

- Notre Dame All-American George Gipp played his last game at Northwestern (won 33-7 Nov. 20, 1920), died 24 days later of strep throat, and football's "Win One for the Gipper" legend was born.

- On Valentine's Day 1921, IU senior Everett Dean of Salem scored 21 points as Indiana whipped visiting Ohio State, 33-11. It was the last of at least seven times when for IU Dean outscored the opposing team. Four times when a beaten opponent's score was so low it might have happened the box scores were lost to history. At season's end, Dean was named IU's first basketball All-American.

- Robert "Fuzzy" Vandivier was the star of Franklin teams that won three straight state basketball championships (1920-22), a feat unmatched by any school for 65 years. Vandivier, his team's leading scorer in all three championship games, scored 1,540 points in his career, the unofficial state record until well into the 1950s. Later a star – a Chicago Tribune first-team All-American – on strong college teams at Franklin and after that a successful coach, he is the only one from Franklin's "Wonder Five" era in the Springfield, Mass., Basketball Hall of Fame.

- Les Mann, an outfielder who was on a World Series champion with the "Miracle Braves" in 1914 and drove in a run against Babe Ruth for the losing Cubs in the 1918 Series, was named IU's basketball coach prior to the 1922-23 season. Mann, the last non-IU graduate to coach Hoosier basketball until Bob Knight 49 years later, replaced George Levis, a Wisconsin All-American who coached the Hoosiers for two seasons but left to enter sales for his father-in-law's company, Nurre, which built (and introduced at IU) basketball's first successful glass backboards. Mann coached two seasons, his teams finishing 8-7 and 11-6.

- Golfing legend Walter Hagen won the 1924 Professional Golf Association (PGA) on the Donald Ross-designed championship course at French Lick.

- On Oct. 18, 1924, Notre Dame edged Army, 13-7, at the Polo Grounds in New York and sportswriter Grantland Rice wrote in the New York Herald Tribune: "Outlined against a blue-gray October sky, the Four Horsemen rode again," immortalizing for all time the Irish backfield of Don Miller (148 yards that day), Jim Crowley (102), Elmer Layden (60) and quarterback Harry Stuhldreher. That Knute Rockne team finished 10-0 and national champion for the first time in school history after beating Stanford in the Rose Bowl, 27-10 – the only bowl game played by Notre Dame until 1969.

- Basketball inventor James Naismith presented the championship awards after Frankfort won it first state title by beating Kokomo, 34-20, at the Indianapolis Exposition Building March 21, 1925. Naismith, who drew up the rules and supervised the first game played at the Springfield, Mass., YMCA Dec. 10, 1891, said after his state tourney experience that despite the factual site of the sport's birth, "Basketball really had its origins in Indiana, which remains the center of the sport."

- Rivals Indiana and Purdue, at IU's new stadium, played the first Old Oaken Bucket football game and tied, 0-0, Nov. 21, 1925.

- Everett Dean, at 25, took over as Indiana's new (and youngest-ever) basketball coach Oct. 15, 1924. On Dec. 18 that year, in his first road game, Dean coached the Hoosiers to a 20-18 victory at Lexington in the first basketball game between Indiana and Kentucky. On March 9, 1926, Dean's Hoosiers beat Wisconsin, 35-20, at IU to clinch the school's first Big Ten basketball title, a co-championship with Purdue.

- Butler University ran away from Notre Dame in overtime March 7, 1928, to win the first game played in its 15,000-seat basketball fieldhouse, 21-13. The vast arena – Butler Fieldhouse by name until it became Hinkle Fieldhouse in 1966 to honor longtime coach Tony Hinkle – was built at a cost of $1 million with agreement that it would be the site of future state high school tournament championship games. Ten days later, capping the first state tournament played there, Muncie center Charles Secrist controlled a last-minute jump ball, then hit a shot from center court to give the Bearcats a 13-12 win over defending champion Martinsville and its three-year star guard John Wooden.

- Junior center Branch McCracken of Monrovia scored the first two points but Indiana lost to Washington University of St. Louis, 31-30, Dec. 8, 1928, in the first game played in the Hoosiers' new 10,000-seat Seventh Street Fieldhouse. Five days later in the building's official dedication game, the Hoosiers whipped Eastern power Pennsylvania, 34-26.

- Purdue won the Old Oaken Bucket for the fourth straight time, 32-0, at IU Nov. 23, 1929, to complete an 8-0 season and win what is still the Boilermakers' only outright Big Ten championship.

1930s

- Center Dave Dejernett scored 11 points to lead Washington to a 32-21 victory over Muncie and become the first African American to play on an Indiana state high school basketball champion (1930). Muncie's center, Jack Mann, became the second when the Bearcats won the 1931 title.

- Idolized football coach Knute Rockne of Notre Dame was one of eight people killed when their TWA flight from Kansas City to Los Angeles crashed in a Kansas field March 31, 1931. Rockne, born in Norway, played at Notre Dame before a 13-year coaching career that included a 105-12-5 record with five unbeaten, national-championship seasons.

- Billy Herman of New Albany, 22 when called up by the Cubs Aug. 29, 1931, in his first major league time at bat fouled a ball off home plate that hit him in the head and knocked him out. He came back to hit .314 in helping the Cubs to the 1932 World Series, made 10 All-Star teams, hit .304 in a war-interrupted 16-year career, and in 1975 was inducted into the Baseball Hall of Fame.

- Guard John Wooden of Martinsville was a consensus All-America for a third straight year and led Purdue to the 1932 Big Ten championship and 17-1 season that, seven years before the first NCAA tournament, led to Helms Foundation recognition as national champion.

- In the 1932 Games at Los Angeles, Ivan Fuqua of Brazil became IU's first Olympic gold medalist, leading off America's 4x400 relay team that set a world record which stood for 20 years.

- Purdue football players Carl Dahlbeck and Tom McGannon were killed and four injured in a locker room explosion Sept. 12, 1936.

- IU distance star Don Lash of Auburn was named the 1938 winner of the Sullivan Award, given annually to the person chosen as America's top amateur athlete. He was the first of four IU athletes to win the award (distance runner Fred Wilt, 1950; swimmers John Kinsella, 1970, and Mark Spitz, 1971). All were Olympians.

- 5-5 guard Rex Rudicel of Huntington scored 13 points as Ball State, coached by former Hoosier Branch McCracken, for the first time beat Indiana in basketball, 42-38, Dec. 11, 1938, at Muncie.

- In the last game for 14-year IU coach Everett Dean before starting a new tenure at Stanford, junior guard Ernie Andres of Jeffersonville set a Big Ten record with the league's first 30-point game as IU won at Illinois, 45-35, March 4, 1938. In mid-summer, after a number of leading Indiana high school coaches had sought the job, IU hired its 1930 all-American center Branch McCracken as its coach.

- Frankfort became the first four-time State basketball champion in 1939, but runnerup Franklin had the state's first "Mr. Basketball" – George Crowe, later the first African-American to play for the baseball Cincinnati Reds (and older brother of 1950s Crispus Attucks coach Ray Crowe).

1940s

- Indiana, though runnerup to Purdue in the 1940 Big Ten basketball standings, beat the Boilermakers twice for the first time, got an invitation to the second NCAA championship tournament, and won it, beating Kansas in the finals at Kansas City, 60-42. Branch McCracken, at 31, became – and still is – the youngest coach ever to win the NCAA championship.

- Tom Harmon, who made Indiana Halls of Fame in basketball, track and football for his stardom at Gary Horace Mann, won the 1940 Heisman Trophy playing for Michigan. Harmon was runnerup to Nile Kinnick of Iowa in 1939, the first of now five Heisman runnersup who played high school football in Indiana (Bob Griese, Evansville/Purdue, 1966, to Steve Spurrier, Florida; Mike Phipps, Columbus/Purdue, 1970 to Steve Owens, Oklahoma; Anthony Thompson, Terre Haute/IU, to Andre Ware, Houston, 1989; Rex Grossman, Bloomington/Florida, to Eric Crouch, Nebraska, 2001).

- Tony Zale of Gary reigned as world middleweight boxing champion from 1941 to '47, lost the title to Rocky Graziano, then won it back by knockout. His nickname was "Man of Steel."

- With major league baseball fearing a possible shutdown because of a World War II manpower shortage, the All-American Girls Baseball League began play May 30, 1943, and the South Bend Blue Sox were one of four charter members. In 1945, the Fort Wayne Daisies joined, and the two Indiana teams remained in the league through its final season in 1954. South Bend won championships in 1951 and '52. The league was the inspiration for the 1992 movie "League of Their Own," filmed in Evansville.

- After going 1-8 in 1942, the Purdue football program received an influx of 26 marines and 9 navy officer candidates as a World War II military training program and the 1943 Boilermakers went 9-0, still Purdue's only unbeaten season and the NCAA record for one-year improvement. Illinois teammates Alex Agase (a first-team All-America guard voted to Purdue's all-time team and later the school's football coach) and halfback Tony Butkovich were among the reassigned additions. Despite missing the last two games when called into the Marines for World War II duty, Butkovich led the Big Ten in scoring and rushing – his 16 touchdowns still Purdue's record. He was killed in action in Okinawa April 18, 1945, the same day Hoosier-born war correspondent Ernie Pyle was killed at Ie Jima.

- Bob Hamilton of Evansville upset favored Byron Nelson 1-up in the 36-hole final match to win the PGA championship Aug. 15, 1944, at Spokane, Wash. It was one of five tour victories for Hamilton.

- War heroes Pete Pihos, Howard Brown and Russ Deal (Bicknell) and freshman George Taliaferro (Gary) led Indiana to its (so far) only clear-cut Big Ten football championship and undefeated season: 9-0-1 in 1945. The Hoosiers finished the season ranked No. 4 in the country (behind Army, Navy and Alabama).

- In the only college football game ever that featured four Heisman Trophy winners, powerhouses Army and Notre Dame fought to a 0-0 tie at packed Yankee Stadium Nov. 9, 1946. Army had backs Doc Blanchard (Heisman '45) and Glenn Davis ('46), Notre Dame had quarterback Johnny Lujack ('47) and freshman two-way end Leon Hart ('49). In the fourth quarter, Blanchard broke free outside but safetyman Lujack knocked him out of bounds at the Irish 37. Both teams finished unbeaten and Notre Dame edged out Army in the final polls for the national championship.

- Dick Piper scored 30 points as unbeaten Chester Township of Wabash County ran away from Marion, 76-54, to win its first regional championship March 6, 1948, at Kokomo. It completed a "power double" for little Chester, which had beaten Kokomo in the afternoon, 48-46. The same day, another small-school upstart, Monroeville, won its first Fort Wayne regional, but the little guys ran out of gas and lost one round short of the Final Four.

- Senior center Lee Hamilton scored 16 points but injured his knee while leading Evansville Central over Muncie Central in afternoon play at the state high school finals March 20, 1948. Hamilton had just 3 points in a restricted role when the Bears lost the state championship game 54-42 to a Lafayette Jeff team they had beaten in December at Lafayette, 65-51. Hamilton received the prestigious Trester Award and went on to a distinguished career as a 17-term congressman and statesman. In 2015 he was brought to the White House and presented by President Barack Obama the nation's Presidential Medal of Freedom.

- Roy Cochran came back from World War II to become IU's only Olympic track and field double-gold medalist, setting a world record in the 400-meter hurdles and running on the 4x400 relay team at the 1948 London Games.

- Bill Garrett led Shelbyville to the 1947 state high school basketball championship, then at IU shattered a long-standing Big Ten racial barrier and opened the league to African American players with a three-year career in which he made first-team All-America and set IU's career scoring record.

- The Fort Wayne Zollner Pistons, Indianapolis Kautskys and Anderson Packers were charter members when the 17-team National Basketball Assn. was formally formed in a meeting at the Empire State Building in New York Aug. 3, 1949.

1950s

- Notre Dame came into the decade riding a four-year unbeaten streak that was snapped at 39 when Purdue and sophomore quarterback Dale Samuels upset the No. 1-ranked Irish at South Bend, 28-14, Oct. 7, 1950.

- Outmanned by a Minneapolis Lakers team that was dominating the NBA behind center George Mikan, the Fort Wayne Pistons on Nov. 22, 1950, angered the crowd at the Minneapolis Armory by stalling from the opening tipoff on, strategy that paid off when Pistons center Larry Faust scored in the final seconds to beat the Lakers, 19-18. It took three years, but that lowest-scoring game in league history led to NBA adoption of basketball's first shot clock, 24 seconds from the outset.

- The Indianapolis Olympians, an NBA franchise built around 1948 U.S. Olympic stars Alex Groza and Ralph Beard of two-time NCAA champion Kentucky, were one of the league's powerhouses until the 1951 college basketball point-shaving scandal got both stars banned for life. The franchise soon folded and pro basketball didn't return to Indianapolis until the ABA Pacers more than a decade later.

- Fort Wayne's brand new Coliseum was the site of the third NBA All-Star Game Jan. 13, 1953, and 10,322 watched the West win for the first time, 79-75, behind 22 points by game MVP George Mikan. It was the first All-Star game played anywhere but Boston.

- Three buzzer-beating baskets gave Indiana its only losses in 1952-53, when Branch McCracken's Hoosiers, with scoring leaders Don Schlundt and Bobby Leonard and no senior starters, went 17-1 in winning their first outright Big Ten championship. Ranked No. 1 in the nation for the first time, they beat Kansas, 69-68, March 18, 1953, for the NCAA championship.

- The Dodgers' Carl Erskine of Anderson set a World Series strikeout record with 14, including Mickey Mantle four times, in beating the Yankees Oct. 2, 1953, but New York still won the Series.

- Sixteen days after Briton Roger Bannister broke through track's four-minute mile barrier, little Max Truex of Warsaw broke the national high school mile record with 4:20.4 in winning the state championship at Indianapolis May 22, 1954. Truex was an NCAA champion at Southern California and a U.S. Olympian.

- Minnesota edged Purdue, 59-56, in a six-overtime game Jan. 29, 1955, still the Big Ten record for longest game. Purdue starters Joe Sexson, Denny Blind, Dan Thornburg and Don Beck played all 70 minutes.

- In back-to-back years, Indiana's historic high school basketball tournament hit a zenith – little Milan and all-time last-second hero Bobby Plump beating Muncie Central 32-30 for the 1954 title, and Indianapolis Attucks with blossoming all-timer Oscar Robertson outran Gary Roosevelt, 97-74, in 1955. That was (1) the first integrated state basketball tournament won by an all-African American team (in a finals between two of them), and (2) the first state title for an Indianapolis team. Robertson had 30 points in that game, 39 the next year when Attucks became the first unbeaten champion in state history by routing Lafayette Jefferson, 79-57.

- Future Purdue coach George King scored the tie-breaking free throw with 12 seconds left as the Syracuse Nationals turned back the Fort Wayne Pistons, 92-91, in the seventh game of the championship-round playoffs at Syracuse April 10, 1955 – still the closest an Indiana team has come to winning the NBA championship. Two years later, the Pistons franchise moved to Detroit.

- Charging for an unprecedented third straight Indianapolis 500 victory, driver Bill Vukovich was killed in a crash in the 1955 race, won by Bob Schweikert.

- Gil Hodges, a high school basketball star at Petersburg, drove in both runs as Brooklyn beat the New York Yankees, 2-0, in Game 7 Oct. 4, 1955 – the "Wait Till Next Year" Dodgers' first World Series championship. They had lost in the Series seven times.

- In Game 5 Oct. 8, 1956, Michigan City native Don Larsen of the Yankees beat the Dodgers, 2-0, in what still is the only World Series no-hitter. Larsen struck out 7, including pinch-hitter Dale Mitchell to end the game.

- Greg Bell of Terre Haute won the Olympic long jump title Nov. 24, 1956, at Melbourne, Australia, five days before IU teammate Milt Campbell won the decathlon.

- Oklahoma's still-record 47-game winning streak ended on the Sooners' home turf Nov. 16, 1957, when Notre Dame's Dick Lynch scored from the 3 on a fourth-down sweep with 3:50 left for a 7-0 Irish victory.

- In a 2-8 season, Notre Dame's Paul Hornung in 1958 became – still – the only Heisman Trophy winner from a losing team.

- Rockport overwhelmed Perrysville, Ky., 58-6, to win the national championship in the first 8-man high school football playoff.

1960s

- Oscar Robertson, after being named College Basketball Player of the Year three straight years at Cincinnati, combined with Jerry West, Jerry Lucas, Purdue's Terry Dischinger and IU's Walt Bellamy to lead the U.S. to a gold medal at the 1960 Rome Olympics. The team, coached by Pete Newell, is usually considered the greatest amateur basketball team ever.

- Junior Jimmy Rayl of Kokomo set IU and Big Ten records with 56 points in a 105-104 overtime victory over Minnesota Jan. 8, 1962. A year later against Michigan State, Rayl tied the record – the only 50-point performances ever by a Hoosier. Against Michigan State, Rayl set IU records that still stand with 23 field goals and 48 shots.

- Identical twins Dick and Tom Van Arsdale of Indianapolis and IU set an unofficial NCAA scoring record for twins – and maybe brothers – with 76 points (Dick 42, Tom 34) in a 108-102 victory over Notre Dame Dec. 4, 1963, at Fort Wayne. It was the IU career high for both, who finished their 72-game IU careers 12 points (1,252 and 1,240) and 4 rebounds (723 and 719) apart – Tom with the edge. In high school at Indianapolis Manual, they were the first to be named co-Mr. Basketball, and in 12-year NBA careers, they were both 3-time All-Stars, twice playing in the same game – the first brothers, let alone twins, in the NBA to do that.

- After Notre Dame went through five straight non-winning football seasons that included four losses to his Northwestern teams, coach Ara Parseghian relit the fuse at Notre Dame in 1964 with a 9-0 start that fell 93 seconds short of a national championship when Southern Cal rallied to win the season finale at Los Angeles, 20-17. Irish quarterback John Huarte won the year's Heisman Trophy.

- In a lightly attended meet with almost no national media coverage, Kansas freshman Jim Ryun set his first world record, winning the 880-yard race in 1:44.9 at the 1966 U.S. Track and Field Federation championships at Terre Haute June 10, 1966. A week later, the NCAA outdoor championship meet was at IU's new Billy Hayes Track, but Ryun as a freshman was ineligible to compete.

- A.J. Foyt won Indianapolis 500 titles in 1961, '64 and '67 in becoming the hard-charging hero of the Brickyard. Foyt also won in 1977 to be the 500's first four-time champion. Since then Al Unser and Rick Mears have joined him.

- Foyt's 1964 victory came after the Memorial Day race was black-flagged – stopped – after one of the Speedway's most horrific crashes. Drivers Eddie Sachs and Dave MacDonald were killed in a second-lap wreck that involved seven other cars and sent up a wall of flame.

- After years of domination by big front-engine-powered roadsters, native Scot Jimmy Clark, a star of Europe's Formula 1 circuit, drove a rear-engined car to victory in the 1965 Indianapolis 500. Every winning car since has been rear-engined.

- Gary's Orsten Artis and Harry Fluornoy played key roles as Texas Western upset Kentucky, 72-65, in the historic 1966 NCAA championship game – the first time a team with five African American starters won the title. Artis scored 15 in the championship game, 22 as the team's leader in a semifinal victory over Utah. Fluornoy was an off-the-bench contributor in both Final Four games of the team later featured in a major movie, Glory Road – the win over all-white Kentucky credited with bringing down the last racial barriers in Deep South college basketball.

- In a head-on collision of the year's two mightiest college football teams, unbeatens Notre Dame and Michigan State played to a 10-10 tie Nov. 19, 1966, at East Lansing. It was the last game of the year for the Big Ten champion Spartans, but Notre Dame crushed Southern Cal 51-0 in its final game and led the season-ending polls to win the national championship.

- Quarterback Bob Griese of Evansville led Purdue – Big Ten runnerup to Michigan State, which under rules of the day couldn't go back for a second straight Rose Bowl – to a 14-13 victory over Southern Cal Jan. 1, 1967, in the Boilermakers' first Rose Bowl.

Indiana Sports Through the Years

When quarterback Mike Phipps was edged out by Oklahoma fullback Steve Owens (1,488-1,344) for the 1969 Heisman Trophy, it gave Purdue three Heisman runnersup in a four-year stretch. Bob Griese (1966) and Leroy Keyes (1968) lost by wider margins.

Unsung senior fullback Terry Cole of Mitchell exploded for two long runs to cap a dream season for Indiana with a 19-14 upset of Purdue that gave the 1967 Hoosiers a Big Ten championship share (with Purdue and Minnesota) and their first Rose Bowl trip. National Coach of the Year John Pont's Hoosiers lost at Pasadena to No. 1 Southern Cal, 14-3. Homegrown tailback John Isenbarger (Muncie) and receiver Jade Butcher (Bloomington) teamed with Ohioan quarterback Harry Gonso as the irrepressible offensive sparks to repeated comeback victories in the all-time storybook season for IU football.

After years of near misses, Indiana blew away the field to win the 1968 NCAA men's swimming and diving championship at Dartmouth. Backstroker-medleyist Charley Hickcox led coach Doc Counsilman's Hoosiers by winning three events. Jim Henry won his first of five NCAA diving championships for Counsilman's coaching partner, Hobie Billingsley. It was the first of a still-record six straight team championships for the Counsilman-Billingsley program.

Rick Mount scored 28 points to launch his Purdue basketball career Dec. 2, 1967, outscoring three-time All-American Lew Alcindor (17) of UCLA. But, the Bruins won the first game ever played at Purdue's new arena, 73-71, on a shot by sub Bill Sweek at 0:02.

Purdue opened the 1968 football season ranked No. 1 and stayed there until a 13-0 loss at No. 4 Ohio State Oct. 12. The five-week run is the only time a Purdue football team was ever No. 1-ranked, and that sophomore-loaded Ohio State team went on to finish unbeaten and win the national championship.

Guards Rick Mount of Lebanon and Billy Keller of Indianapolis led Purdue to the 1969 Big Ten championship and all the way to the NCAA finals before losing to UCLA and Lew Alcindor – and Purdue alumnus John Wooden, the UCLA coach.

George McGinnis, after leading Indianapolis Washington to the fourth unbeaten state championship in history and first in 12 years, set still-standing series records of 53 points and 30 rebounds before 17,875 at Freedom Hall in Louisville June 28, 1969, capping a 114-83 victory and a summertime sweep for the Indiana All-Stars over Kentucky.

1970s

All-American Austin Carr scored 50 points and teammate Collis Jones 40 as Notre Dame edged Butler, 121-114, at Hinkle Fieldhouse Feb. 23, 1970 – the last game for 41-year Butler coach Tony Hinkle. Butler's Billy Shepherd, "Mr. Basketball" for Carmel in 1968, scored 38. Hinkle retired with 561 basketball coaching victories.

Rick Mount set a still-standing Big Ten record with 61 points Feb. 28, 1970, but Purdue lost 108-107 to an Iowa team that went 14-0 and averaged more than 100 points a game while winning the 1970 league championship. Mount set other Purdue records with 27 field goals and 47 shots in the game.

17 seasons before the 3-point shot was introduced to college basketball, Austin Carr of Notre Dame set the NCAA tournament record with 61 points when the Irish beat Ohio, 112-82, in first-round play at Dayton March 7, 1970. It still stands.

Roger Brown scored 45 points as the Indiana Pacers won at Los Angeles, 111-107, on May 25, 1970, to beat the Stars 4-2 and clinch the Pacers' first American Basketball Assn. playoff championship. The Pacers, who brought pro basketball back to Indiana in 1967, added hometowner George McGinnis in 1972 and under Hall of Fame coach Bobby Leonard won two more ABA titles before merging into the NBA in 1977.

Pete Trgovich scored 40 points in a 102-88 semifinal shootout with Floyd Central, then came back hours later with 28 to lead unbeaten East Chicago Washington past Elkhart, 70-60, March 20, 1971 – the last state championship game played at Hinkle Fieldhouse. The 29-0 Senators, the tournament's fifth unbeaten champion, rank with the best teams ever. Starters Trgovich (UCLA), Junior Bridgeman (Louisville) and Tim Stoddard (North Carolina State) all went on to play in the NCAA Final Four, Bridgeman had an outstanding NBA career, and Stoddard is the only man in history to play on an Indiana state champion, an NCAA champion, and – as a relief specialist – a World Series champion (Baltimore 1983). The Fieldhouse hosted 41 state finals before the tournament was moved in 1972 to IU's new Assembly Hall.

IU played its first season at 17,700-seat Assembly Hall with a new basketball coach in place, 31-year-old Bob Knight. The Hoosiers dedicated the Arena Dec. 18, 1971, with a still-record (for winning margin) 94-29 victory over Notre Dame, in which junior forward John Ritter of Goshen became the only Hoosier in now more than 85 years of IU basketball to outscore the opposing team. Ritter had 31 points.

- Mark Spitz of IU had an Olympics for the Ages, going 7-for-7 in gold-medal and world-record swimming performances at the 1972 Games in Munich. In the overnight hours after Spitz's last victory, eight Palestinian invaders came over the Olympic Village fence, seized the building where the Israel Olympic team was quartered, and the subsequent standoff, then shootout at the Munich Airport left 17 people dead, 11 of them the full Israeli team and 5 of the attackers.

- Officially the 1973 race was the shortest Indianapolis 500 ever: 133 laps, 332½ miles. But it was excruciatingly long. It started May 28, and was suspended by rain. Already by then driver Salt Walther had suffered major injuries in a mainstretch crash that spewed fuel into the crowd, causing some injuries, and left Walter pinned in his car on the track, gravely injured. The race stopped, was resumed, rain came, the race was to go the next day but more rain set it back another day. May 30, on Lap 59 in nearly the same Turn 4 area where drivers Eddie Sachs and Dave MacDonald had been killed in 1964, another wall of flame went up in a crash that injured driver Swede Savage, who weeks later died. A firetruck speeding uptrack to the accident – in full spectator view – blindsided and killed pit crew worker Armando Teran, who crossed into the truck's path while running to the scene. The race restarted and Gordon Johncock was leading when rain came again, after enough laps had been finished to make the race official.

- Mike Miller broke a 13-13 tie with a 22-yard touchdown run with 3:15 left to give South Bend Washington a 19-13 victory over Indianapolis Cathedral for the 3A (highest enrollment group) championship in the first state high school football playoffs Nov. 17, 1973. The game drew 12,000 people at School Field in South Bend. Greenfield (2A) and Mishawaka Marian (1A) were the other first-year champions.

- In a New Year's Eve 1973 Sugar Bowl battle of unbeatens for the national championship, Tom Clements completed a 38-yard third-down pass out of the end zone in the fourth quarter to ease Notre Dame out of trouble in a 24-23 victory over Alabama that won coach Ara Parseghian his second national title.

- At 31, winner of 124 major league games, pitcher Tommy John of Terre Haute underwent a revolutionary surgical procedure Sept. 25, 1974 (Dr. Frank Jobe replaced an elbow ligament in John's pitching arm [left] with a tendon from his right). He sat out a season, then won 164 more games for the Dodgers and Yankees and gained lasting identity as the guinea pig for the "Tommy John surgery" that has extended hundreds of baseball careers ever since. Despite a 26-year career, 288 career victories, 2,245 strikeouts, a 3.34 career earned run average and the most frequently mentioned name in modern baseball, Tommy John is not in the Cooperstown Hall of Fame.

- Jane Amlin's shot rolled along the top of the net and dropped just over for the point that gave Muncie North a 15-13 third-set victory over South Bend Clay and the fourth state high school girls' volleyball championship Nov. 15, 1975. North's victory, completing a 25-1 season under coach Debbie Millbern, was doubly historic: the first repeat title, and it came over a Clay team that included two boys, including 6-2 Brian Goralski who had played on the U.S. Junior Olympic team – allowed to play under a court ruling because Clay had no boys' volleyball team. The next year, South Bend Adams with three boys won the girls title, and two days later the IHSAA passed a rule banning boys from girls competition. Millbern, leading scorer on IU's first official women's basketball team in 1971-72, wrote of the '75 championship match in her 2014 book Meeting Her Match.

- Senior captain Judi Warren broke a 52-52 tie with two free throws that edged Warsaw out to a 57-52 victory over Bloomfield in a battle of unbeatens for the first state girls' basketball championship Feb. 28, 1976. Warren scored 17 points and sophomore teammate Chanda Kline 19 for Warsaw, which came back two years later with Kline scoring 29 final-game points to win its second undefeated championship. Both Warren and Kline were named "Miss Basketball" for the Indiana All-Stars as seniors. Bloomfield's stars, twins Melinda and Melissa Miles, went on to collegiate careers at West Point.

- Indiana University climbed to the top of college basketball in the mid-1970s. The Hoosiers won a Big Ten title and made a Final Four run in 1973, had to settle for a Big Ten co-championship in '74, then went on a 63-1 two-year run unmatched in Big Ten annals. The 1974-75 Hoosiers, No. 1-ranked from early January on, had the first 18-0 season in Big Ten history and were 31-0 when upset 92-90 by Kentucky in the Mideast Regional finals. Scott May, first-team All-America the year before but a non-factor the last five weeks after breaking his left arm, came back to be National Player of the Year as the 1975-76 Hoosiers went 32-0, stretched their still-record (by 10 games) Big Ten winning streak to 37, and beat Michigan 86-68 in the national championship game to be – still – the nation's last perfect-record men's national champion. In 2013, marking the 75th year of NCAA tournaments, the '76 Hoosiers and coach Bob Knight were brought to the Final Four in Atlanta and honored as the winner of a national poll picking the all-time best NCAA champion.

Swimmer Gary Hall of IU carried the United States flag in opening ceremonies at Montreal July 17, 1976. Hall was selected by a vote of U.S. team captains, a group that included men's basketball captain Quinn Buckner. Buckner and IU teammate Scott May won gold medals with the U.S. basketball team, and Hall medaled in his third Olympics by finishing third in the 100-meter butterfly.

Two months past her 15th birthday, Jennifer Hooker of Bloomington swam in the 200-meter freestyle finals and in qualifications with the U.S. 4x100 freestyle relay team at Montreal. When that team upset the favored East Germans to win the gold medal, Hooker ultimately was awarded a gold of her own for her qualifying role, making her the youngest Olympic gold medalist in Indiana history.

Jim Montgomery of IU won three gold medals and broke through what coach Doc Counsilman called swimming's last milestone by winning the 100-meter freestyle in 49.99 seconds at Montreal.

Captain Anita DeFrantz of Indianapolis won a bronze medal when the U.S. team she captained finished third in eight-oared shell with coxswain competition at Montreal July 24, 1976. In 1986, DeFrantz became the first black woman on the International Olympic Committee.

Future hockey all-time great Wayne Gretzky made his professional debut at 17 with the Indianapolis Racers in the World Hockey Assn. He played just eight games with the Racers before he was dealt to Edmonton in the 1978-79 season, the last year for the Racers and the WHA.

Down 34-12 with 8 minutes left in history's coldest Cotton Bowl game, Notre Dame beat Houston, 35-34, as Joe Montana introduced his name to national heroics by running for a touchdown, passing for two two-point conversions, and hitting Kris Haines from the 8 with 0:00 on the clock and 20 on the thermometer Jan. 1, 1979.

Larry Bird was the consensus College Player of the Year while leading Indiana State to No. 1 ranking and an unbeaten regular season in 1978-79. The Sycamores were 33-0 when they lost to Magic Johnson and Michigan State in the NCAA championship game at Salt Lake City March 26, 1979. They were the only team to make it to the championship game unbeaten in the first 40 years after Indiana's perfect season in 1976.

1980s

All-America center Joe Barry Carroll became the first Purdue player taken No. 1 in the NBA draft June 10, 1980. The day before, Golden State traded center Robert Parish and the No. 3 draft pick to Boston for Nos. 1 and 13. Boston, which had improved a record 32 games in its first year with Rookie of the Year Larry Bird, used the third pick to add Kevin McHale of Minnesota and set in place the Bird-McHale-Parrish front line that was best in the league for the next decade.

Sophomore point guard Isiah Thomas opened the second half with two steals and layups, then played most of the half in a surprise assignment in the post as IU ran away from North Carolina 63-50 for the 1981 NCAA championship. Thomas, who scored 23 points in his last game before starting a Hall of Fame professional career, won the Final Four's Most Outstanding Player Award.

Freshman Steve Alford scored 27 points and unranked Indiana eliminated No. 1-ranked North Carolina and national Player of the Year Michael Jordan, 72-68, in an NCAA regional first-round game March 22, 1984, at Atlanta.

An American-record basketball crowd, 67,596, turned out July 9, 1984, as the 1984 U.S. men's and women's Olympic teams opened the new $77-million Hoosier Dome with exhibition victories over all-star opposition. Coach Pat Head Summitt's women's team won 97-54, before Indiana coach Bob Knight's men's team topped a strong NBA all-star group, 97-82. IU's Steve Alford (New Castle) was with future pro all-timer Michael Jordan on the men's team, and Larry Bird (French Lick) and IU's Quinn Buckner and Isiah Thomas were on the NBA team. Both the men and women went on to win gold medals at the Los Angeles Olympics.

Fuzzy Zoeller of New Albany won the 1984 U.S. Open to become just the 12th golfer to win both the Open and the Masters (which Zoeller won in 1979). Through 2016, there now have been 16.

A Hoosier Dome crowd of 61,148 watched the Indianapolis Colts score first but lose 23-14 to the New York Jets Sept. 2, 1984, in the first National Football League game in Indiana.

Isiah Thomas scored a team-high 22 points and Larry Bird 21 as the Indiana collegiate heroes came home for the NBA All-Star game played before 43,146 at the Hoosier Dome Feb. 10, 1985. Their return wasn't triumphant; their East team lost 140-129 to the West, led by game MVP Ralph Sampson's 24 points. Rookie Michael Jordan started but scored just 7.

- Incensed by an early-game official's call, Indiana coach Bob Knight threw a folding chair onto the court during a game with Purdue Jan. 24, 1985, at Assembly Hall. Knight was ejected, Purdue went on to win 62-52, and Knight was sentenced to a lifetime of watching that chair fly whenever mention of his name on television needed visual accompaniment.

- Maicel Malone of North Central set records by winning state championships in the 100 (:11.52), 200 (:23.12) and 400 (:52.42) May 31, 1986, to cap the greatest track and field career by an Indiana high school girl. Malone, who went on to win an Olympic gold medal in the 4x400 relay at Atlanta in 1996, won 11 state high school titles – as the only two-event four-time winner ever (400 and 100), with three more in the 200 (beaten as a sophomore). She won seven NCAA titles at Arizona State.

- With a premiere showing in Bloomington, hometown of screenwriter Angelo Pizzo and college home of producer David Anspaugh, the low-budget movie "Hoosiers" opened Nov. 14, 1986. A fictionalized story linked in theme to Milan's 1954 state championship, the film won Oscar nominations and ignited audience response across the country with its message of small-school triumph and a state's love for basketball and its tournament. Almost instantly, and long years later, it gained inclusion with the greatest sports movies ever.

- Marion did the unthinkable: 65 years later matched Franklin's 1920-22 run of three straight state championships and did it with its own "Wonder Two." Jay Edwards scored 35 points and Lyndon Jones 23 as Marion topped North Central Conference rival Richmond 69-56 to win the state championship March 29, 1987 – old stuff for the two. Each had 18 points as sophomores when Marion beat Richmond for the 1985 title, then Edwards had 25 and Jones 19 when the Giants beat another NCC team, Anderson, for the 1986 championship. The two, named Indiana's co-Mr. Basketball in '87, combined for 264 career Final Four points – 133 by Jones, 131 by Edwards, an average of exactly 44 points a game together – as Marion and coach Bill Green achieved their "3-peat."

- Indiana broke a 10-10 halftime tie with three second-half touchdowns to win at Ohio State, 31-10, Oct. 10, 1987, ending history's longest winless streak in a Big Ten football series: 36 years, 31 games, since a 32-10 IU win at Columbus in 1951. After that '51 game, first-year Buckeye coach Woody Hayes' first OSU loss, the

Bucks beat IU 7 straight games, tied 0-0 in 1958, then won 23 more. IU coach Bill Mallory, who sat in the stands as a high school junior in the 1951 game, became the only Indiana coach ever to beat both Ohio State and Michigan in the same season when, two weeks after the Columbus victory, the Hoosiers whipped Michigan in the rain at Memorial Stadium, 14-10.

- 1967 and '68 All-American Leroy Keyes edged out Bob Griese, Rod Woodson and Otis Armstrong in votes cast by more than 3,000 fans to be named Purdue's all-time best football player as the 100th anniversary of Purdue football was celebrated in 1987. "Moderns" dominated the 24-man team, but linemen Elmer "Red" Sleight (1925-27), Ned Maloney (1945-47) and back Duane "Scooter" Purvis (1932-34) made it.

- Keith Smart's baseline jump shot with five seconds left gave Indiana a 74-73 victory over Syracuse and the 1987 NCAA championship. Smart had 15 of his 21 points in the last 12 minutes to earn the Outstanding Player Award he received. Two-year All-American Steve Alford's 23 points included seven 3-point baskets, still tied for most in a championship game. Two days earlier, Alford scored 33 points when IU outran No. 1-ranked UNLV 97-93 to get into the final game.

- Florence Joyner's stunning world-record :10.49 time in winning the women's 100-meter dash highlighted the U.S. Olympic Trials at IU Stadium in Indianapolis July 16, 1988. The time, never since even threatened, is considered a rare track and field record likely never to fall.

- Senior Anthony Thompson of Terre Haute set an NCAA record with his 60th career touchdown Nov. 4, 1989, then set another the next Saturday at Wisconsin with 377 rushing yards on 52 carries in a 45-17 Hoosier victory. Thompson, only two-time consensus All-American in IU history, finished a close runnerup (to Houston's Andre Ware, 1,073-1,003) in Heisman Trophy voting. Thompson's jersey number, 32, became the first one in any sport officially retired by IU. He is in the College Football Hall of Fame.

- In the decade's final hours, high school basketball titans Damon Bailey of Bedford North Lawrence and Eric Montross of Lawrence North met as opponents for the only time in their high school careers – in the championship game of the Indiana Basketball Hall of Fame Classic, played before 10,716 Dec. 26, 1989, at IU's Assembly Hall. Montross delivered the tie-breaking free throw with 4 seconds left in LN's 51-50 victory, but Bailey, with a game-high 26 points (to Montross's 16, was named the Classic's MVP. Lawrence North had won the 1989 state title, and BNL went on to win in '90, but the two never met in tournament play.

1990s

- Damon Bailey, a national sports figure since being featured in Sports Illustrated and a national best-selling book for his play as an eighth-grader, scored his Bedford North Lawrence team's last 11 points for a come-from-behind 63-60 victory over Concord for the 1990 state basketball championship before a national-record crowd of 41,046 at the Hoosier Dome March 25, 1990. Bailey scored 30 points to close his still-record state boys' career scoring record at 3,134. Concord, unbeaten going into the game, led 58-52 with 2:38 to play.

- Glenn Robinson, 1991 "Mr. Basketball" for state champion Gary Roosevelt, scored his Purdue career high of 49 points in his last home game as the Boilermakers beat Illinois, 87-77, March 13, 1994, to close out their Big Ten championship run under coach Gene Keady. Robinson was named College Basketball Player of the Year and was the first player taken in the 2004 NBA draft.

- In what still is the closest finish in Indianapolis 500 history, Al Unser Jr. held off charging Scott Goodyear by 43 thousandths of a second – about one-seventh of the time taken for a blink of an eye – to win on May 24, 1992. The race was historic in other ways: a record 10 former champions were in the field, and it was the last 500 for Speedway legends A. J. Foyt and Rick Mears, and former champions Tom Sneva and Gordon Johncock.

- Larry Bird was the only Hoosier on the U.S. "Dream Team" that – in the first Olympics when professionals could compete in basketball – overwhelmed Croatia 117-85 Aug. 8, 1992, to win the gold medal at the Barcelona Olympics.

- Calbert Cheaney hit a baseline jump shot early in the game against Northwestern March 4, 1993, at Assembly Hall to make the IU forward from Evansville the Big Ten's career scoring leader. Cheaney went on to become the College Player of the Year for the No. 1-ranked Big Ten champion Hoosiers, finishing his career with 2,613 points – almost a quarter-century later still the IU and Big Ten records.

- Reggie Miller gave basketball an all-time memory by scoring 8 game-changing points in 9 seconds to pull the Indiana Pacers past the New York Knicks, 107-105, in Game 1 of their Eastern semifinal playoffs at Madison Square Garden May 7, 1995.

The Pacers won that series, 4 games to 3, but lost in the Eastern finals to Orlando in seven games.

- 16-year-old Jaycie Phelps of Greenfield was one of the "Magnificent Seven" who captured America's hearts by winning the first women's gymnastics gold medal for the U.S. at the 1996 Atlanta Olympic Games.

- Bloomington North shut out Delta in the first quarter and cruised to a 75-54 victory in the 87th and last one-champion state high school basketball tournament March 22, 1997, before 26,187 at the RCA Dome in Indianapolis. Bloomington North, 28-1 under coach Tom McKinney, became the 47th school to win the title in the first finals trip for both it and Delta. Three Saturdays earlier, Martinsville (26-1) closed out on a 24-game winning streak by beating Crown Point, 66-59, in the last open girls' tournament. Coach Jan Conner's team, 16th different winner in the 22-year-old girls' tourney, had only one senior on its roster and came back to win the first 4A championship in the 1998 four-class girls tournament.

- Leigh Anne Hardin had an eagle on her way to a record-tying 69 and medalist honors with a two-day 143 total to lead Martinsville to its third straight state high school girls golf championship Oct. 11, 1997, at Avon. Martinsville's record-setting team score of 623 won by 43 strokes, another meet record. Besides winning her third team championship, Hardin added two more state team titles by helping the Artesians' basketball team to the 1997 and 1998 championships – five in all, surely a record of its own.

- Four-year star Stephanie White went down with a severe ankle sprain with four minutes left and Purdue up just 47-42 in the NCAA women's basketball tournament championship game at San Jose, Calif., March 28, 1999. The No. 1-ranked Boilermakers scored the next 14 points to blow out Duke, 62-45, and win the school's – and the Big Ten's – first women's title. Ukari Figgs scored all 18 of her team-high points in the second half and won the Most Outstanding Player Award. She, White (from Seeger) and Katie Douglas (Perry Meridian) made All-Tournament. Purdue finished 34-1, on a 32-game winning streak, in national Coach of the Year Carolyn Peck's last year before moving to a professional position.

2000-2009

- In the Pacers' first run to the NBA championship series, the Los Angeles Lakers "broke serve" by beating the Indiana Pacers at Indianapolis 120-118 in overtime

151

June 14, 2000 – the only road win in the tightly contested series – and five days later closed out a 4-2 NBA championship-series victory. Shaquille O'Neal outscored Pacers star Reggie Miller, 36-35, in the Game 4 thriller, then had 41 points in a 116-111 Game 6 victory at Los Angeles to clinch series MVP honors.

• Citing insubordination, IU President Myles Brand ended the 29-year tenure of basketball coach Bob Knight by announcing his firing Sept. 10, 2000. Assistant coach Mike Davis was named his successor.

• Drew Brees hit Seth Morales for a 64-yard touchdown play with 1:55 left to give Purdue a 31-27 victory over Ohio State at Ross-Ade Stadium Oct. 28, 2000. It was a key victory in a season that sent Big Ten co-champion Purdue to the Rose Bowl. Brees closed his career with virtually every passing record at the Cradle of Quarterbacks: 1,026 completions, 11,792 yards, 90 touchdowns. As a senior, he won the Maxwell Player of the Year Award and finished third in Heisman voting before a pro career capped when he was named Super Bowl MVP after leading the New Orleans Saints past Indianapolis 31-17 at Miami Feb. 7, 2010.

• Sophomore Jared Jeffries of Bloomington, the Big Ten Player of the Year, had 24 points and 15 rebounds as Indiana overcame a 13-point halftime deficit and upset No. 1-ranked Duke, 74-73, in the NCAA regional at Lexington, Ky., March 21, 2002. The Hoosiers, with guard Tom Coverdale of Noblesville also playing a primary role, went from there all the way to the national championship game before losing to Maryland, 64-52.

• Jack Butcher announced his retirement June 5, 2002, after 45 years of coaching at his high school alma mater, Loogootee. His 806 victories still is the state record.

• Florida sophomore Rex Grossman of Bloomington was consensus All-America quarterback and Southeastern Conference Player of the Year but he was edged out by Nebraska quarterback Eric Crouch (770-708) in 2002 Heisman Trophy balloting. Grossman was the Chicago Bears' first-round draft pick in 2004 and in his third pro season was their Super Bowl quarterback.

• Luke Zeller's buzzer shot from just across the center line gave Washington a 74-72 overtime victory over Plymouth in the 3A state championship game March 26, 2005, at Conseco Fieldhouse in Indianapolis. Zeller, who had 27 points, 9 rebounds and 11 assists in the game, was named "Mr. Basketball" as the leadoff man in an unmatched Indiana basketball family story. Brother Tyler came along next, winning

two state championships and "Mr. Basketball" in 2008. Brother Cody left with three championship rings, 2011's "Mr. Basketball." All were about 7-feet tall, all virtually straight-A students, all played in the NBA, Tyler (ACC Player of the Year for North Carolina) and Cody (an All-American on Indiana's 2013 Big Ten champions) as first-round draft picks.

• Lawrence North joined Franklin (1920-22) and Marion (1985-87) as winners of three straight state high school basketball championships with an 80-56 breeze past Muncie Central before 18,483 at Conseco Fieldhouse in Indianapolis March 25, 2006. National Player of the Year Greg Oden scored 26 points and guard Mike Conley 21 as coach Jack Keefer's team finished 29-0 and tied Oscar Robertson's Indianapolis Attucks teams' state-record winning streak, 45 games. A year later, Oden and Conley – stars of all three LN state champions – led Ohio State to an NCAA-runnerup finish, then went 1-4 in the NBA draft. Lawrence North, without the two, won its first five games before losing to Indianapolis Arlington, 46-44, Dec. 15, 2006, to cap its record winning streak at 50.

• In their 23rd year, the Indianapolis Colts withstood rain at Miami and a strong Chicago Bears defense to win, 29-17, in Super Bowl XLIV Feb. 4, 2007 – the first major league professional sports championship for Indianapolis and Indiana. Quarterback Peyton Manning was named MVP, hitting 25 of 38 passes for 247 yards and a touchdown. The game-clincher was Colts cornerback Kelvin Hayden's interception and 56-yard touchdown runback in the fourth quarter.

2010s

• Butler and young coach Brad Stevens introduced themselves to college basketball celebrity with a 25-game winning streak that took them all the way to the national championship game before Gordon Heyward's halfcourt buzzer shot barely missed and the Bulldogs lost to Duke, 61-59, at Lucas Stadium in Indianapolis April 5, 2010. The No. 5-seed Bulldogs, trying to become the smallest school to win the title since Holy Cross 63 years earlier, beat a 1-seed (Syracuse), 2-seed (Kansas State) and Big Ten tri-champion Michigan State before losing to No. 1-seed Duke.

• Christian Watford's 3-point basket at the buzzer gave Indiana a 74-73 victory over No. 1-ranked Kentucky and sent thousands rushing onto the Assembly Hall court Dec. 10, 2010, signaling the Hoosiers' arrival back from three-year 8-46 Big Ten doldrums. A year later, coach Tom Crean's Hoosiers opened the season ranked No. 1 in the nation and won their first Big Ten championship in 20 years.

- The "Butler Miracle of 2010" got an unexpected rerun when Brad Stevens and the Bulldogs did it again: This time an 8-seed and minus Gordon Heyward who had gone on to the NBA, the Bulldogs beat a 1-seed (Pittsburgh), a 2 (Florida) and 4th-seeded Big Ten power Wisconsin but went ice-cold with .188 shooting and lost the NCAA championship game to Connecticut, 53-41, at Houston April 4, 2011 – fourth anniversary of his signing as Butler's surprise new coach. On July 3, 2013, the Boston Celtics hired Stevens as their new coach.

- Almost as heady for Indianapolis as getting the Colts into a Super Bowl was bringing the Super Bowl to Indy, which happened with No. 46 – XLVI, to Romantics. Indiana in February rarely is as sunny and pleasant as Indianapolis was Feb. 5, 2012, when a grand and gala week was capped off with the next-happiest outcome the locals could have imagined, short of a Colts victory. Hated rival New England, hoping to avenge their Super-disappointment four years earlier when the underdog Giants stopped them a game short of joining the '73 Dolphins with a perfect run to the championship, led into the last minute but lost on a 6-yard Ahmad Bradshaw run, 21-17. This time it was the Giants' record that set a record: they were 9-7, worst regular-season record ever for a Super Bowl champion.

- David Boudia of Noblesville and Purdue nailed his difficult final dive to come from behind and win the 10-meter Olympic diving gold medal at London Aug. 12, 2012. Boudia barely squeezed into the semifinals, last of the 16 qualifiers, but he was third entering the finals and won America's first platform title since 1988. Boudia won a state high school title as a sophomore and was Big Ten male Athlete of the Year for winning six NCAA championships at Purdue.

- Junior Jackie Young scored 36 points to lead 30-1 Princeton to a 72-44 victory over Tippecanoe Valley March 7, 2015, for the 3A state high school girls basketball championship. Bidding for a second title, Princeton was upset by Southridge 34-33 in the 2016 sectional despite 26 points by Young. "Miss Basketball" Young finished her four-year career with a state-record 3,268 points – 134 more than boys recordholder Damon Bailey's, set 26 years before. She was named the Naismith National Player of the Year.

- Pike junior Lynna Irby swept the sprints for the third year in a row June 3, 2016, at IU to continue her challenge to 1990s star Maicel Malone's Indiana girls track and field supremacy. Malone went 11-for-12 in winning the 100 and 400-meter titles four years in a row and the 200 three times for North Central, setting records in each. Irby kept her 12-for-12 hopes alive and went 11.50 in the 100 to tie the one record she has taken from Malone.

- Months after he had been inducted into the College Basketball Hall of Fame, 1976 Indiana captain Quinn Buckner was named an IU trustee by Gov. Mike Pence June 3, 2016. Only Buckner and two other Big Ten players, Jerry Lucas of Ohio State (1960-62) and Magic Johnson of Michigan State (1978-79) achieved basketball's Grand Slam of team championships: high school, college, Olympic and NBA.

- Lilly King of Evansville and IU provided the 2016 Olympics with one of its most dramatic moments when she won the women's 100-meter breaststroke championship Aug. 8, 2016. The race became a showdown between drug-free swimmers worldwide and Russians who had entered the Rio de Janeiro games facing a possible teamwide ban that narrowed to individual cases. King's match-up was with Yulia Efimova, who had twice been banned for using illegal drugs but was cleared to compete at Rio. In a tense atmosphere that included booing, rare in swimming, King – who had spoken out publicly against Efimova and swam beside her in the finals race – pulled out to win by a half-second in setting an Olympic record of 1:05.70. She added a second gold swimming the breaststroke leg on the U.S. medley relay team. When Canadian Derek Drouin won the high jump Aug. 16, it marked the first Olympics when athletes from IU – or any other Indiana school – won individual golds in both swimming and track.

Index

154

If your sports organization or business would like to purchase books for fundraisers or bulk orders, please contact M.T. Publishing Company, Inc. at 1-888-263-4702 or www.mtpublishing.com for volume pricing.

*Dust jackets can be branded for your business. Ask us for details!

25 Greatest Sports Stories in the History of Indiana™